CREATING THE CODING GENER
PRIMARY SCHOO

Creating the Coding Generation in Primary Schools sets out the what, why and how of coding. Written by industry innovators and experts, it shows how you can bring the world of coding to your primary school practice.

It is packed with a range of inspirational ideas for the cross-curricular teaching of coding, from demystifying algebra in maths, to teaching music, to designing digital storytelling, as well as an insight into the global movement of free coding clubs for young people such as *CoderDojo* and *Girls Learning Code.*

Key topics explored include:

- what we mean by 'coding'
- understanding and teaching computational thinking
- building pupils' passion for and confidence with technologies
- artificial intelligence systems
- how gender impacts on coding
- STEM learning and Computer Science
- using Minecraft to improve pupil engagement
- fun projects using a Raspberry Pi.

Designed to be read from cover to cover or dipped into for ideas and advice, *Creating the Coding Generation in Primary Schools* offers all teachers a deeper knowledge and understanding of coding that will help them support and inspire the coding generation. It is cool to code!

Steve Humble MBE is Researcher and Teaching Fellow for Primary and Secondary PGCE Maths at Newcastle University, UK, with extensive experience working as an educational advisor to both government and schools.

CREATING THE CODING GENERATION IN PRIMARY SCHOOLS

A Practical Guide for Cross-Curricular Teaching

Edited by
Steve Humble

Routledge
Taylor & Francis Group

LONDON AND NEW YORK

First published 2018
by Routledge
2 Park Square, Milton Park, Abingdon, Oxon OX14 4RN

and by Routledge
711 Third Avenue, New York, NY 10017

Routledge is an imprint of the Taylor & Francis Group, an informa business

British Library Cataloguing in Publication Data
A catalogue record for this book is available from the British Library

Library of Congress Cataloging in Publication Data
A catalog record for this book has been requested

ISBN: 978-1-138-68118-7 (hbk)
ISBN: 978-1-138-68119-4 (pbk)
ISBN: 978-1-315-54581-3 (ebk)

Typeset in Times New Roman
by Swales & Willis, Exeter, Devon, UK

Printed and bound by CPI Group (UK) Ltd, Croydon, CR0 4YY

CONTENTS

CONTENTS ▪ ▪ ▪ ▪

ILLUSTRATIONS

FIGURES

ILLUSTRATIONS ▪ ▪ ▪ ▪

TABLES

CONTRIBUTORS

Sam Aaron is a researcher, software architect and computational thinker with a deep fascination surrounding the notion of communicative programming. He sees programming as one of the many communication channels for descriptions of formalised process of any kind, be it a business process, a compiler strategy or even a musical composition.

Yasemin Allsop worked as an ICT Coordinator in primary schools in London for almost ten years. She is currently employed as a Lecturer in Primary Education at the Institute of Education, University College London. Her research focus is children's thinking, learning and metacognition when making digital games. She is the founder and co-editor of the online magazine *ICT in Practice*, where educators from around the world share their experiences of using technology in education, and the co-editor of the *International Journal of Computer Science Education in Schools*.

Tim Bell is a professor in the Department of Computer Science and Software Engineering at the University of Canterbury, New Zealand. His main current research interest is computer science education. His "Computer Science Unplugged" and related projects are widely used internationally, and their books and videos have been translated into about 20 languages. He has received several awards for his work in education, including the University of Canterbury's Innovation honorary medal for fundamental contributions in Computer Science education in 2013. Since 2008 he has been actively involved in the design and deployment of the new Digital Technologies curriculum in New Zealand schools.

Quinn Burke is an Assistant Professor at the College of Charleston (South Carolina) Department of Education. Quinn's research examines the particular affordances of different coding activities (e.g. digital storytelling, video game making) and different introductory programming languages (e.g. Blockly, Scratch, Python, Java) in successfully integrating computer science into the core curricula in classrooms. Quinn's research has been supported by a number of state and federal grants, most recently a National Science Foundation grant to investigate alternative post-secondary computing education options. He has written a number of articles around integrating computing into the school day, and he recently completed a book (with co-author Yasmin Kafai) entitled *Connected Code: Why Children Need to Learn Programming*, which was published by MIT Press in July 2014. A new book, *Connected Gaming* (MIT Press), is forthcoming in the spring of 2017.

Chris Carr is a primary school teacher and STEM (science, technology, engineering and mathematics) coordinator in Gosforth, Newcastle upon Tyne. Having graduated with a BSc in Psychology and MSc in Applied Psychology from Ulster University, he furthered his studies with a PGCE from Newcastle University. His interests are in the design of learning activities in which meaningful opportunities are provided for pupils to design the programme content and choose the medium in which they work. Through this locus of control, pupils discover and assemble knowledge independently by developing their own understanding of concepts and relationships.

Paul Curzon is a Professor of Computer Science at Queen Mary University of London. His research interests are computer science education, human–computer interaction and formal methods. He was awarded a Higher Education Academy National Teaching Fellowship in 2010 and won the EPSRC (Engineering and Physical Sciences Research Council) Non-professional Computer Science Writer of the Year in 2007 in addition to several teaching prizes. He co-founded Teaching London Computing, providing continuing professional development support for teachers. Paul first taught himself to program on a beach in the South of France.

Caitlin Duncan is a PhD student from the University of Canterbury, New Zealand, working in the Computer Science Education Research group. Her research area is the integration of computational thinking, computer science and programming into the primary school curriculum, and the impacts of this on both teachers and pupils. She is a Google Anita Borg Scholar, is active in supporting diversity in the computer science community, and has authored several papers on computing education.

Alan Gleaves is a lecturer in Educational Computing and Learning Technology at Durham University. An award-winning teacher, he has worked as a schoolteacher and further education lecturer, and before entering higher education was a college vice-principal. He has been a school governor with responsibility for technology development and investment; a technology consultant for the Department for Education; and a regional schools' advisor for various technology programmes including the National Grid for Learning, Building Schools for the Future and the City Technology Colleges' Trust. He has published widely in the areas of mobile technology use in informal learning and for assessment purposes.

David Hill has been playing with technology all his life, from ZX81s to 3D printers to using augmented reality – with a habit of taking things apart to see how they work, which he inherited from his dad. He's always been interested in how technology can used to enable learning. After working in industry, he spent several years as a primary school teacher leading computing and science. He is currently the Technology Faculty Outreach Coordinator for the University of Portsmouth, working with schools and colleges to help inspire the next generation of students to take up STEM subjects. Through this, and as a Computing At Schools Hub leader, he supports local teachers in methods of delivering these subjects, such as project-based learning, and demonstrating how technology can be used to effectively support teaching and learning. He occasionally tweets what he's doing on @TecOutreach.

Mark Horneff is a talented business strategist with more than a decade of global experience harnessing innovation to ensure technology is leveraged as a competitive tool in the creation of high-quality platforms and products, including computer games and application development. He is a Managing Director at Kuato Studios. He is a high-energy leader who blends passion for progressive social media and emerging technologies with an impressive portfolio of successful project management with industry giants Sony and Sega, and a record of guiding and infusing large teams and staff with the tools and capabilities to achieve high performance. He presents with ease to large groups, and is experienced in the management of multi-million pound budgets, whilst accurately identifying critical business objectives and value drivers. He ensures technology adoption decisions are made for the optimal support of both the immediate and long-term business strategy.

Steve Humble MBE works at Newcastle University, UK. He was the awarded his MBE (Member of the Most Excellent Order of the British Empire) for services to education in the 2016 New Year's Honours list. His interest in coding started in the 1980s, when, as a teacher of mathematics and computing, he taught students how to write computer games (Space Invaders, Breakout, Pac-Man and Asteroids) for their coursework. In these early days, computers such as the ZX Spectrum and BBC Micro ran slowly, and so he spent many hours waiting for beautiful Julia Sets to appear. His first book, *The Experimenter's A–Z of Mathematics: Maths Activities with Computer Support* (2002), uses snippets of code to allow the reader to uncover mathematical secrets within a historical setting. Around this time he also wrote a series of educational research papers that use code to support the reader's mathematical understanding. He is a fellow of the Institute of Mathematics and its Applications (IMA), and to promote public interest in mathematics he wrote fortnightly newspaper columns for eight years as @DrMaths. He also has written a range of puzzles "explorer" books and a number of classroom resources. Humble's book *How to Be Inventive When Teaching Primary Maths* was published by Routledge (2015), and he was Routledge education author of the month for March 2015. He is editor with Professor Pauline Dixon on the *Handbook of International Development and Education* (2015) and is one of the editors for *50 Visions of Mathematics* (OUP, 2014).

Michael W. Kessinger has served Morehead State University, Kentucky, as an adjunct instructor for 17 years and has been a full-time faculty member for the past three years. His background includes 37 years with the Martin County School System in Kentucky. He received his EdD from the University of Kentucky, EdS (Education Specialist) and Masters from Morehead State University, and Bachelor of Science from the University of Wisconsin–Eau Claire. In addition to this interest in education technology and school leadership, Michael is also involved in gifted education research. He currently serves as programme leader for the Instructional Leadership programme.

Ahmed Kharrufa's background is in the software industry, but since starting his PhD in Computing Science in 2007 he has been very interested in the potential of technology to support learning. After finishing his PhD and spending a few years in the educational technology industry, he switched to being a full-time researcher. He leads the educational technology research strand in Open Lab, exploring the role of technology in supporting communities to play a more effective role in formal education towards a more community-driven curriculum. This also involves looking at the support of technology for creating engaging digital content, the means by which content usage information can be fed back to creators and educators, and new ways of understanding the impact of technology use in education. He is also interested in interaction design and interactive surfaces, looking at the use of wearable sensors to enhance pen-and-touch interactions.

Shaimaa Lazem earned her PhD from the Department of Computer Science, Virginia Tech, USA, in 2012. She then returned to Egypt, where she holds an academic position at the City for Scientific Research and Technological Applications, to establish a research programme in Human–Computer Interaction (HCI) with a particular focus on the intersection between HCI and education. Her programme aims at developing a robust assessment for the national agenda of integrating technology in formal education, exploring critical alternatives and providing recommendations for policy makers. Her research interests include educational technologies, game-based learning and computer science education.

Bill Liao is an Australian entrepreneur and co-founder of CoderDojo, a not-for-profit organisation that teaches children how to code. It aims to teach children creative problem-solving skills and practical creative skills and was launched in Ireland in mid-2011. Bill and his co-founder James Whelton hope that CoderDojo will provide an outlet for children who know how to code to meet other children with similar interests and work on projects in an environment with their peers – similar to a co-working space but less formal. One of Bill's other great passions is combating global warming, and he has a goal to plant two trillion trees by 2020 through WeForest.org, an organisation he founded in 2009. Bill is dedicated to the vision that business and enterprise, conducted fairly and with respect for the environment, can and will create a better environment for work, life and the world that we all share. This vision is captured in his book *Stone Soup: A Secret Recipe for Making Something from Nothing.*

Simon Marsden really became interested in computers during his teacher training, particularly with the amazing RiSC OS Archimedes. He became very interested in using control and monitoring to enhance his science teaching and soon became more interested in teaching ICT and computing. He embarked on a Masters degree in computing and became passionately interested in open-source software and Linux. By the end of his classroom teaching career, his whole school was run on Linux servers, with Linux clients for the pupils. He now works as course leader in Initial Teacher Training (Computing) and in the School of Computing at the University of Portsmouth. Alongside David Hill, he is a Computing At Schools Hub leader. He is interested in all aspects of computing but loves tinkering around with physical computing, solving problems and making things work. Follow @sipmar if you wish to see his occasional computer- and education-related musings.

Sylvia Martinez is a maker, mom, engineer and co-author of the book *Invent to Learn: Making, Tinkering, and Engineering in the Classroom*, called "the bible of the classroom maker movement". Sylvia speaks to and works with schools around the world evangelising authentic, inclusive use of technology across the curriculum. She is president of Constructing Modern Knowledge Press, creating books and professional development advocating using modern technology for learning. Sylvia is also the principal advisor to the FabLearn Fellows programme at Stanford University, funded by the NSF (National Science Foundation). Prior to that, Sylvia ran the educational non-profit Generation YES, designed and programmed educational software and video games, and was an aerospace engineer specialising in GPS navigation and high-frequency receiver systems.

Peter W. McOwan is a Professor of Computer Science at Queen Mary University of London. His research interests are in computer vision, artificial intelligence and robotics. He was awarded a Higher Education Academy National Teaching Fellowship in 2008, and the IET Mountbatten medal in 2011 for his work in promoting computer science to diverse audiences. Peter is an amateur magician with a healthy interest in science fiction. Paul Curzon and Peter co-created the internationally known ComputerScience For Fun project (www.cs4fn.org) and were original members of the UK Computing At School network (CAS).

David Miller is the Director of Learning at Kuato Studios. This is a vibrant London start-up, out to challenge the perception of educational gaming. Backed by Horizon Ventures and SRI International, Kuato Studios boasts a mix of educators, game designers and artificial intelligence specialists, all of whom harbour a strong passion for learning. David believes strongly that technology must be used to promote and equip people of all ages with relevant skills for the future. He was the Guardian/ Pearson UK Teacher of the year for 2008.

Joel Mills saw his first computer in 1977 aged five – a Sinclair calculator – and has been playing computer games ever since, starting with Pong and working through a gaming history in the 1980s arcades playing Space Invaders, Donkey Kong, Asteroids and Galaxian in the early days. His gaming knowledge continued at home on Sega Mega Drive, Super Nintendo, PS1, PS2, Xbox and PC gaming, providing him with an established pedigree in computer game history. He began teaching in Higher Education in 1997, and when *Minecraft* was released he quickly took it into his classroom to explore how it could be used in further and higher education for game-based learning. In 2015 he won the award of Learning Technologist of the Year for his work in *Minecraft* in higher education, and he has developed award-winning projects in chemistry, history, archaeology, business studies and also a recreation of the University of Hull's Brynmor Jones Library. Joel is currently working at the University of Hull as a lecturer and advisor on all aspects of technology-enhanced learning and pedagogy, and has been selected by Microsoft as a 2017 Minecraft Mentor.

Sugata Mitra is Professor of Educational Technology at the School of Education, Communication and Language Sciences at Newcastle University, UK. He is best known for his "Hole in the Wall" experiment, and widely cited in works on literacy and education. He won the TED Prize 2013. Mitra's TED Talk "Build a School in the Cloud" was featured in NPR's *TED Radio Hour* on "Unstoppable Learning". Mitra claimed that children in the rural slums of India, many of whom had never seen a computer in their lives, had, when left with computers in kiosks, taught themselves everything from "character mapping" to advanced topics such as "DNA replication" on their own, without adult assistance. He suggested this would lead to "unstoppable learning" through a "worldwide cloud" – where children would pool their knowledge and resources in the absence of adult supervision to create a world of self-promoted learning. The "Hole in the Wall" experiment inspired Indian diplomat Vikas Swarup to write his debut novel, *Q & A*, which later became the film *Slumdog Millionaire*.

Kimberely Fletcher Nettleton earned an EdD in Curriculum and Instruction, with an emphasis on Instructional Design and Technology, from the University of Kentucky. She holds a Masters in Elementary Education from Georgetown College, Kentucky, and another MA in School Administration, also from the University of Kentucky. She is currently an Associate Professor at Morehead State University, Kentucky. In addition to teaching at Morehead State, she is the Director of the Professional Partnership Network, a pre-service teacher professional development school programme. As both a former classroom teacher and school principal, she is a firm believer in the healing power of chocolate.

Patrick Olivier leads Open Lab, Newcastle University's centre for cross-disciplinary research in digital technologies. He is the principal investigator for the EPSRC Centre for Doctoral Training in Digital Civics and the EPSRC Digital Economy Research Centre. He is an expert in the application of social and ubiquitous technologies in education, health and wellbeing, and in the development of new approaches for interaction and human-centred design methods. He is committed to the pursuit of processes by which people can be involved in creation of technology and digital services, both in the design processes and in their actual production. Most recently he has been exploring the concept of the "commissioning platform", including citizen-commissioned information services (e.g. App Movement), events (Event Movement) and media (Bootlegger). For Patrick, digital civics is about truly empowering communities and how digital technologies can underpin a new era of participatory citizenship.

Anne Preston PhD FHEA is a lecturer in Technology Enhanced Learning at the Centre for Higher Education Research and Practice (CHERP) at Kingston University, UK. With Anne's background in educational linguistics, her research focuses on the different ways in which teachers and students make sense of technological innovation, how they develop an evidence base for the kinds of decisions they enact through practice, and how technology itself can be designed to better support this reflective process.

Bradley Pursglove is a software developer. His main research interests are based around machine learning, activity recognition and user identification on touchscreen devices. His work has also focused on leveraging these techniques within Self Organised Learning Environments.

Austen Rainer is Associate Professor in Software Engineering, and Head of Department of Computer Science and Software Engineering, at the University of Canterbury in New Zealand. His main research interests are in the area of behavioural software engineering, e.g. investigating the actual practices of software engineers. Much of his research is conducted with industrial and societal stakeholders. He co-authored the first discipline-specific book on the design, conduct, analysis and reporting of case studies, entitled *Case Study Research in Software Engineering*.

Gary S. Stager PhD is an internationally recognised educator, author, speaker, journalist and consultant, and the founder of the Constructing Modern Knowledge summer institute. Gary has helped learners of all ages on six continents embrace learning-by-doing, and the power of computers as intellectual laboratories and vehicles for self-expression. He led professional development in the world's first laptop schools and has taught students from pre-school through doctoral programmes. Gary curates the website "The Daily Papert" to help educators understand his colleague Seymour Papert's enormous influence on the field of education.

Caroline Walker is a Professor of Education and Head of the School of Education, Communication and Language Sciences at Newcastle University. A former physicist working in the field of vehicle engineering, she has also been a secondary school teacher with specialisms in Physics and Music, and has worked in schools and further education colleges in the UK and overseas. She has received many awards for teaching excellence and scholarship, including a UK National Teaching Fellowship, an award for Innovative Excellence in Teaching and Learning with Technology from the US Association of Colleges of Education, and Vice-Chancellor's Awards for Excellence in Teaching & Learning and Doctoral Supervision from Durham University.

'THE CODING DREAM'

Do while else
Repeat
End
Do while else
fuzzy
Repeat
Do while fuzzy
Repeat end
The Sun drifts shadows
across a binary shore
Glistening on open code
Responsive fingers slip
and the metallic dream of days gone
slides into the ocean foam
Reflection grasps but cannot hold
Binary digits explode
Rippling onto the sun-drenched shore
The coding generation is free
to tread and explore
Do while
Repeat

by Steve Humble (2017)

INTRODUCTION

Steve Humble

■ **Figure 0.1** Julia's monster footprints

This book sets out the what, why and how of coding. Experts have written chapters to create a stimulating book that can be read from cover to cover or taken one section at a time. This book has been written for a wide audience. Whether you're a teacher, parent or academic, or just interested in coding, this book will have something to your liking.

There's a chapter dedicated to the history of why we need to code, to set the scene and give some understanding of where we have come from. This provides a foundation that is always a good place to build from. But why do we need to code? Well, ask some of the most influential businessmen and women around the world and their answers are clear. It's obvious: if you're developing smartphone apps or running e-commerce platforms, coding is essential. However, most businesses deal with data, such as customer details, and websites: this is where basic knowledge of coding really sets you apart.

Learning code will provide skills that can put you in a good place in the job market and provide a solution to the growing "skills gap"; however, there's more to coding than improving your CV. Just like learning to play an instrument or learning a new language, coding provides a new set of skills that benefit the learner. Coding provides the tools that allow an understanding in order to grasp the accelerating nature of technology.

Learning how to code can be an exciting journey, and this book provides examples of exploring the coding revolution through story, music, games, science and maths to name just a few ways. The new "coding generation" needs to adapt to the fast change of technology, developing their skills to code, design, interact, monitor and participate to the maximum in their everyday lives. This book provides a start for the new coding generation, focusing on the why, what and how.

Chapter 1 explores what the term "coding" is intended to mean, focusing on the general context of programming. The use of the term "coding" to refer to programming has risen sharply since 2012, and has developed a new meaning that embraces many aspects of computing and programming. In this chapter, the authors distinguish the concepts of a program and an algorithm, and the problems that they solve. The notion of a "Turing-complete" system provides a guide to the range of tools needed to realise the full power of programming, and also helps to distinguish between teaching a particular language and teaching programming in general. The authors also explore the steps needed to analyse a problem and implement a program that solves it, including testing and debugging. The relationship of "coding" to the broader idea of "computational thinking" is clarified, highlighting how they are highly connected but not the same thing. Finally, the chapter considers how coding and computational thinking relate to the skills required in industry to produce programs that work well in real situations. In conclusion, the authors suggest that programming is a highly social task.

The theme of computational thinking and how it can be taught is explored in greater depth in Chapter 2. Computational thinking has been called the most important skill that any child in the twenty-first century could ever acquire, with the same life-skill significance as reading, writing and arithmetic. But standing behind these developments are educational issues that are not yet clear, and that need a much closer look in order for teachers, schools, universities and teacher educators to understand what pedagogic and curriculum claims are being made for computational thinking and whether these are realistic and evidence-based. In addition, it is critical to understand what may be the most effective ways for teachers to develop their own knowledge and skill in computational thinking, and to help clarify and reduce impediments to teaching it effectively to pupils. Examining this from the perspective of technological innovation and curriculum development, the chapter then goes on to adopt a conceptual approach to understanding how computational thinking could be taught across subjects and key stages. Specific examples are given, with key critical reflections and the latest research into how computational thinking could be taught. The underlying ethos of this chapter is the idea that computational thinking can be an enabling and empowering skill that will benefit all children in the way that they approach learning.

Chapter 3 contains ten considerations for teaching coding as a new liberal art, rather than as training for a "STEM [science, technology, engineering and mathematics] job". The authors believe that with fluency and access, programming allows children to make sense of the world and express themselves as they master difficult concepts. Thirty-five years after computers were introduced into classrooms in the UK and US, there is a rediscovery of what those early pioneer teachers knew – that the best use for computers in the classroom is learning to program them. Despite an educational technology industry that seems bent on depriving children (and teachers) of agency by making coding "simple", Seymour Papert's concept of "hardfun" is the more estimable goal. The materials and tools of the maker movement extend the digital to the analogue. This physical computing creates extensive opportunities for "instrumental coding", where coding is a means to end, solving problems both personal and global with interactive materials, robots and real-world mathematics. Using iterative methods, teachers can scaffold student understanding of coding with projects that build interest and skills as students gain fluency. The global interest in computer science is a gift we must not waste by making programming boring and out of touch with the real world.

Chapter 4 investigates the philosophy, biology and technology behind artificial intelligence systems. We are living in a shared world, a world increasingly inhabited by robots and artificial intelligence. Home robot vacuum cleaners, self-driving cars, automatic financial trading systems, video game-playing avatars, automatic milking robots on farms, sat nav car systems, production line robots and autonomous military drones are all current examples of the application of artificial intelligence.

The authors look at the fundamentals of software that exhibits a range of behaviours we would call "intelligent". The exploration starts with simple rule-following systems, and also covers bio-inspired computer systems that can learn, along with simple forms of robotics. Each type of artificial intelligence is introduced through an unplugged classroom activity. These activities are used to demonstrate the underlying ideas, and are followed by a discussion that includes the principles of the code for implementing such systems in the classroom. As artificial intelligences and robots develop further, and start to permeate every aspect of our lives, the ethical, social and legal implications for a world cohabited with artificial intelligence become increasingly important. The media mainly paints a futuristic picture of doom in relation to the development of artificial intelligence in computing with films such as *Blade Runner*, *The Terminator* and *Westworld*. But is that future inevitable, and will humans end up being "managed" (terminated) by a superior android species? Therefore the chapter concludes by posing a range of discussion topics that can be debated in the classroom, such as "Would an artificial intelligence be a better politician than a human?" and "If a self-driving car crashes who is responsible? Is it the occupant or the computer programmer who wrote the car's driving code?" These ethical and philosophical questions[1] regarding artificial intelligence have been posed by many science fiction writers, such as Philip K. Dick, around the issue of "What it really means to be human".

In Chapter 5, the authors discuss how gender impacts on coding and how computer science seems to be a male-dominated field. At first glance, the number of women interested in games and computer programming appears to be low. Gender differences in game choice, colour and characters have been observed. For years, males have overwhelmingly represented the gaming and programming arena, with female participation in each being relatively low. Changes are emerging. Women are becoming actively engaged in games and are marshalling their talents to storm the citadel of computer programming. While gender differences are indicated, questions surface as to whether there are true differences or merely bias.

As a watchword in digital learning, the DIY moniker ("do-it-yourself") is increasingly being used to describe the use of Web 2.0 applications in and around schools. But despite the DIY name, to what extent does the scrappy, "can-do" autonomy associated with Web 2.0 media actually mesh with the nature of schools – institutions that historically have been "top-down" and largely conformist in both design and practice? Investigating youth's use and perception of the introductory programming language Scratch, Chapter 6 reports on a two-month design study involving two groups of middle-school youth. The first group were introduced to Scratch in a language arts course, composing their own digital stories within the setting of a writing workshop. In this setting, participants followed a scripted curriculum tied to statewide academic standards. The second group created Scratch projects in an after-school fan-fiction club. Considerably more "loose" in nature, the club involved participants sharing their work and offering feedback but entailed no scripted lessons nor requisite submissions. Reporting on each learning environment, this study contrasts the two social and technical infrastructures and examines how design processes and remixing took on different meanings based upon each setting. Seventy-one per cent of the club members – versus 90 per cent of the classroom students – completed a project in Scratch, though, on average, club participants produced twice as many projects than those in the class. Classroom students, however, generally produced longer projects entailing clearer narrative structures. The conclusion focuses on finding a balance between structure and autonomy in children's use of digital media in and around schools.

Chapter 7 discusses the use of coding in a mathematics classroom through the use of snippets of code to help pupils explore order and pattern in whole numbers. Mathematical activity involves creating algorithms, experimenting, writing algebraic generalisations and establishing proofs. Coding can help, and allow time for, children to develop these skills in the classroom. This allows them greater ownership in the development of concepts. When children formulate ideas in this way, a corresponding construction is made in their minds. This in turn stimulates both short- and long-term memory. It is therefore possible, using this abstract-to-concrete concept, to organise coding tasks to enhance the pupil's mathematical knowledge and understanding. In terms of teaching pedagogy, once these various constructs have been created and used in the classroom, it can be useful to reflect on what they are and how children can be engaged through these processes. This chapter looks at a series of number patterns in mathematics, and considers how children can construct algorithms and code to help them understand the processes involved. The simplicity of the code considered in this chapter demonstrates that one can exploit the computer mathematically without being an expert programmer. There are four parts to the chapter. The first discusses what is meant by "pattern" and "order". The next section investigates well-known number patterns through coding, incorporating historical contexts and number facts to allow for a more in-depth further exploration. The third part discusses the means to determine the level of order existing in finite number patterns.

This allows pupils to have a more comprehensive discovery around number patterns and the use of coding. Finally the chapter ends with a summing up and conclusion.

The subject of teaching STEM is considered in Chapter 8, along with its links to coding. Recent technological advances have influenced not only the way we communicate but also the way we think and learn. There has been a shift in the anatomy of thinking and learning from a ready static to an interactive-dynamic experience. We are now aware that in order to learn, the learner has to be at the centre of the learning experience and also have opportunities to learn the same material in different contextual settings. Therefore the traditional way of teaching subjects in isolation may not be seen as the best way of teaching, and teachers may need to explore the opportunities for integrating learning into different sub-jects. STEM learning gives learners opportunities to investigate an idea in a different context and connect the learning across disciplines. It is often said that computer science is the silent "C" in STEM, as it has very strong links with mathematics and science, and with design and technology; therefore it can be defined as a STEM discipline. In this chapter, we discuss the relationship between STEM learning and computer science and provide some example projects that can be used for teach-ing both STEM and computer science skills.

Chapter 9 considers the use of Sonic Pi to teach music in a school setting through live coding. Sonic Pi is a powerful new kind of musical instrument with a novel interface. Instead of plucking strings, blowing into mouthpieces or hitting things with sticks, you write and modify code. This new style of music-making has been termed "live coding", and the number of musicians producing music in this way is growing dramatically. Through the act of writing and modifying code, a live coding musician can convert thoughts into musical events in a similar way to how jazz musicians improvise. The chapter tells the story of how Sonic Pi music was developed through a school-based case study over a period of seven weeks. It looks at the hardware and software developments, the pure delivery aspects and the motivational impact on the pupils. The software design principles at the heart of this project focus on the concepts of core simplicity, effective communication, fast feedback and clear learning pathways. The chapter mainly focuses on using music as a mechanism to engage users with coding concepts, but it also can be said that computer science could be used to engage, and create new avenues for, pupils' involvement and interest in music.

The purpose of Chapter 10 is to look at how *Minecraft* can be used as a frame-work for engagement. The chapter is aimed at teachers, public engagement teams, bid-writers and volunteers involved in working with young people. Three projects were set up through the University of Hull that used *Minecraft* to engage young people with aspects of the university: the Hull History Centre (HHC) Archives, the Chemistry Department and the library. Each of these projects involved students and staff creating a map, or "world" as it is known in *Minecraft*, that encouraged explora-tion, interaction and creativity all under the umbrella title of "HullCraft". The projects were undertaken to engage audiences in higher education, specifically the University of Hull, through the use of game-based learning theory using *Minecraft*. Each project was separate but had common themes: student and staff collaboration; student-led learning; the University of Hull.

Each of the projects engaged its audience in different ways. All were well attended and received positive feedback. The engagement with the HHC project was evidenced through the creative builds that the participants did on the server. The MolCraft project with the Chemistry Department was released to a global audience and has been used at science fairs by hundreds of players. The library project has been toured by staff and students alike and is being used by the library staff as a form of virtual induction.

The results, in theory, mean that through creativity and play in *Minecraft*, new ways of engaging audiences with higher education can be developed and achieved. In practice, this means that the University of Hull is gaining a reputation in academia on the use of game-based learning in higher education. This has opened up new audiences who might otherwise not have thought about the university as a study or career path.

The key benefit for readers is that they will be able to see how a *Minecraft* project works from inception to completion, and learn about how creativity and play using *Minecraft* can provide a framework for an engagement strategy within an organisation.

Some things remain unresolved: the effective impact of *Minecraft* on engagement projects, the lifespan that it has as an engagement tool, the longer-term impact that Microsoft's purchase of *Minecraft* will have on licensing costs, and how it can be used in wider access groups.

In Chapter 11, we ask a big question: "What are the implications of Self Organised Learning Environments (SOLE) for creating the coding generation?" The concept of SOLE and "big questions" grew out of research commonly referred to as the "Hole in the Wall experiments", pioneered by Professor Sugata Mitra and his colleagues. These experiments demonstrated that children could learn in groups, with the Internet and without a teacher. This chapter charts the development of a group of children and their teacher in the North East of England, who had very little experience or knowledge of computing, using SOLE to develop a more holistic and deeper understanding of coding through computational thinking. Through reflective first-hand accounts over time, it zooms in more specifically on how a non-computing specialist teacher was an agent for change and how SOLE more specifically was adopted and appropriated as both the object and subject of pupil *and* teacher self-development. Central to our approach is that non-computing specialist teachers can be the agents for change in creating the coding generation. We invite you to consider the notion of the absence of direct teacher intervention and control in how children prepare themselves for the coding generation, as a way to engage in deeper discussions about the pedagogical implications of curriculum change in the Primary Computing Curriculum.

Chapter 12 practically discusses how you can develop projects in school using a Raspberry Pi. The chapter looks at projects that take several hours, days or weeks from concept to realisation, not just one-off lessons – arguing that more meaningful lessons create greater engagement from the children. The chapter then goes on to describe how you can scaffold these projects into meaningful lessons and long-term work with the children. Projects discussed in the chapter include a weather station, a bird box camera and a robotic arm. The chapter discusses how these projects can follow an engineering design process that is not just tethered to the computing curriculum. It is suggested that these projects can help towards children's attainment targets in other areas, and help develop skills such as resilience, resourcefulness, reflection and reciprocity. The chapter ends by looking at different ways in which networking and communication can be achieved with the Raspberry Pi.

Chapter 13 starts by looking at the recent change in the world view of coding. It then discusses how Kuato Studios have developed coding game stories which addressed the issue of students wishing to code using a real programming language. In *Code Warriors*, students see their code at all times, rather than having it encoded into graphical blocks. The game takes a chess-like mechanic, and gives students two different views. One, the code editor view, is where students plan and execute their moves. The other is the arena view, where students watch their, and their opponents', code play out. Depending on how they have coded their robots, they will see their *Code Warriors* move across atmospheric arenas taking out enemy robots, or moving towards their opponents' core to delete it – the ultimate aim of the game. In the arena view, students see an animation of their coded algorithms running in the background, so that the code and its execution are visible at the same time. Like a story, students can "read" their code as it plays out in dramatic narrative fashion! The chapter suggests that designing learning experiences that teach computational thinking, or delivering programmes that teach coding skills to young people, must ensure that participation, collaboration, creativity and sharing are at the heart of the experience.

Finally, Chapter 14 looks at CoderDojo's imaginative vision for the future of coding education. This was established in Cork in Ireland in 2011 to be a low-cost, high-efficacy, scalable methodology to produce collaborative coders who have the highest levels of creative skills in coding languages and are also possessed of economy of expression in those languages. Creative language, economically expressed, is the definition of poetry, and collaboration is the *sine qua non* of CoderDojo; thus it is set up to produce generations of collaborative young coder poets. What has been demonstrated, though, is that within the appropriate learning context, kids can step up and learn even the most complex programming abilities; and that the younger they begin the journey with real programming tools and languages, the faster they progress. It is also vital that iteration and computational tools are embraced, and thus instead of asking why something was done the way it was done, the focus is on how can you do it better and then pass that on. Indeed, it is not uncommon in CoderDojo to see an 11-or 12-year-old girl leading a session of older boys who have come to programming just a year or two later and who find it much more difficult to make progress.

The world needs a coding generation.

Ask the Executive Chairman of Google, Eric Schmidt, why we need to code, and he puts it succinctly: "For most people on Earth, the digital revolution hasn't even started yet. Within the next 10 years, all that will change. Let's get the whole world coding!"[2] And the CEO and co-founder of PayPal, Max Levchin, says that learning code is a must as it "will be a huge booster for your future, no matter what your professional plans may be. Learning to code will also make you extremely cool!"[3]

The authors hope that this that this book will help to inspire the coding generation. We welcome your comments and questions.

email:
steve.humble@ncl.ac.uk

NOTES

1 https://www.fi.edu/understanding-artificial-intelligence
2 http://www.academy-cube.com/coding-programming-necessary-skills-to-survive-in-the-digital-world/
3 https://www.kidstinker.com/why-code

PART I
TEACHING CODING

CHAPTER 1

WHAT IS CODING?

Tim Bell, Caitlin Duncan and Austen Rainer

"CODE" AS A BUZZWORD

The idea of school pupils learning to "code" has been widely talked about in recent years, and the media discussions around this idea have almost redefined what we mean by "coding". We can see increased public interest in coding by simply counting Google searches on the phrase "learn to code", which increased rapidly from 2011 (shown by the black line in Figure 1.1), when industry, governments, and media started talking about this being an important aspect of children's education. Traditionally this skill might have been referred to as "computer programming"; the grey line in the figure shows the corresponding number of searches for "learn to program", which is being searched less often (relatively) over time.

The spikes in the "learn to code" queries (along with smaller spikes from "learn to program") correspond to significant publicity events. January 2012 marked the release of the "Shut down or restart?" report from the Royal Society in the UK, which led to programming becoming a compulsory topic for all pupils in England; it was also when the Code.org organisation was announced and the first Raspberry Pi was being launched. The March 2013 spike corresponds directly to Code.org releasing their viral video "What Most Schools Don't Teach"; and December 2013 was the month of the first "Hour of Code", promoted by Code.org, which included a message from US president Barack Obama – although, interestingly, the verbs used in the president's speech are "make", "design" and "program", not "code".

The word "code" has also started appearing in the names of many organisations that have promoted learning to program publicly. With all this publicity, it isn't surprising that the idea of "coding" has been raised in the public's consciousness. In this chapter we explore what "coding" really is, and why it has had so much attention.

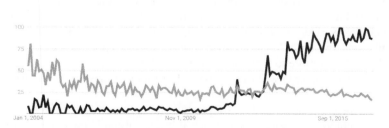

Figure 1.1 Number of Google searches for "learn to code"[1]

> ## REFLECTION ACTIVITY
>
> Is "coding" the appropriate term to use in your context for teaching programming?

As the trends in the Google searches show, "coding" hasn't always been this commonly used to refer to computer programming, and in the world of computing, the term "code" has many meanings, making it highly ambiguous. One of the earliest applications of computers was during World War II for "codebreaking", which is in the context of cryptography being used to hide secret messages. A somewhat broader meaning of coding developed as fundamentals of data representation (binary code) and information theory (including source coding and channel coding) developed to describe how data could be represented digitally. "Coding" can also refer to assigning codes to data to make it faster to enter into a computer, and "code" is used in a similar way to refer to the kinds of metadata that can be attached to information, such as the time and location of a photo. All of these meanings of "code" are about the information, and not the programs that process the information.

As compiled computer programs appeared, a distinction was drawn between "source code" (what a human would write) and "machine code" (a translated version that a computer could run). In the context of programming, traditionally "coding" would refer only to the last stage of the process of programming: translating the design of a program into a programming language (source code). Therefore in the broader context, "coding" is only a small part of developing a computer program.

The more recent use of "coding" to be synonymous with computer programming, while not entirely faithful to the historical use of the term, invokes a sense of mystery and excitement that has clearly served well in getting the public's attention, and this informal use of the term has effectively changed its meaning. The word "code" has so many legitimate definitions that its meaning may catch the reader's attention for a variety of reasons, and this can be useful for promoting the discipline of programming.

Even taking into account a wider meaning of "coding" or "programming", they are not an end in themselves, and are part of a broader discipline around computational thinking and computer science, which is becoming more and more visible in education systems.

In this chapter we focus on the meanings typically intended when "coding" is discussed in the public arena around computing education. In kindergarten, primary, secondary and twelfth grade (for 17- to 19-year-olds), and in formal discussions, the general area in which coding is central is referred to using terms such as "computing", "computer science" and "digital technologies". In several European countries, "informatik" and the term "computational thinking" have also been adopted, to emphasise that there is a lot more to these disciplines than just coding.

To explore how these all connect, we look at these different aspects of "coding":

■ programming: writing source code for software such as an app;
■ computer science: the broader discipline around how to write effective and efficient programs;

■   computational thinking: a term that captures the broader intentions of having "coding" in the curriculum by considering how pupils can use computational concepts for problem solving, even if the solution doesn't involve implementation on a digital device;

■   software engineering: the discipline in industry that enables large software systems to be developed and maintained effectively.

We will see that the skill of "coding" touches on a range of issues, from more technical concepts (including the minimum understanding one needs to do something that could be considered programming) to social practice (such as how to develop software in a team environment, and how to design it in a way that is sympathetic to the needs of the end user). For the remainder of this chapter we will focus on the use of the word "coding" to mean "programming", and will use the two terms interchangeably.

Although the term "coding" has many meanings, there are also several things that it is not. In particular, the term reflects a shift from broad terms such as "ICT", "computer literacy" and "digital literacy" that had evolved in many school curricula to focus on preparing pupils to be *users* of computing technology, rather than enabling them to be makers or developers. A common complaint about traditional computer courses is that they have reinforced the role of a user at the mercy of the system they are using, rather than empowering them to change and create new systems (Bell, 2015).

PROBLEM-SOLVING ON COMPUTERS

The intention of programming is to solve a problem, and although coding is an interesting intellectual exercise in its own right, in an educational or industrial context we are generally concerned about the skills needed to develop software that is useful for people. Coming up with ideas for what might be useful is a creative activity, but it also needs to be built on a foundation that enables us to write programs that are reliable, efficient and usable. You don't need to look far to find software that fails at least one of those criteria! These considerations and more are the ambit of computer science and software engineering, which are discussed later in this chapter.

In the meantime, as a concrete example to illustrate details of what programming is, but still maintaining a wider context, we use an example based on a "Computer Science Unplugged" activity. These are a free collection of activities for engaging pupils with the ideas in computer science without necessarily using programming. The CS Unplugged site[2] includes a range of strategies for teaching coding, even one involving magic tricks based on error correction. For this chapter, we use a follow-up example, which detects whether an error occurs when a barcode (Universal Product Code – UPC) on a product is scanned. In passing, we note that the appearance of the word "code" in "barcode" is yet another use of the term that isn't related to the meaning of coding that we're focusing on!

The final digit on commonly used barcodes is chosen so that all the digits can be combined using a simple formula, and the total will be a multiple of 10 (e.g. 80 or 110, but not 83 or 92). This is done so that if any digit is read or typed incorrectly, or if two of them are transposed, this will usually be detected because the result isn't a multiple of 10. This example exercises many key ideas from programming and computer science, but is fairly short, and is something that pupils may be familiar with from buying products in a shop. It is very important for efficient commerce: without it, barcodes would commonly scan as the wrong product without any warning, and both customers and shops would need to check dockets very carefully for such errors.

The "unplugged" version involves manually checking some barcodes. The following formula works for most commonly used codes (including EAN-8, EAN-13 and UPC-13), but not some eight-digit codes (UPC-E).[3]

To check a barcode, we multiply alternate digits by 1 and 3 respectively, starting at the *right-hand* digit in the code. In the example in Figure 1.2, the rightmost digit is 4, so that contributes 4×1 to the total; the second-to-last digit is 5, so that contributes 5×3, then 2×1, 3×3, 3×1, 8×3, 5×1 and 6×3. Adding these up gives $4 + 15 + 2 + 9 + 3 + 24 + 5 + 18 = 80$. Because 80 is a multiple of 10, this indicates that we can be confident that the digits were read correctly.

If there had been an error while scanning or typing in the number, and suppose the leftmost digit was read as a 5 instead of a 6, the total would be $4 + 15 + 2 + 9 + 3 + 24 + 5 + 15 = 77$. This is not a multiple of 10, and so the scanning would be rejected. If any single digit is incorrect, the sum cannot remain a multiple of 10 and the error will be detected. Another common error when typing digits is to swap two adjacent digits. For example, if the code had the first two digits swapped and was changed to 5683 3254, the total would be 78, and again an error would be detected.

Figures 1.3 and 1.4 show programs to implement this method (or algorithm) in Scratch and Python respectively. These coding languages have been chosen because they are commonly used programming languages in education. The programs have been written to correspond to each other closely, as well as to the algorithm for checking the barcodes described above. There are many different ways the task could have been programmed, and this highlights that there is not a single correct answer to the problem. As long as the program correctly applies the formula to find erroneous barcodes, it is a correct solution, even if not the most efficient solution. In the figures, we have kept the structure of the two programs very similar; one slightly confusing difference is that Scratch numbers the digits in the input from 1, whereas Python numbers from 0, which is why Python uses "position_in_code - 1" for the current digit.

■ **Figure 1.2** A sample barcode to show how errors reading the digits can be detected[4]

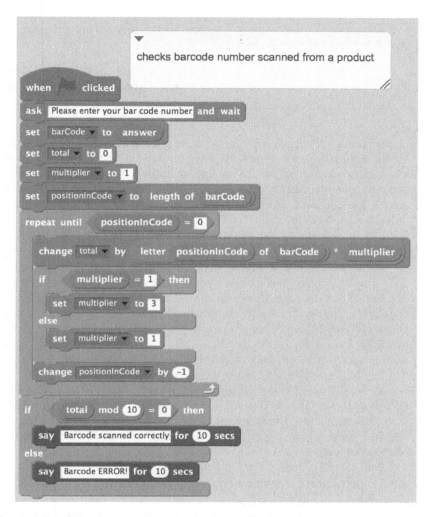

Figure 1.3 A Scratch program to check a barcode number for errors

```
1  # checks barcode number scanned from a product
2  barcode = input("Please enter your barcode number: ")
3  total = 0
4  multiplier = 1
5  position_in_code = len(barcode)
6  while position_in_code != 0:
7      total += int(barcode[position_in_code - 1]) * multiplier
8      if multiplier == 1:
9          multiplier = 3
10     else:
11         multiplier = 1
12     position_in_code -= 1
13 if total % 10 == 0:
14     print("Barcode scanned correctly")
15 else:
16     print("Barcode ERROR!")
```

Figure 1.4 A Python program to check a barcode number for errors

---

REFLECTION ACTIVITY

What are some other ways that the two programs could have been written to solve exactly the same problem (same input and output), but using a different approach?

Putting programming style aside, the main point is that these two programs essentially do the same task in the same way. They both begin with a comment, which is ignored when the program runs, but is very important for someone coming across the code later to enable them to quickly determine what its purpose is. They then prompt the user to enter a barcode, and set up some variables ("total" and "multiplier") to keep track of the running total of the digits. The "position_in_code" variable starts by referencing the last digit in the barcode, and in the loop ("repeat until" and "while" respectively) the "position_in_code" has 1 subtracted from it each time, to gradually work back through the barcode. Each time around the loop, "multiplier" alternates between 1 and 3.

Having two programs for the same task in different languages enables us to clearly distinguish the *algorithm* (the method implemented by the programs) from the program code itself. They both embody the same algorithm, and although they might look completely different, they behave in essentially the same way. Apart from Python numbering the digits from 0, the main other significant differences are that they use opposite loop conditions, with Python continuing while the position is *not* 0 (i.e. at the start of the code), and Scratch repeating until the position *is* 0. The only other semantic differences are minor: Scratch always stores input into "answer", from where it must be retrieved, and Python treats the digits as characters, which are converted to integers using "int()".

This task also illustrates some of the computer science behind the idea of transferring data reliably. The big questions are around how likely the system is to detect data entry errors, such as:

■ Will it detect every time a digit is typed incorrectly?
■ What if two digits are typed incorrectly?
■ Are there any digits that can be swapped without the error being detected?

And then, from a human–computer interaction point of view, the method for typing input isn't ideal (e.g. adding a space might be an obvious thing for the user to do, but the programs currently fail if we type "6583 3254" for the above barcode instead of "65833254"). The output also has issues – just displaying "ERROR!" isn't very helpful, and in a supermarket situation, it's better to have audible feedback since the operator may overlook the message on the screen. There's a lot to know to produce a reliable and usable program! These topics are addressed by the disciplines of computer science and software engineering, which are discussed further later in this chapter.

From this example, we can now illustrate some of the common terms surrounding coding that have a widely used technical meaning in the field of computer science:

■ **Problem**: the task that needs to be done. In this case, checking that the data entry of a number is correct.

■ **Algorithm**: the particular method used to find a solution to the problem. In this case, multiplying alternate digits by 1 and 3, and checking the sum. There can be multiple algorithms for solving the same problem; one simple variation would be to add up the values from left to right instead of right to left; another would be to extract the alternate digits and add them first before multiplying. These algorithms all solve the problem correctly in different ways.

■ **Program**: a particular implementation of an algorithm in a chosen language; both of the programs above do the same thing, even though the details look different.

■ **Coding**: taking the algorithm and converting it to a working program. Although, as we have noted, the term "coding" is also used loosely for the entire process of solving the problem.

PROGRAMMING

Even if we clarify that "coding" means "computer programming", there are still a lot of different ideas about what that might mean. In a school context, programming is typically an individual skill learned by writing small programs, whereas in industry programming is a heavily social skill (it can be thought of as a multi-agent cognitive activity) that involves finding out what kind of program (or modification to a program) is needed by its users, and then working with a team to bring that about (Blackwell, 2002). We might think of a program as being written for a computer, but in a commercial setting it is usually more important to focus on writing it for the next person who will read it, which is why there is such an emphasis on practices such as good design, putting helpful comments in the code, and choosing variable names that are meaningful. This social aspect isn't so obvious in the school setting because the program is typically being written as a one-off assessment, requiring a fairly short program that may well be discarded when it is complete.

In industry, being aware of social context is crucial, as digital technology affects everyone in some way, across different countries, cultures and social classes. A key reason why employers value diversity in software development teams is the variety of perspectives, experiences and skills that diverse team members can bring to the task. Diversity can improve the products and innovations a company produces, and make these technologies more accessible. While programming is a highly technical activity, we can't lose sight of the social context needed for it to be effective.

In general use outside the world of computing, the word "programming" means to create a sequence of activities, such as songs in a radio show or tasks in a building project. However, *computer* programming must take into account the capability of computational devices, which go beyond the ability to follow a fixed sequence of instructions, because computers are able to follow instructions that depend on input from the external world, and can be instructed to execute sub-sequences of a task many times. For example, a program to make a single colour stored on a computer brighter might be only a few lines long, but it can be applied to each of the millions of pixels (megapixels) in a photograph by adding one extra command in the program. Thus, a few lines of "code" can result in millions – or billions – of actions.

If a program is what makes computers perform certain operations, it's useful to know exactly what sorts of operations a computer can do, and especially what it couldn't be expected to do. This leads us to the notion of a "Turing-complete" system, a well-established idea in computer science used to describe any computational device that is equivalent to an imaginary computational system called a "Turing machine". The Turing machine is a mathematical concept proposed by Alan Turing in the 1930s that essentially can simulate *any* computer algorithm using very minimal features. The remarkable thing is that Turing's imaginary machine captured the essence of all modern computers, from the ones he was about to use to crack ciphers during World War II to the latest smartphone, tablet, laptop or microprocessor in a child's toy. In other words, the idea of what a "computer" is has been very well established, and it defines what a computer *program* needs to be able to do.

It turns out that very few elements are required to have a fully functioning programming language; most programming languages have lots of instructions to make programming more convenient, but you can exploit the full power of a Turing machine (i.e. any computer) with just a few types of instructions. Böhm and Jacopini (1966) established that any programming language provides the level of computational power of a Turing-complete system as long as it can store values, read input and write output, and has the three control structures in Table 1.1.

In most languages, a *sequence* is achieved by typing statements in order from first to last (typically one per line); in block-based languages it is done by clipping one instruction under the previous one. *Selection* (sometimes referred to as "branching") is usually an "if . . . else" or "case" statement, and iteration (also called "repetition") is typically a "for", "while", "repeat" or "do" statement.

The elements required for a system to be Turing-complete can be seen in the programs in Figures 1.3 and 1.4 as follows:

■ **Storing values**: In Scratch, the "set" command saves values into variables such as "total" and "multiplier". In Python, the same is achieved with the "=" symbol.

■ **Read input and output:** In the Scratch program, "ask" and "say" are used to read input and deliver output respectively. In the Python program, the "input" and "print" commands are used.

■ **Sequence:** In the Scratch program, execution of commands starts at the top and moves down through the list. Likewise, the Python program starts at line 1 and then carries on to line 2, then 3 and so on.

■ **Selection:** In both Scratch and Python, the "if" command checks a condition and selects an action. For example, at the end of each program the "if" command checks whether the sum is a multiple of 10, and based on that it chooses which message to give the user.

■ **Iteration:** In Scratch, the "repeat until" structure is used to process each digit, stopping when the position in the barcode has hit the left-hand end; in Python, the "while" command serves the same purpose. The same loop would process every digit in a barcode, regardless of whether the user typed in eight digits or 13; for that matter, the program for processing a very long barcode found on shipping packages needn't be any longer than our sample program.

■ **Table 1.1** The essential control structures for any programming language

• **Sequence**	Execute one subprogram (which might be a single instruction) after another.
• **Selection**	Check a true/false condition to choose which of two subprograms (or instructions) to execute.
• **Iteration**	Repeat a subprogram until some true/false condition is met.

The point of thinking about the minimal set of commands needed to write *any* program is that once pupils have mastered just one example of each of these few concepts, in principle they have the tools that give them access to the full power of programming. This helps us to focus on teaching pupils *programming*, rather than seeing coding lessons as teaching all the commands in some particular language such as Scratch, Python, Java, JavaScript or PHP.

Of course, in practice, using particular tools can help to implement a program more easily – JavaScript is useful in web pages, Java is good for building large, reliable systems, and Scratch is popular for teaching beginners. Being aware of this definition of what programming fundamentally means also helps us to identify "coding" systems that aren't Turing-complete. In particular, HTML (HyperText Markup Language) is a code, yet it doesn't (in its normal form) have selection or iteration, and so writing HTML is not computer programming.

In many international curricula, the junior years (typically five to seven years old) tend to focus on just *sequence*, without necessarily offering *iteration* and *selection*. This is often in the context of "turtle graphics", where an avatar (such as the cat in Scratch or ScratchJr, or the Beebot bee) moves around following simple sequences of instructions such as "forward", "left" and "right". This is clearly foundational to computer programming, and is likely a good match for the cognitive level of young pupils, so is appropriate for this age range – but we need to be aware that it's not until pupils have used a system that provides selection and iteration that they have accessed the full power of programming.

If we aren't aware of this, one consequence can be what one teacher called a "spritefest" – pupils focus on choosing sprites and moving them around the screen. This can result in extremely complex and even impressive programs, but if they don't exercise the subtle logic of commands such as "while" or "if . . . else", they aren't becoming familiar with the full power of computer programming. If they miss learning the full power of programming, "coding" becomes an awkward tool just for making simple animations – it has value, but it isn't really programming. Similarly, learning HTML is good background to programming, but no matter how skilled a pupil is with HTML, they won't have had the opportunity to explore the real power – and demands – of programming.

A positive consequence of this view of programming is that learning these key ideas in just one or two languages provides pupils with a solid underpinning should they need to adapt to a new language that perhaps hasn't even been invented yet. If we see ourselves as teaching programming, rather than a particular language such as Java or Python, the pupils' learning is far more future-proof. Learning a few different languages provides them with a variety of experiences, and is likely to help them to see what is in common to the activity of programming, and what is just a feature of a particular language.

From the example above, we can now articulate the steps needed to develop a program for a given problem. These are typically broken down into several phases as follows:

■ **Analysis:** determining what the problem is, e.g. with the barcodes, we need to decide what the input will be and how the output should be presented.

■ **Programming/design:** this formulates the algorithm (process) that is needed to come to the solution, with enough precision that it is clear how it should be done, e.g. the process for adding up the multiplied values in the barcodes.

■ **Coding:** this involves converting the design to a computer language, e.g. producing the "code" shown in Figures 1.3 and 1.4.

■ **Testing:** determining if the program does what is required. There are many aspects to this: from making sure the program is technically correct, e.g. checking that all correct barcodes are accepted and vice versa, to making sure it's easy to use, e.g. whether the interface confuses the user; and, of course, determining whether it's even what the user required.

■ **Debugging:** if the program fails a test, a lot of skill can be required to track down where it's incorrect – this could range from something as simple as forgetting to display the result, to a very subtle error that occurs with only certain inputs.

In an educational context, typically all of the above steps are regarded as a part of programming, whereas in a commercial setting the whole process might be referred to more broadly as "software engineering", with programming being just a relatively small component. Thus, the definition of what "programming" is depends a lot on the context: a six-year-old who has instructed an image of a cat to move across the screen could be congratulated for being a "programmer" in the same way they might be considered a "musician" if they perform a simple tune using only a few notes. But to truly be a programmer, the programmer needs at least to have the full power of a Turing-complete system in their toolkit, and beyond that they need additional skills around analysis, design, testing and debugging to ensure that their program fully meets the needs of its users.

The remarkable thing about coding is that we are effectively creating something out of nothing. A programmer can start with a blank screen and craft something completely new, which could be a game, an interactive website, an educational system, a social media app or a tool to help other programmers. This is one thing that makes programming digital systems different from building things in the physical world: the raw resources in our digital world are essentially digits, which represent both data and programs. These can be created, manipulated and shared at very little cost, and the same device can be used for many different purposes, which means that programming as an activity is fundamentally different to the techniques used for creating physical artefacts, and therefore requires different pedagogies and contexts to enable pupils to learn it.

COMPUTER SCIENCE

The field of "computer science" is often viewed as being primarily about programming. However, this is not the case: Mike Fellows has pointed out that computer science is as much about programming and computers as astronomy is about telescopes.[5]

Programming is essential to setting the ideas of computer science in motion, but computer science tells us how to write effective programs by providing underpinning knowledge such as designing efficient algorithms, usable interfaces, reliable and secure systems, efficiently networked programs, and programs that make intelligent decisions. You don't even need a computer to be doing computer science – a point demonstrated in history, as programs existed before computers did, such as Ada Lovelace's programs for Babbage's "analytical engine", and Alan Turing's exploration of computation through what became known as the Turing machine.

In the barcode "program", we began with the idea that adding up the digits could help us to determine whether the data had been entered accurately. This is a concept that appears in many forms in computer science, and the general principle of a "check digit" can be generalised to a "checksum" or "hash total", which can be used to check whether an entire file has been downloaded correctly, or track down and correct faulty storage devices in a large computer installation. A pupil who is aware of the range of techniques available in computer science is in a much better position to design and implement fast, reliable and efficient systems.

A good example of computer science concepts at work can be seen in action on the world's most popular website: the Google search engine. The main interface on this is just one text box and a search button. Writing a program that searches a small amount of data with a simple interface like that isn't very complex from a programming point of view. But to do it in a way that it searches billions of documents in a fraction of a second so that the user doesn't get frustrated waiting for it, and can handle such requests from all over the world, keeping the searches private to the user, while often predicting what the user will search for as they type, requires many aspects of the broader disciplines of computer science and software engineering.

For school pupils, understanding all of these concepts in depth is beyond what can reasonably be put into a curriculum. Being aware of these ideas is very important, though, and initiatives such as CS Unplugged make it possible for them to get first-hand experience with them without even having to learn to program – or even to use a computer.

The field of computer science doesn't just provide ideas for writing better programs: it also warns about programs that can't be written in any effective way. For example, the optimal solution for some problems – such as timetabling, finding optimal delivery routes and minimising the number of vehicles needed to deliver a range of goods – can be found only by effectively trying out every possible solution and choosing the best one. In many cases this isn't feasible, even on the fastest computer, and it's important to know that one shouldn't attempt to write a program like this in the first place, as one might eventually find out – after implementing it – that it takes far too long to solve the problem. Other problems can be solved much more easily than might be expected; again, it's important to know the techniques for solving these, otherwise time might be spent implementing an ineffective solution that wastes time, or a solution might not even be attempted because it doesn't sound possible.

Thus, it's important that programming isn't taught as an isolated skill. As a programmer develops the ability to create complex programs, they also need to develop an awareness of the tools and techniques available in computer science and software engineering, to design effective programs.

REFLECTION ACTIVITY

By teaching coding in schools, what are we preparing pupils for?

Should teaching of coding be linked with other subjects?

COMPUTATIONAL THINKING

One of the core motivators for teaching pupils to code is the development of computational thinking (CT) skills that it supports. There is concern that teaching all pupils to code may not be worthwhile, because this work may become automated or outsourced, and so not be a required skill in the future; or because coding will become a "white collar sweatshop" type of job. History, however, does not support this concern, as any automation of programming tasks has only seen an increase in demand for expertise. More importantly, the goal of teaching children to code is not to simply produce coders, or to ensure they all go on to be computer scientists or software engineers, although it is hoped it will increase enrolments in these degrees. Rather, the goal is to equip children with the CT skills required to understand computing technology, use it effectively and be informed consumers and citizens in our increasingly digital world. Having a complete and deep knowledge of computer science and software engineering concepts is not necessary – rather, it is important to have enough understanding of these to be aware of how these might impact the world around us. The computational thinking skills and knowledge of technology that pupils can gain are highly valuable on their own.

Computational thinking can loosely be described as a problem-solving approach based on core concepts of computer science, and programming is an important skill to use in the teaching of CT. Coding can be thought of as the technique that brings CT to life. It turns a theoretical computational solution for a problem into a program, and running a program is a good method for testing whether your CT ideas and process are right.

The phrase "computational thinking" was coined by Seymour Papert in his 1980 book *Mindstorms: Children, Computers, and Powerful Ideas*, and mentioned again in 1996, but was not described or defined. The CT concept was not widely used until 2006, when the concept was reintroduced to the computing community by Jeannette Wing in her article "Computational thinking" (Wing, 2006). She identified it as a "fundamental skill . . . something every human must know to function in modern society", and has since referred to it as the "new literacy of the 21st century" (Wing, 2010). The definition was refined in 2008 to: "Computational thinking is taking an approach to solving problems, designing systems and understanding human behavior that draws on concepts fundamental to computing" (Wing, 2008).

Since then, the idea has been widely adopted by the computing education community (Grover and Pea, 2013), and being a computational thinker is seen by many groups of educators, the computing industry and politicians as highly desirable for the next generation (Voogt et al., 2015).

The concept of computational thinking has evolved since 2008, and now many definitions have been published, covering a wide range of target audiences, contexts and uses for different age groups. In this chapter, we will make use of those relating to pre-tertiary education only. There is a great deal of overlap between most definitions, but there are still areas where they do not agree.

Two of the most prominent definitions for pre-tertiary education have been published by the Computing at Schools (CAS) community, in 2014, as part of their "Barefoot Computing" resources,[6] and by the Computer Science Teachers Association (CSTA) in 2011.[7] They agree that at its core CT is a problem-solving skill set, although the definitions differ slightly in the precise descriptions of the skills. In Table 1.2 we have grouped what we see as the core skills from CAS and the CSTA, and to illustrate these we have used examples from the barcode example from earlier in this chapter. The skill definitions are paraphrased from the CAS and CSTA definitions.

There are many elements of coding that require CT skills to solve, and learning to program, whether on a computer or using "unplugged" methods, can be an extremely effective and engaging way to develop these skills. Many pupils begin with creating simple

▓ Table 1.2 Computational thinking skills

Skill	Definition	Barcode example
Logic and analysis	Logic is the study of reasoning. The purpose of logic is to help us try to make sense of things. It helps us establish and check facts.	Logic is required to follow the program and understand why it works. Reasoning is also used to predict what will happen when correct or incorrect barcodes are checked. At the lowest level, Boolean logic is used to determine whether the checksum is correct.
Algorithms and algorithmic thinking	An algorithm is a sequence of instructions, or set of rules, for performing a task. Algorithmic thinking allows us to formulate instructions that a computer can use to solve a problem.	Understanding and/or creating the sequence of instructions that validate the barcode using the formula. There are different algorithms that can be used for this same problem, even within the constraints of the particular formula.
Decomposition	Decomposition is the process of breaking a problem or system down into smaller, more manageable parts. It helps us solve complex problems, as each part can be solved separately and built up to a full solution, without needing to consider the entire problem at once.	Breaking the overall problem of "find the errors in the barcode" into smaller parts, such as decode the stripes into numbers, multiply and add these numbers, check the numbers, give error messages if there is a mistake or problem. Each of these can be broken down further: for example, decoding the stripes will involve working out the width of each stripe and converting groups of stripes to a digit.
Patterns and generalisation	Using patterns means spotting similarities and common differences. By identifying patterns we can make predictions, create rules and solve more general problems. This is called generalisation.	Identifying typical errors in barcodes, identifying repetition and removing this (for example, multiplying alternate values by 1 and 3); and generalising the concept of using an algorithm to validate data.
Abstraction	Abstraction is simplifying things by identifying and discarding unnecessary details. It allows us to manage complexity. Data can be represented through abstractions (digits represent text, images, sound etc.). Simulations provide an abstraction of real situations.	Understanding that the stripes represent different numbers, and the numbers themselves represent a product in a database. Also, the program multiplies alternate digits by 3, but other checksums use different systems (for example, credit card numbers are checked by multiplying alternate digits by 2, and ISBN-10 numbers multiply each digit by a different value), so the abstract principle is to use different multipliers for digits.
Evaluation	Evaluation is concerned with making judgements, in an objective and systematic way, and evaluating possible solutions to a problem. The goal of it is to achieve the most efficient and effective solution using the resources available.	Asking and answering questions such as: will this find all possible errors? How long does it take? Is it efficient enough for a small machine to perform this quickly?

programs or sets of instructions that incorporate sequencing only, but even at this stage they will learning valuable CT skills. For example, they can use a grid on the ground and create a series of instructions, like "Forward, Forward, Turn left, Forward", that can be given to move a toy across the grid. Though these programs seem very simple, children must use their logic skills to decompose each problem into steps, understand these steps and figure out where the toy will be after each instruction is carried out. Once they have tested their program, they must debug any problems it has by tracing through the instructions and thinking logically about where something went wrong. There will be alternative algorithms to get to the same location, and these can be evaluated and compared.

As pupils progress, and work on coding more complex tasks, they continue to practise these skills and introduce more to their problem-solving process, including the following:

- ▦   They must *decompose* the problems they are solving. To create a program to perform a task, they need to break it down into every individual step it must perform so they can identify the instructions they need to give to the computer. They will also use their *logic* skills to identify what these steps must be, and what order they need to be performed in.

- ▦   They learn about *algorithms*, how to implement these in code, and how to evaluate them. For almost any problem you want to solve with programming, there will be many different algorithms and instructions you could use which would solve the problem. Therefore you need to be able to understand and evaluate different algorithms for the same task, and make a judgement on the best one to use.

- ▦   They learn to *recognise patterns* in their programs. If they are using the same piece of code, or the same pattern of code (e.g. iterating over a set of data and modifying it) multiple times throughout a program, they can create modules that take these pieces of code and *generalise* them so they can be used to solve a range of similar problems.

- ▦   If they are tackling large and complex problems, they will need to practise *abstraction* to help them effectively create their programs. Abstraction is used to hide complexity. If you are coding part of a large project, it is difficult and unnecessary to try to hold in your head how every segment of code works all at once. We use abstraction to hide this unnecessary information so we can focus on the particular task at hand.

- ▦   No matter what programming task someone is working on, they will almost certainly be working with some form of data. Working with different types of data, and different data structures, is a necessary part of programming, and teaches valuable skills about the nature of information and representing it, particularly taking advantages of *patterns* in the data (such as what type of data it is).

- ▦   Through all this, they will be performing large amounts of *debugging*. Debugging is a technique that coders must practise from day one. From syntax errors to logic problems, there are inevitably bugs in code that must be located and resolved. Debugging is something any programmer will have to spend time on whenever they write a new program or modify an existing one. They must evaluate the program to determine whether there are bugs: does it do what it is meant to do? Should it be accomplishing this faster? Using logical thinking, the coder can step through the program and recognise what it is doing at each step, determining whether this is the logical thing to do, and whether it is algorithmically correct. As people become more practised at this, they can begin to identify patterns that often lead to bugs, or are common errors that are made.

Although programming is an excellent tool for scaffolding the development of CT skills, it is unlikely to work if it is taught without a specific focus on these skills. It is very easy for pupils (and educators) to slip into using "copy and paste" coding exercises only, where pupils will be following instructions, rather than working through a problem-solving process. Without a focus on these skills, it is also common for pupils to default to "spritefest"-style programming that doesn't demand good problem-solving skills.

SOFTWARE ENGINEERING

Much of this chapter has talked about the nature of coding – of what coding is. In this section, we briefly consider the contribution of coding outside of, or beyond, the classroom. Software engineering is concerned with developing software, i.e. one or more programs, to satisfy real-world problems such as controlling traffic flow across a city, automating detection of objects in a photograph, or social gaming over the internet using augmented reality. In very simple terms, software engineering is scaled-up coding. This scaling is not just about producing more code, or larger programs, but about ensuring software possesses a range of other attributes, such as reliability and meeting users' needs. We discuss these attributes later in this section of the chapter.

To illustrate the relationship of coding to software engineering, we extend our earlier example of barcode scanning. Earlier in this chapter, we discussed two implementations of an algorithm to detect errors in a barcode for a supermarket product. Figure 1.5 presents a very simple process that occurs in a supermarket. A customer selects a product [1] and takes it to the self-checkout for it to be scanned [2]. In that earlier section, we discussed how the barcode scanner would detect a valid barcode. In this context, "valid" means the barcode has the correct number of digits and they have been recognised correctly. Once the scanner has detected a valid barcode, it then communicates with a server [4], over a network [3], to get information on the product that is associated with that barcode, such as its description and price. The server comprises a *stack* of programs, from an operating system that all programs run on, through to a database. Each of these programs satisfies a different problem or problems (see the definitions in Table 1.2); each will contain implementations of many algorithms (such as search algorithms) and data structures (such as searchable lists of products); and each will communicate with the other programs.

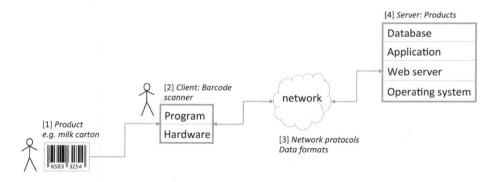

■ **Figure 1.5** Simple representation of the broader process around scanning a barcode at a supermarket checkout

■ **Table 1.3** Attributes that should be addressed when building a software system

Attribute	Brief description
• Security	A customer could potentially seek to use false barcodes to fool the system; or a third party could seek to access the database to change the data, or could attempt a denial-of-service attack to prevent product scanning.
• Performance	The system needs to be responsive, providing timely information at various points in the system, e.g. if each product took ten seconds to scan, no one would want to use the system and it would take too long to check a basket of products.
• Reliability	The system should be sufficiently reliable to either not fail, or recover quickly from failure, e.g. if a barcode scanner breaks, or there are errors in transmitting data across the network.
• Concurrency	The system should be able to handle thousands of products being scanned in a short period, by multiple customers, possibly across multiple supermarkets.
• Currency of information	The system should provide up-to-date information, e.g. a price for a product might be updated centrally, and all checkouts should use the new price.
• Maintainability	The design and implementation should allow for maintenance work (e.g. introducing replacement scanners), changes to functionality (e.g. changing the system to accommodate a new tax law requirement) and recovery after system failures.
• Extensibility	The system should support the addition of new features, e.g. the introduction of self-service checkouts, or the use of barcode scanners by customers as they move through the supermarket.
• Usability	The system should be usable and useful for humans, e.g. the barcode scanner should be easy to use and deal with typical errors that people make; the database should be easy for an appropriate administrator to access.
• Exception handling	The system should be capable of handling exceptions, e.g. damaged barcodes.

For the network, there is a range of protocols for network communication, and these protocols provide standards for communicating data between programs. Each of these programs will be written using the three fundamental constructs in programming: sequence, selection and iteration. For example, a sequence of instructions would detect a barcode and then send information to the server; selection could be checking for an entry in the database for the respective barcode; and repetition would be used to continue to scan with the reader until a barcode is detected.

In some situations, the barcode may be valid but there may not be a matching entry in the database, perhaps because the database was not updated correctly. In other situations, a product may only be purchased by adults – the barcode scanner will then need to alert the customer as well as the supermarket staff. Software engineering is concerned with ensuring that a software system, such as that illustrated in Figure 1.5, should address a range of attributes, summarised in Table 1.3.

The table indicates that, in software engineering, coding is not just about implementing an algorithm, but about integrating multiple algorithms (and data structures) and implementing each algorithm in a way that addresses the attributes in the table. Indeed, the purpose of some algorithms is primarily, or even solely, concerned with addressing the attributes, e.g. error detection.

Software engineering comprises a mix of disciplines. *Software Engineering 2014: Curriculum Guidelines for Undergraduate Degree Programs in Software Engineering* (IEEE/ACM, 2015) is an international document developed by experts who have considered the areas of expertise needed to do a good job of software engineering. It recognises a number of reference disciplines for software engineering, including computing; mathematics and statistics; engineering; psychology and social science; and management science. As software engineering has matured, so it has taken on increasingly large and complex problems, thus requiring increasingly large and complex software engineering tools and processes. Software is now developed by globally distributed teams; it may comprise a "mash-up" of third-party software services; the software itself may be distributed over a global network. The software development processes and tools may include distributed control of the source code, continuous integration of software components, continuous automatic building of the software, deployment of the software, issue and bug (defect) tracking, and collection of usage statistics. Each of the items listed above hints at how software engineering is so much more than "just" coding.

A software engineer may be understood as a professional coder who has responsibilities much greater than just producing code. A software engineer works in a large social system of other software engineers and other stakeholders, and their primary role is to communicate with these engineers and stakeholders in order to produce software (programs) that satisfies the needs of those engineers and stakeholders. Code is one artefact, and coding is one process, in the execution of that primary role.

REFLECTION ACTIVITY

Can we, and should we, teach *software engineering* in the school environment?

What aspects of software engineering can we, and should we, teach in a school environment?

CONCLUSION

The term "coding" has many meanings, but even when we restrict ourselves to the widely used sense of "programming" it has a range of implications depending on the context it is being used in, from solving small logic problems to developing large software systems. "Coding" invokes all the ideas discussed in this chapter, even if technically it is really just a tiny part of any of the contexts mentioned.

To adapt George Bernard Shaw's observation about England and America, we could even consider computer science and software engineering to be two disciplines separated by the common language (programming); it is central to both, but is approached in subtly different ways in each. When viewed properly, these disciplines are strongly intertwined, but a practitioner immersed in the needs of one or the other of them may well be seen as not paying attention to the aspects of importance to the other, and it is challenging for an educator to maintain a broad view for their pupils while focusing on specific techniques and skills.

The public's view of "coding" may be that it is a highly technical subject that is an individual pursuit, but through the points raised in this chapter we hope that it can be recognised as being a very *social* pursuit. Programmers are communicating with the end user by building something they will use, and with other programmers who must make sense of the program that has been written. Furthermore, the closely allied areas of computational thinking and computer science have relevance even if we don't use computers, again emphasising that it isn't completely about the machine, but about important skills for thinking and participating in a digital society.

Despite its ambiguity, "coding" is a useful word for summing up the many ideas mentioned in this chapter in one word, and in education it unpacks to a wealth of ideas, skills and issues that can be explored.

REFLECTION ACTIVITY

What could be the negative effects of teaching "coding" to all school pupils, and how do we mitigate them?

Should we teach programming so that pupils can do computer science, or computer science so that pupils can do programming?

Should we teach programming so that pupils can progress to software engineering, or so that pupils can develop their computational thinking?

If we don't need computers to do computer science, do we need computers to develop computational thinking?

NOTES

1 https://www.google.com/trends/explore#q=%22learn%20to%20code%22
2 csunplugged.org
3 UPC-E is mainly used in North America, and won't work for this example; you can tell a UPC-E code because it has six digits in the middle, with a single digit at each end. More details about barcode formulas are available at http://www.gs1.org/how-calculate-check-digit-manually
4 From https://upload.wikimedia.org/wikipedia/commons/thumb/2/26/Barcode_EAN8.svg/800px-Barcode_EAN8.svg.png [CC licence]
5 http://csfieldguide.org.nz/en/chapters/introduction.html
6 http://barefootcas.org.uk/barefoot-primary-computing-resources/concepts/computational-thinking/
7 http://www.csteachers.org/

REFERENCES

Bell, T. (2015). Surprising computer science. In A. Brodnik & J. Vahrenhold (Eds), *8th International Conference on Informatics in Schools: Situation, Evolution, and Perspective* (pp. 1–11). New York: Springer.

Blackwell, A. (2002). What is programming? In *14th Workshop of the Psychology of Programming Interest Group*, 204–218.

Böhm, C. and Jacopini, G. (1966). Flow diagrams, Turing machines and languages with only two formation rules. *Communications of the ACM,* 9(5), 366–371.

Grover, S. and Pea, R. (2013). Computational thinking in K-12: A review of the state of the field. *Educational Researcher*, 42(1). 38–43.

IEEE/ACM. (2015). *Software Engineering 2014: Curriculum Guidelines for Undergraduate Degree Programs in Software Engineering – A Volume of the Computing Curricula Series*, 23 February. Accessed from: http://www.acm.org/education/se2014.pdf.

Voogt, J., Fisser, P., Good, J., Mishra, P. and Yadav, A. (2015). Computational thinking in compulsory education: Towards an agenda for research and practice. *Education and Information Technologies*, 20(4), 715–728.

Wing, J.M. (2006). Computational thinking. *Communications of the ACM*, 49(3), 33–35.

Wing, J.M. (2008). Computational thinking and thinking about computing. *Philosophical Transactions of the Royal Society A: Mathematical, Physical and Engineering Sciences*, 366(1881), 3717–3725.

Wing, J.M. (2010). Computational thinking: What and why? Accessed from: https://www.cs.cmu.edu/~CompThink/resources/TheLinkWing.pdf.

CHAPTER 2

TEACHING COMPUTATIONAL THINKING

Caroline Walker and Alan Gleaves

INTRODUCTION

Computational Thinking (CT) has been called the most important skill that any child in the twenty-first century could acquire, with the same life skill, personal development, economic prospects, and even well-being and prosperity status as reading, writing and arithmetic (Wing, 2006; CSTA, 2013). As a result of the all-pervasive nature of technology in everyday life, along with the ubiquity of computers and mobile devices, the 'computational thinking movement' has infiltrated all ages and sectors of education in the industrialised world (Yadav et al., 2011). Globally, many national curricula have been reformed and rewritten over the last five years, with Computational Thinking playing an increasingly major role – as an organising principle across many other disciplines and subjects; as a skill to inform thinking and problem solving; as a discipline in ways of planning, working and organising learning; and, not least, as an academic subject in its own right (Grover and Pea, 2013).

But standing behind this are educational questions and issues that are not yet clear, but that need a much closer look in order for teachers, schools, universities and educators who are teaching the new curriculum to understand what claims are being made for CT and whether these are realistic or evidence-based. Also, it is critical that teachers, schools and teacher educators alike understand the historical, conceptual and practical basis of CT when it is taught.

COMPUTATIONAL THINKING: A BRIEF HISTORY

It has been over a decade since Jeannette Wing, a Professor of Computer Science in, and the Head of, the Computer Science Department at Carnegie Mellon University in Pittsburgh in the US, wrote a viewpoint article entitled 'Computational Thinking', published in the *Communications of the Association for Computing Machinery* (Wing, 2006), in which she argued that Computational Thinking represented a 'universally applicable attitude and skill set that everyone, not just computer scientists, would be eager to learn and to use' (2006: 33). Wing argued that computational methods and models would give people the courage and capability to solve problems and design systems that no one person would be capable of tackling alone. She argued this on the basis of three main assumptions about the world:

- that computing machines now occupy such an essential and embedded place in the world that we need to think more carefully than ever about questions such as what humans can do better than computers and what computers can do better than humans;
- that the extent of convergence of human computation and artificial intelligence is such that we need to better understand what is computable and what is necessary and desirable to be computed; and
- that problems in the world are increasingly complex and require specific forms of thinking (Computational Thinking) to reformulate them into soluble problems.

DEFINING AND UNDERSTANDING COMPUTATIONAL THINKING

In other words, Computational Thinking is at its core about three concepts, what we could call the 'three As':

- *audacity* – the willingness to think about things in different ways and experiment;
- *abstraction* – the ability to develop mental pictures and structures to represent things in different ways; and
- *automation* – the act of a using processes and techniques to solve practical problems in diverse circumstances and contexts.

In other words, Computational Thinking can be summed up diagrammatically using some of the original terminology that Jeannette Wing used, as shown in Figure 2.1.

These three ideas are critically important in developing ideas to teach about and learn Computational Thinking, and we will develop them again and again as we go through this chapter.

Well, as we said before, it's now been over a decade since Wing published her paper in that professional journal, and it turns out to have something of a seminal paper – indeed, a game changer in the field of computing, and in the whole discipline of education, across countries, cultures and curricula. Why? And what does this mean for teachers who are tasked with teaching Computational Thinking?

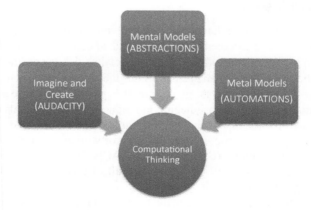

■ **Figure 2.1** Terminology of Computational Thinking

COMPUTATIONAL THINKING: 11 YEARS ON

In an article that Wing published in the Microsoft Research Blog in March 2016, she said the following:

> 'Not in my lifetime.'
> That's what I said when I was asked whether we would ever see computer science taught in K-12 [16–18 year old students in the UK]. It was 2009, and I was addressing a gathering of attendees to a workshop on computational thinking convened by the National Academies. I'm happy to say that I was wrong.

Wing went on to say:

> Think back to 2005. Since the dot-com bust, there had been a steep and steady decline in undergraduate enrolments in computer science, with no end in sight. The computer science community was wringing its hands, worried about the survival of their departments on campuses. Unlike many of my colleagues, I saw a different, much rosier future for computer science. I saw that computing was going to be everywhere.
> I argued that the use of computational concepts, methods and tools would transform the very conduct of every discipline, profession and sector. Someone with the ability to use computation effectively would have an edge over someone without. So, I saw a great opportunity for the computer science community to teach future generations how computer scientists think. Hence 'computational thinking.'
> I must admit, I am surprised and gratified by how much progress we have made in achieving this vision:
> Computational thinking will be a fundamental skill used by everyone in the world by the middle of the twenty-first century. By fundamental, I mean as fundamental as reading, writing and arithmetic.
>
> (Wing, 2016)

THE IMPACT OF COMPUTATIONAL THINKING ON EDUCATION AND EMPLOYMENT

Since then, Wing's ideas have indeed been revolutionary, but not necessarily for the reasons that even she had foreseen. First, the financial crisis of 2007–2008, also known as the 'global financial crisis' and the '2008 financial crisis', is considered by many economists to have been the worst financial crisis since the Great Depression of the 1930s. As a result, and over the next five years, governments began to invest in developing workforces for economic advantage and privileging individuals with high levels of transferable skill and knowledge. It's true to say that the push for all pupils to learn computer science in general therefore also comes from market demand for workers skilled in computing, and not just information technology (CSTA, 2013; NAACE, 2013). Car manufacture, manufacturing engineering, pharmaceutics and genetics: all of them are requiring increasing levels of computing expertise in their workforce.

But such changes have been the function of individuals' experiences as well: after the crash, millions of people the world over reconsidered their life prospects, their skills and employability and took the opportunity that the devastation of the crash had imposed upon them to retrain, enter education and take advantage of programmes conferring high-level skills in computing and programming. And most of all, educational institutions across the world initiated a series of major curriculum reforms that not only reflected Wing's initial ideas about the difficulty of being prepared to solve increasingly complex problems, but also reflected the imperatives that had been exposed by the crash – economic stability, development and advantage, and individuals' preparedness, flexibility and adaptability.

Of course, since 2006, we have also seen a huge increase – some would say a superfluity – in the amount of data that we generate as a global society. Social networking, evidence-based practice, the increasing use of analytics, and the outputs of computation itself: all have created very significant data sets that have the capacity to be used to understand and solve problems – but, critically, only if the problems can be understood and the utility of the solution can be realised.

It is this last sentence that lies at the heart of Computational Thinking. And it is this idea, of questioning ideas *behind* processes and practices, which in turn stands *behind* the coverage of Computational Thinking in the English National Curriculum.

COMPUTATIONAL THINKING IN THE NATIONAL CURRICULUM

In September 2014, ICT (Information and Communications Technology) was replaced by Computing as a key subject within the English National Curriculum at all key stages (Department for Education, 2013). The British Computer Society identified three distinct strands within computing, each of which is complementary to the others:

■ Computer Science (CS) – the scientific and practical study of computation: what can be computed, how to compute it, and how computation may be applied to the solution of problems;

■ Information Technology (IT) – how computers and telecommunications equipment work, and how they may be applied to the storage, retrieval, transmission and manipulation of data; and

■ Digital Literacy (DL) – the ability to effectively, responsibly, safely and critically navigate, evaluate and create digital artefacts using a range of digital technologies.

Computational Thinking is core to the programme of study across all key stages. In the National Curriculum, it is defined as the process of recognising aspects of computation in the world that surrounds us, and applying tools and techniques from computing to understand and reason about both natural and artificial systems and processes. As such, the National Curriculum makes it clear that Computational Thinking not only is able to provide a powerful framework for studying computing, but also has wide application beyond computing itself: for both the development and betterment of society, for personal development and for becoming an informed citizen who is able to contribute to the world in diverse ways. It states that:

> A high quality computing education equips pupils to use Computational Thinking and creativity to understand and change the world.
>
> (Department for Education, 2013)

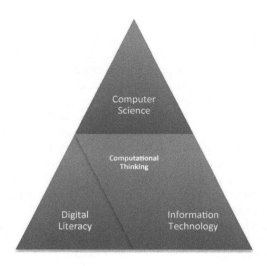

■ **Figure 2.2** Computational Thinking

THE STRUCTURE OF THE COMPUTATIONAL THINKING CURRICULUM

The National Curriculum approach to Computational Thinking is based on the notion of looking at a problem in such a way that a computer can help us to solve it. In other words, and using the terms that we introduced earlier, it is:

■ using *audacity* (being imaginative and creative) to
■ develop *abstractions* (models and representations) to
■ create *automations* (use practical tools to solve problems).

However, there is a great deal of vocabulary and terminology that is associated with each of these ideas within the National Curriculum: for example, the following words crop up throughout it at various key stages, and each one can be confusing for teachers teaching Computational Thinking for the first time, often because of existing beliefs about particular words and the way that they are used in other subjects, and also sometimes because of the ways that words are used in films and other popular media.

In addition, it is very important for teachers to begin to understand whether and how each of these areas can be taught using software, computers, hardware and equipment. Also, of course, it is critical for teachers to understand how and where these three themes fit into the National Curriculum, and to ask whether they should be regarded as *concepts* to be taught, *approaches* to be taken, *skills* to develop or *processes* to be learned. Perhaps the best way to think about how the Computational Thinking coverage links together is to examine the actual curriculum content itself and the words and ideas that are used, as shown in Table 2.2.

A good source of materials to help illustrate links between the Conceptual-basis and the Approach-led elements of Computational Thinking can be found in the Barefoot Computing project (Barefoot Computing, 2013).

Table 2.1 Computational Thinking and the National Curriculum[1]

Key Stage in the National Curriculum	Computational Thinking-related statement
• **EYFS**	Understanding order, doing tasks and sorting objects
• **KS1**	Understand what algorithms are, how they are implemented as programs on digital devices, and that programs execute by following precise and unambiguous instructions
• **KS2**	Solve problems by decomposing them into smaller parts
• **KS2**	Use logical reasoning to explain how some simple algorithms work and to detect and correct errors in algorithms and programs
• **KS3**	Design, use and evaluate computational abstractions that model the state and behaviour of real-world problems and physical systems
• **KS3**	Understand several key algorithms that reflect computational thinking
• **KS3**	Use two or more programming languages, at least one of which is textual, to solve a variety of computational problems
• **KS4**	Develop and apply their analytic, problem-solving, design and computational thinking skills

Table 2.2 Vocabulary in the National Curriculum[2]

Term	What it is	Examples of what it isn't
• Algorithm	A precise method for solving a given problem. Programs *contain* algorithms. But algorithms exist all around us. For example, a *recipe* is an algorithm.	A program; something that is only done with a computer.
• Decomposition	The process of breaking a problem or system down into its component parts. In a recipe, that might be a flat surface to cook on, an oven to cook the food, a set of plates to serve the food on, and so on.	A list of everything that you will use in a task: a shopping list of ingredients for a pizza, for example.
• Logic	A set of principles or statements that guide a device in performing a particular task. For example, in cooking a pizza, logic would suggest turning on the oven *before* cooking the pizza.	Always doing things in the same way: for example, laying the table before you start to cook the pizza.

(continued)

▦ **Table 2.2** *(continued)*

Term	*What it* is	*Examples of what it* isn't
● Code	A generic term for any set of statements written in a programming language. These might equate to the individual numbered recipe steps in making the pizza.	A program. Code consists of the building blocks that make up a program.
● Program	A series of instructions that are put in order to make a computer perform an operation. This could be likened to the whole of the recipe to make a pizza.	A general recipe to cover *all* pizzas; each program is written to perform a particular task and so when the task or the circumstances have changed, the program must be changed. This might mean changing a part of the program (a line of *code*).
● Programming	The process of writing programs; using the principles of *algorithms*, *logic* and *decomposition* for example, to write programs for particular contexts and to solve particular problems.	Easy! Programming doesn't require a special sort of brain (contrary to the way that it is often presented in films and books!), but it *does* require staying power, tenacity, resilience and, above all, *practice*.
● Programming language	A formal and structured computer language, with its own structure, rules, grammar, syntax, words etc, that can be used to express algorithms, write code and construct programs.	Not necessarily similar to everyday spoken language; doesn't use familiar words in the same, or even similar ways.

THINKING ABOUT THE ORDER IN WHICH YOU WILL TEACH CONCEPTS AND IDEAS

The most important questions to consider when teaching Computational Thinking are what computer science concepts should be taught when, and how? Of course, the National Curriculum is central to answering this question, because it suggests that the order in which to teach it is based on the idea of building blocks that are assembled gradually into a more complex conceptual understanding of what is happening. A conceptual map might look like the one shown in Figure 2.3:

▦ **Figure 2.3** Key stage building blocks

But, of course, such a structure doesn't help teachers to know exactly where to start, or what the building blocks of progression in Computational Thinking should actually look like. Put simply, and using the language of Computational Thinking itself: how should teachers 'decompose' the Computational Thinking curriculum? To answer this question, it's useful to think in terms of a subject with which we are all familiar – mathematics.

In most school systems around the world, including the UK, mathematics education, despite the volume of research into its structure and content, is quite uniform in its coverage of topics (Kahan et al., 2003). We teach numbers to 5-year-olds, algebra to 12-year-olds and calculus to 18-year-olds. Over hundreds, if not thousands, of years of mathematical educational development, we have somehow figured out that the best and most natural and productive progression of concepts to teach in mathematics is a hierarchical one, where the learning of each new concept builds on, and is necessarily therefore linked to, understanding the previous concept. As a key part of this, the curriculum progression reflects the progression of mathematical sophistication of a child as he or she matures, along with aspects of child development, such as the ability to understand abstract ideas, the ability to manipulate formal operations, and the ability to understand the difference between logic and intuition (Bers et al., 2014).

So think about how this mathematical structure has emerged: what is that progression in computer science? For example, when is it best to teach concurrency? Children are frequently taught in school to focus on one topic at a time, and to complete tasks before they move on. So is this a better concept to teach in KS3 and KS4, when they can understand its significance? We frequently teach very young children particular ways of subtraction based on decomposition, and although the method is algorithmic, teachers rarely, if ever, teach children that this is an algorithm. But should they? Or is the concept of algorithms too difficult for primary-school children? What is clear from Figure 2.3 is that even the complex concepts have real examples and clear roots in everyday life. It is possible, but arguable, that there are many concepts in computing that are innate, and simply need to be highlighted where they occur, as frequently as possible, so that children become accustomed to thinking computationally as a natural and automatic process.

EXAMPLES OF WHAT TO TEACH AND HOW

So Computational Thinking shouldn't just be seen as a new name for 'problem-solving skills' or 'creative approaches'. It *does*, of course, help to solve problems, and it has very wide applications across other disciplines. Likewise, it *is* important to help pupils and students to think imaginatively, and to think 'out of the box'. But Computational Thinking is most obviously apparent, and probably best learned, through the process of writing code. In this way, pupils will very quickly learn the basic ground rules of all Computational Thinking, that it is:

- creative;
- systematic; and
- rigorous.

And that you can improve by:

- thinking;
- persistence; and
- practice.

COMPUTATIONAL THINKING THROUGH THE NATIONAL CURRICULUM AT EACH STAGE

1. Early Years Foundation Stage (EYFS)

Computational Thinking in the EYFS is about starting to understand that following instructions (algorithms at their most basic level), doing little jobs in a sensible order (logic at its basic level) and splitting tasks up into different parts (decomposition) are part and parcel of everyday life; and, as such, these concepts can become themes for early-years activities in communication, playing and making things. Important ideas to remember at this stage are:

- using everyday contexts to explain ideas (e.g. taking a dog for a walk involves decomposing a problem into parts, including getting a lead, putting the dog's harness on, getting food for treats);
- that teaching should focus on the most important elements rather than on lots of extra detail.

2. Key Stage 1 (KS1)

Computational Thinking at KS1 should be about starting to understand the ideas behind it, and importantly, wondering whether a problem always needs a computer to actually solve it at all. Moving on from teaching pupils the parts of an activity or process, pupils can begin to link computational ideas with tasks and structures that they have initiated. For example, if they wanted to find a programme on TV, what would be the best way to find it? Would they ask a friend, search the web, find an app? Important ideas to remember at this stage are:

- In designing such activities, *always* link them to the *conceptual* ideas and approaches that stand behind the activities and processes.
- Give pupils plenty of time to think and to work together and to practice these activities, so the *ideas of collaboration, persistence and iteration are reinforced.*

3. Key Stage 2 (KS2)

At KS2, Computational Thinking should be about demonstrating increasing understanding and independence in relation to patterns, decomposing into greater numbers of levels, and understanding relationships between concepts in CT. Such developments should go hand in hand with cognitive abilities, and greater emphasis on pupils taking responsibility for thinking through what they are doing. Also at this stage, however, it is critically important to note that as advancing ability and skill are assumed, they are not always apparent or even present in many pupils. For many reasons, emotional, social, cultural and linguistic, it is entirely probable that children will be at varying levels of metacognitive maturity. For this reason, at KS2, whilst it is a critically important transition stage as Computational Thinking progresses to more advanced levels of complexity, the following ideas are very important to remember:

■ A culture of collaboration, community and collective activity should be fostered, where children talk through and discuss ideas, to improve understanding at a deeper level.

■ An environment of risk, practice, trial and error and persistence should be encouraged, where it is acknowledged that Computational Thinking is sometimes difficult, but that perseverance and resilience are important cognitive and affective qualities.

4. Key Stage 3 (KS3)

At KS3, Computational Thinking should begin to be embedded in other topics, such as representations of data, variables and functions, relationships, algorithms and of course, more complex problem solving. For pupils progressing to KS4 and beyond, KS3 provides a common core that teachers are free to develop and augment depending on their own capabilities and resources, as well as the needs and abilities of the pupils that they teach. What is important, though, is that in conceptual terms, KS3 is another turning point for Computational Thinking, and preparing for a full and detailed coverage will mean that KS4 can be devoted to practising coding techniques. It is important to remember the following ideas for KS3 Computational Thinking:

■ The topics in KS3 should be increasingly taught with explicit links between them, and this should be made clear to pupils.

■ It is critical that, at this stage, teachers make the curriculum 'their own' by adapting resources and designing activities to suit their own interests. This is an important element in the development of any deeply conceptual area of study, since it emphasises to pupils that it is the *ideas* and *abstractions* that are important, rather than simply the processes and practicalities.

5. Key Stage 4 (KS4)

At KS4, Computational Thinking should have become an intuitive way of thinking about the whole range of concepts that we have discussed in this chapter, and the approaches to problem solving should be deeply ingrained in the ways that both teachers and pupils encounter problems in a wide range of contexts and circumstances. Whilst the basics of these ways of thinking and working are important for all pupils to acquire, it will not, of course, be the case that all individuals are able to tackle problems with the same skill and aptitude, It is very important to remember, therefore, that becoming an independent and discerning computer scientist, whilst desirable, is a journey in which practice is a key component.

COMPUTATIONAL THINKING ACROSS THE CURRICULUM

As we have already established, Computational Thinking is a problem-solving method that can be applied to create solutions that are often implemented using digital technology. When teachers and teacher educators think critically about the purpose of Computational Thinking, it is the start of a process of developing learners' ability to recognise Computational Thinking elements in their current and future teaching and learning.

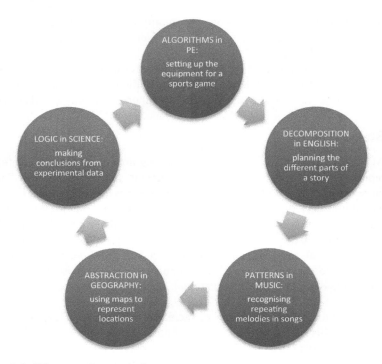

▪ **Figure 2.4** CT across the curriculum

This is paradigm-shifting step for many teachers, since it opens up 'possibility' thinking, as well as the important need for Computational Thinking to be developed in all learners, including those with disabilities and learning difficulties; it is also the start of developing a more sophisticated pedagogic imagination in relation to how and why particular contexts may be suited to thinking computationally (Israel et al., 2015). Figure 2.4 gives some examples of CT across the curriculum.

REFLECTIONS ON LEARNING HOW TO TEACH COMPUTATIONAL THINKING

In this chapter, we have discussed many ideas and questions surrounding Computational Thinking and its place in the English National Curriculum. Whilst it is an important and integral component of the Curriculum, however, practical challenges and research opportunities remain, for teachers, teacher educators, pupils and learners alike. Perhaps the main practical challenge is that we do not have enough teachers trained to teach Computer Science at all levels and in all educational contexts. We have begun to have cohorts of primary teachers since the new curriculum was introduced in 2014, but such cohorts are still small, and, at the moment, insufficient to share practice at the intensive level required for all teachers and all schools (Kahan et al., 2003). Similarly for secondary teachers: the diversity of traditional entry degrees for postgraduate training in ICT has been found wanting for many teachers who are now required to teach Computing (Wilson et al., 2010). We also don't have enough teacher educators who are specialists in Computer Science and have the levels of profound, and systematically and gradually acquired, pedagogic content knowledge (Zohar, 2004) that it takes to fully and deeply understand conceptual coverage of many topics (CSTA, 2013).

There are many developments in training and education for existing staff, in-training teachers, and teacher educators, however (Barr and Stephenson, 2011). Online workshops, intensive self-organised working groups and social networks based on principles of communities of practice and distributed knowledge, have adopted a range of methods, both digital and unplugged, to explore Computational Thinking across the curriculum, and to develop specific disciplinary approaches.

But it is critically important to invest properly and deeply in both teachers and their practices and technology, in parallel. We know from other innovations in the past, such as with thinking skills, creativity and learning styles, that evidence relating to them is frequently misinterpreted and appropriated in ways that are not supported in the research – and, as a result, do not support sustained pedagogical impact (Leat, 1999). Furthermore, we know from other research that information technology teachers' practices are frequently neither altered nor more transparent as a result of pedagogical development that doesn't engage with the teachers' values and their specific working contexts (Zeidler, 2002). In these circumstances, curricular innovations become 'what works' and 'just in time' and, in the worst cases, leave learners with haphazard collections of skills and processes together on an incoherent disciplinary thread (Blin and Munro, 2008).

Finally, we need to understand how best to use computing technology in the classroom. Simply leaving computers in the classroom, together with large-scale investment in kits, gadgets and mobile devices, is never the most effective way to teach Computer Science concepts. A key element of teaching Computational Thinking is to ask how a problem can be solved at all, with and without technology. So in turn, all teachers and teacher educators are required to ask: how can we use technology to enhance the learning of *all* children, and reinforce the understanding of Computer Science concepts in the most productive and inclusive way, including, of course, Computational Thinking? Put simply, it is too important not to consider these most profound of questions, because the use of Computational Thinking has life-changing implications:

> Computational thinking makes it possible for transplant surgeons to realise that more lives can be saved by optimising the exchange of organs among pools of donors and recipients. It enables new drug designs to be analysed so that they are less likely to create drug-resistant strains of diseases. Artists, when given the tools to think and express themselves computationally, can create totally new modes of human experience. Users of the Internet, when empowered with computational thinking, can demystify privacy technologies and surf the web safely.
>
> (Carnegie Mellon University, 2016)

QUESTIONS THAT WE HAVE ASKED AND ANSWERED IN THIS CHAPTER

- Is CT a skill that can be taught using problem-solving activities?
- Is it a way of working that applies to particular types of subject?
- Is it an overall approach, like creativity and exploration, that needs teachers with a particularly adventurous mindset?

▨   Is it thematic, and can it therefore be adopted when teaching particular subjects that may use similar analytic approaches, like music and language?

▨   Is it only a higher-level skill that can be taught in secondary education, but not in primary schools?

▨   Are teachers who can teach CT different from other teachers – do they need particular technical knowledge and skill, for example?

▨   And finally, is CT an academic concept in its own right, or part of the computing curriculum; or should it go hand in hand with all sorts of other approaches, and themes across the curriculum?

This chapter has answered all these questions with examples of how to teach, with different approaches that schools might take when teaching CT. It has also presented case studies and the latest research into teaching CT. Standing behind the chapter is the idea that CT can be an enabling and empowering skill that will benefit all children in the way that they learn all subjects within the school curriculum, not just coding.

REFLECTION ACTIVITY

What is the place of CT in the National Curriculum?

Would you agree that CT is a critical-concept twenty-first-century school curriculum, as an enjoyable and empowering discipline, as a first step in preparing future computer scientists, and as an important element of future employability?

Can CT be thought of as a concept, a process, a skill and an approach?

Why is it important to understand why we teach topics in particular ways when thinking about how best to teach CT?

Do you think that CT is good for learning how to learn, and for disciplining and helping all learners to think more carefully, effectively and productively?

NOTES

1 www.gov.uk/government/publications/national-curriculum-in-england-computing-programmes-of-study/national-curriculum-in-england-computing-programmes-of-study
2 www.gov.uk/government/publications/national-curriculum-in-england-computing-programmes-of-study

REFERENCES

Barefoot Computing. (2013). The Barefoot Computing project: Computing readiness for primary school teachers. Accessed from: http://barefootcas.org.uk/.

Barr, V. and Stephenson, C. (2011). Bringing computational thinking to K-12: What is involved and what is the role of the computer science education community? *ACM Inroads, 2(1)*, 48–54.

Bers, M.U., Flannery, L., Kazakoff, E.R. and Sullivan, A. (2014). Computational thinking and tinkering: Exploration of an early childhood robotics curriculum. *Computers & Education, 72*, 145–157.

Blin, F. and Munro, M. (2008). Why hasn't technology disrupted academics' teaching practices? Understanding resistance to change though the lens of activity theory. *Computers & Education, 50(2)*, 475–490.

Carnegie Mellon University. (2016). What is Computational Thinking? Carnegie Mellon University: Center for Computational Thinking. Accessed from: http://www.cs.cmu.edu/~CompThink/.

CSTA (Computer Science Teachers' Association). (2013). *Bugs in the system: Computer Science Teacher Certification in the US.* New York: ACM.

Department for Education (DfE). (2013). National Curriculum in England: Computing programmes of study. Accessed from: https://www.gov.uk/government/publications/national-curriculum-in-england-computing-programmes-of-study.

Grover, S. and Pea, R. (2013). Computational thinking in K-12: A review of the state of the field. *Educational Researcher, 42(1)*, 38–43.

Israel, M., Pearson, J.M., Tapia, T., Wherfel, Q.M. and Reese, G. (2015). Supporting all learners in school-wide computational thinking: A cross case qualitative analysis. *Computers & Education, 82*(C), 263–279.

Kahan, J.A., Cooper, D.A. and Bethea, K.A. (2003). The role of mathematical teachers' content knowledge in their teaching: A framework for research applied to a study of student teachers. *Journal of Mathematics Teacher Education, 6(3)*, 223–252.

Leat, D. (1999). *Rolling* the *stone uphill*: Teacher development and the implementation of thinking skills programmes. *Oxford Review of Education, 25(3)*, 387–401.

NAACE (National Association of Advisers for Computers in Education). (2013). *Computing at School*. Nottingham: NAACE Publications.

Wilson, C., Sudol, L., Stephenson, C. and Stehlik, M. (2010). *Running on Empty: The Failure to Teach K-12 Computer Science in the Digital Age*. New York: Association for Computing Machinery and Computer Science Teacher Association.

Wing, J. (2006). Computational Thinking. *Communications of the ACM, March 2006, 49(3)*, 33–35.

Wing, J. (2016). Computational thinking, 10 years later. Microsoft Research Blog. Accessed from: https://www.microsoft.com/en-us/research/blog/computational-thinking-10-years-later/.

Yadav, A., Zhou, N., Mayfield, C., Hambrusch, S. and Korb, J.T. (2011). Introducing computational thinking in education courses. In *Proceedings of ACM Special Interest Group on Computer Science Education*. Dallas, Texas.

Zeidler, D.L. (2002). Dancing with maggots and saints: visions for subject matter knowledge, pedagogical knowledge and pedagogical contend knowledge in Science Teacher education reform. *Journal of Science Teacher Education, 13(1)*, 27–42.

Zohar, A. (2004). Elements of teachers' pedagogical knowledge regarding instruction of higher order thinking. *Journal of Science Teacher Education, 15(4)*, 293–312.

CHAPTER 3

THIRTEEN CONSIDERATIONS FOR TEACHING CODING TO CHILDREN

Gary S. Stager and Sylvia Martinez

There is a "back to the future" quality to the newfound interest in children coding. When microcomputers began entering classrooms in the US thirty-five years ago, programming was what kids and teachers did with them. As the software industry developed, software designed for education emerged. That software was primarily games designed to teach through constant testing of existing knowledge through flashcard-style drill and practice, while a few titles were more constructivist in nature. Things shifted dramatically in the late 1980s, when, seemingly overnight, the emphasis around computers in education shifted to using office applications so that a generation of fifth graders (aged ten to eleven years) would develop terrific secretarial skills. The "one computer classroom" became popular in the early 1990s. Now the teacher was the star of the classroom theater, and the computer was her prop for engaging children in specific activities carefully designed to teach a specific concept.

Beginning in the late 1990s, the five-paragraph essay migrated to the computer screen in the form of "digital storytelling." Kid-Pix-like graphics, simple animation, PowerPoint presentations, and digital video editing were perhaps more expressive than memorizing the menus in Microsoft Word, but no more technically sophisticated. Technology standards authored by organizations such as the International Society of Technology in Education did not mention programming at all and emphasized digital citizenship, communication, and other generic skills better suited for a Computer Appreciation course, rather than computer science.

The twenty-first century has seen microcomputers mostly used for test preparation or standardized testing, with the occasional app thrown in to justify tablet purchases or present an illusion of modernity.

This oversimplification of recent history suggests not only different views of educational technology, but also a shift in agency from the learner, to the teacher, and ultimately to the system. In too many schools, the very same computer that was once used as an intellectual laboratory and vehicle for self-expression (Kohl, 2012; Stager, 2003) has been reduced to a tool of delivery, compliance, and surveillance.

The good news is that programming and computer science are back in vogue in the guise of coding. This presents reason for optimism and opportunities for those of us who have been advocating for all children to develop programming fluency across national curricula for several decades. The current interest in coding is likely rooted in three phenomena:

- economic insecurity addressed by politicians and business leaders calling for better STEM (science, technology, engineering, and mathematics) education in order to create "college- and career-ready" students (United States Department of Education, 2010);
- the embarrassing state of computer science education in the United States, most notably in the low female and minority participation rates in the Advanced Placement (AP) Computer Science exam (Erickson, 2015);
- the emergence of a maker movement combining digital fabrication, physical computing, programming, and timeless craft traditions.

Reintroducing computer science into the intellectual diet of children via the maker movement emphasizes individual creativity, authentic problem solving, and a multitude of contexts for programming through a variety of projects appealing to a diverse population of learners. Such a learner-centered approach to coding empowers students through modern meaningful experiences. The result may even address the first two concerns.

Teachers eager to embrace the promise of coding should seek inspiration from educators with a demonstrated track record of teaching kids to program based on solid progressive traditions, rather than the commercial hucksters, app makers, testing conglomerates, and professional associations who presided over the near extinction of computer science in schools.

Effective computer science education for primary students requires implementation strategies and curricula that move beyond empty rhetoric, mindless cheerleading, or kneejerk criticism. We cannot afford to put the assessment cart before the learning horse and allow those with little or no understanding of computing to set the standards. Therefore, realizing the promise of computer science for all children is predicated on the following ten observations.

COMPUTER SCIENCE IS THE NEW LIBERAL ART

We are horrified by the energy, time, and opportunities wasted by two decades worth of adults arguing against providing each child with the opportunity to learn to program computers. The vehemence with which this case has been argued has been remarkable and destructive. One would be hard-pressed to find a similar example of such anti-intellectualism as, "Not everyone needs to learn to program . . ." when talking about teaching students to read, write, or learn science. Yet curriculum, policy, and classroom practice have been denatured by such ignorance and arrogance. There are plenty of questionable things taught to children, but no one ever proclaims that not every child should learn Haiku or take Advanced Algebra. Why would you even imagine not teaching every kid to program?

While there may indeed be vocational benefits of learning to program, the real reason we should teach all children to program is because it gives them agency over an increasingly complex and technologically sophisticated world (Stager, 2014). It answers the question Seymour Papert began asking a half century ago: "Does the computer program the child, or the child program the computer?" This is a fundamental question of democracy that should concern every parent and educator.

Computer science (CS) is the new liberal art. It is also a legitimate science that students need to learn. However, unlike other branches of science, CS is beneficial in every other discipline. Any vocational pursuit in the arts, sciences, or humanities requires control over the computer. There may also be no more profound way than programming to develop habits of mind like persistence, perspective, or causality. Boys and girls need to experience the joy, creativity, and satisfaction associated with making something out of nothing or bending the computer to one's will. If we are to have computers in education, then learning to program grants the greatest return on investment.

WE HAVE DONE THIS BEFORE

While the use of the term "coding" as a substitute for "programming" may be new, we have taught lots of children and their teachers to program all over the world in the recent past. Such awareness should inspire and support future efforts.

Hobbyist programming flourished prior to the dawn of the maker movement or Computer Science for All (CS4All) efforts. David Ahl, Editor of *Creative Computing* magazine, told Gary Stager that his publication reached a subscriber base of 400,000 in 1984. In the mid-1980s, long before computers were ubiquitous in schools, Dan Watt sold more than 100,000 copies of his book *Learning with Logo*, largely to school teachers interested in teaching programming to children. Beginning in 1989, Australian schools pioneered one-to-one computing when the first schools anywhere outfitted every child with a personal laptop computer. The purpose of those laptops was for children to program across the curriculum, make learning more personal, and realize the progressive visions of John Dewey, John Holt, and Seymour Papert. (Grasso & Fallshaw, 1993; Johnstone, 2003; Stager, 1995, 1998, 2006).

We have also seen how elitist and theoretical approaches to computer science, as demonstrated by the Advanced Placement examination system,[1] can turn droves of students, especially women and minorities, away from computing while leaving most teachers with the impression that their academic subjects have nothing to do with it (Erickson 2015, Herold 2014).

This has happened before. In the 1980s, there was intense interest in computer science, corresponding to the rise of personal computing. Because there were no additional spaces for university computer science majors, introductory courses got harder, to halt the rise in the number of students who were "harder to teach," which really meant those with less experience in high school (Guzdial, 2014). Today, as popularity again drives renewed interest in computer science, the limited numbers of teachers and slots in computer science classes raise the bar, making it even less possible for beginners to find a place to learn. We must find ways to reach all students with programming activities that are interesting and fun, opening doors for all kinds of students, even ones who are interested in programming not to become computer scientists or engineers, but because they want to use the limitless power of the computer to explore areas of their own interests.

Arthur Luehrmann coined the term "computing literacy" in the early 1970s. The term later morphed into "computer literacy", with a focus on the machine, rather than on process. Although many schools have eliminated programming from their computer literacy offerings, Luehrmann was quite specific in defining the term:

> Computer literacy must mean the ability to do something constructive with a computer, and not merely a general awareness of facts one is told about computers. A computer literate person can read and write a computer program, can select and operate software written by others, and knows from personal experience the possibilities and limitations of the computer.
>
> (Luehrmann, 1980)

Even if our primary goals include awareness of the computer, digital citizenship, or basic computer operation, these concepts are best developed in the meaningful context of learning to code.

Educators in the past have demonstrated how to create compelling programming activities for children that offer teachers evidence of curricular relevance. In other words, we *know* how to make programming "hard fun" (Berry & Wintle, 2009; Papert, 1993, 2002) for children while revealing the educational benefits teachers seek. The Logo literature is filled with such ideas.

LEARNING TO PROGRAM TAKES MORE THAN AN HOUR

Advocacy groups, such as Code.org, have done an impressive job of raising the visibility of coding as an important skill young people should acquire, even if their motives are vocational or commercial in nature. In addition to lobbying efforts, their annual Hour of Code campaign has captured the attention of politicians, the media, and school leaders.

Recognizing that the existing US school curriculum is morbidly obese, Hour of Code says to educators, "C'mon, you can find an hour once a year to expose kids to coding." To support this effort, websites like Code.org offer countless little coding games and puzzles that kids can complete in a matter of minutes without the participation of a teacher, who is assumed to know little or nothing about computer programming.

The success of Hour of Code in raising the visibility of coding must be tempered by the schools who congratulate themselves for literally doing the least they can to introduce children to computing. It is too easy to use Hour of Code participation as a substitute for action. Quality work takes time!

FLUENCY IS THE GOAL

Exposure may be a worthy first step as long as substantive plans are clearly outlined for truly learning to code. Exposure itself is insufficient. Fluency must be the goal. We want children to be able to create, invent, dance, sing, write, and debate ideas via programming. Such fluency requires the same levels of dedication necessary to become good at any other time-honored pursuit (Cavallo, 2000).

> Technological fluency will be valued far less as something needed for the workplace than as a language in which powerful ideas can be expressed.
>
> (Papert, 1998)

Websites like Code.org introduce needless confusion, with a smorgasbord of coding options using many different programming languages, each with quite specific syntax. Educators report how we "do a little Scratch, then we do some Java, then some Codestudio. . ." This may be novel, but has little educational value. Sampling programming languages is as foolish as offering a few hours of instruction in multiple foreign languages or reading one page each of a dozen works of great literature. Well-meaning teachers new to coding need guidance in selecting a language appropriate to their student population and programming goals. Then they need to stick with it long enough for some kids to become sufficiently proficient to explore their own ideas and share expertise with their peers.

Jumping around different programming languages may appear sophisticated, but is merely an exercise in false complexity (Squires & McDougall, 1994; Squires & Preece, 1996) with little benefit to learners.

There are programming languages designed with learning in mind (Logo, MicroWorlds, Scratch, Snap!, Turtle Art) and others with a more vocational focus (Python, C++, Java, Processing). Learning to code in any language is better than not coding at all. That said, if we wish to democratize coding and have all students code, it is important to use a language designed for learning (Greenberg, 1991; Harvey, 1982, 2003; Papert, 1999) Such languages have accessible interfaces, consistent syntax and helpful error messages, and contain objects to think with that encourage mathematical thinking and problem-solving skills, even when programming an interactive story or an animation for history class.

The extraordinary popularity of the Scratch programming language is based on its clever design, its online library of more than fourteen million projects, and being free. It follows the old Logo edict of "low threshold" and, with the addition of new dialects and increased functionality, also promises "no ceiling" (Papert & Watt, 1977). Scratch is neither a baby programming language nor a stepping-stone to coding. It *is* a programming language. The block-based interface makes the process of coding more concrete for many learners. The ability to easily share projects, open the hood on those projects, remix them, or borrow the code for use in your own creations inspires lots of young programmers. Scratch is a descendent of Logo and embodies many of its Piagetian and Papertian traditions in its design.

The creation of Scratch dialect Snap!, complete with recursion, first-class objects, and program as data, creates a glide path for young coders to develop real computer science fluency. The fact that Snap! is used in the University of California at Berkeley's Beauty and Joy of Computing course ("Beauty and Joy of Computing", 2016) and as a pathway for the Advanced Placement Computer Science Principles class by the same title, solidifies Scratch's status as a rich environment for learning to code and developing powerful ideas in computer science, mathematics, and other disciplines.

The Scratch dialect Beetle Blocks allows children to program in 3D and export those files to 3D printers. The "secret sauce" of Tickle, a version of Scratch for the iPad, is that in addition to Scratch functionality, the user can now program low-cost drones, robots, LEGO, and even home lighting systems. Being able to program your toys to dance, fly, and speak generates other exciting contexts for learning to code.

If fluency is the goal, students should perhaps spend a year or more learning with a single programming language.

THERE IS NO COMPUTER SCIENCE WITHOUT COMPUTERS

It would appear self-evident that one needs computer access to learn computer science. Computer coding requires a computer, right? Not necessarily if one is to believe the K-12 digital technologies policy statements prepared in the US, the UK, and Australia. These frameworks, policies, and curricula place a greater emphasis on computational thinking than computing or coding. This focus on computational thinking assumes a lack of access to computers, or of teachers capable of teaching coding.

While we appreciate that computational thinking provides valuable opportunities for problem solving, critical thinking, and analysis, such skills would be enriched in the context of computer programming. Computational thinking without programming is just math. Since mathematical knowledge construction is more efficacious when situated in a programming context, we stand by the radical claim that computer programming is better with computers than without them (Harel, 1991; Harel & Papert, 1990; Kafai & Resnick, 1996). We share Piaget's belief that knowledge is a consequence of experience and that the experience of programming computers is richer than learning *about* computer programming (Ackermann, 2001; Duckworth, 1996; Kamii, 2000; Kamii & Joseph, 2004; Papert, 1988; Piaget & Piaget, 1973).

The popular Exploring Computer Science (Goode & Margolis, 2011; Goode, et al., 2012; Outlier Research and Evaluation, 2015) curriculum places a great deal of emphasis on social implications of computing, problem solving, and off-computer activities, while Computer Science Unplugged (Bell, et al., 2009; Bell, et al., 1998; CS Unplugged, 2016; Henderson, 2008) does not use computers at all.

> The activities introduce students to Computational Thinking through concepts such as binary numbers, algorithms and data compression, separated from the distractions and technical details of having to use computers. Importantly, no programming is required to engage with these ideas!
>
> (CS Unplugged, 2016)

This statement from the Computer Science Unplugged website draws focus to several shortcomings of this approach.

- The fallacy that you cannot enjoy dessert without eating your vegetables first.
- The debatable idea that binary numbers, algorithms, or data compression are appropriate or important curricular topics for young people, especially if there will be no actual coding involved.
- The implicit suggestion that these topics are easier to learn without programming or are even relevant in the absence of coding.
- When "distractions and technical details" are used as an excuse for coding without computers, the writer presents an incorrect notion of cognitive development. Introducing these topics without the context of computing makes them more abstract, not less.

Code.org commissioned an online study in the US, with students aged from four to eighteen, to measure the effectiveness of its outreach and curriculum development efforts.

High school students reported dissatisfaction with "off-computer" or "unplugged" activities compared with the actual programming in their Exploring Computer Science (ECS) classes.

Students preferred the programming activities to the unplugged lessons. Many teachers felt that the programming units, especially those that included emphasis on HTML and Scratch, were of the greatest interest to students. Teachers felt that programming allowed students to "just try things out, make mistakes, explore things." Teachers described how the opportunity to create things engaged students, with one teacher noting, "What got them all excited was being able to create in HTML, in Scratch, in making a robot do something" (Outlier Research and Evaluation, 2015).

Several teachers remarked that students were frustrated because they were not doing what they thought of as "real" computer science. As one teacher said, "I heard more than a few times early on in the year, 'Isn't this a computer science class? Where are the computers?' That's part of the ECS shtick. You can kind of play it off and explain it away, but when it comes down to it I also agree with them" (Outlier Research and Evaluation, 2015).

The students also reported displeasure with waiting through several units of study before computers were used (Outlier Research and Evaluation, 2015).

You should avoid a computer science curriculum that delays actual programming for weeks or months while content is covered. Another sign of poorly conceived curricula is when there is a great emphasis on memorizing vocabulary such as "algorithm", "binary numbers", or "data compression" at the expense of actual coding.

THE STANDARDS ARE AT BEST PREMATURE

Educators, publishers, and policy-makers too often resort to the cliché, "We need to teach teachers how to assess this stuff." When the "stuff" is associated with new and powerful ideas like computer science, making, tinkering, or engineering, this desire becomes highly problematic.

Ask any decent fourth grade teacher to show you student writing samples representing below grade level, at grade level, or exemplary work, and they can do so with ease and alacrity. Why? Because they have seen thousands of examples of student writing, and there are decades' worth of experience evaluating writing. This is not so for Scratch programming, Arduino projects, or digital fabrication.

Therefore, it is premature to create benchmarks for judging student work at a specific moment in time, since we have no idea of what kids are capable of doing with these emerging technologies. A teacher's energies would be much better spent supporting her students in creating hundreds of unique and wondrous projects. Only then may we begin to assess such efforts.

This putting of the assessment cart before the learning horse results in the laundry lists of hierarchical skills dictated to teachers by anonymous committees of bureaucrats. Turn to any page in a K-12 digital technologies framework and read a few paragraphs. It will not take long to find empty rhetoric, preposterous sequences, low-level project suggestions, and mountains of nonsensical word salad that fails to drive progress. A lack of imagination and vision is often rooted in ignorance. Too often in education, such ignorance is cloaked in a few hundred pages of bullet points, charts, and graphs that no one bothers to read. This leaves teachers doubting themselves and without any real guidance about how to teach coding.

COMPUTER SCIENCE IS A CONTEXT FOR CONSTRUCTING MATHEMATICAL KNOWLEDGE

If your educational goals are no more ambitious than increasing understanding of the existing math curriculum, then you should teach children to program. After a sixth grade teacher had been observed leading a forty-five minute lesson on absolute value, she was asked, "When would you *use* absolute value?" She shrugged and answered, "Perhaps in seventh grade." Absolute value comes in quite handy when you're trying to land your rocket ship on a planet in the video game you programmed or to teach a robot to navigate unfamiliar terrain.

Absolute value, probabilistic behavior, negative numbers, angle measure, rate of speed, coordinate geometry, Boolean logic, modulo arithmetic, and even inequality are confusing abstractions without the context of computer programming. In other words, much of the US math curriculum has little, if any, application or relevance outside of coding.

While coding, these concepts have meaning and application. Learning them becomes more natural and students engage in the practice of mathematicians rather than being taught math (Cavallo, et al., 2004; Harel & Papert, 1990; Kafai, 1995; Papert, 1971, 1972a, 1972b, 1972c, 1980a, 1980b, 1993, 1997, 1999, 2000, 1991; Papert, et al., 1979; Stager, 1997).

Josh Burker, a teacher in a K-5 school in the United States, created a lesson for grade four students who were studying Islamic tiling patterns as part of a world culture unit. The students used Turtle Art to create patterns following the geometry of Islamic tiles (see Figure 3.1). A few years ago, this project would have ended with this two dimensional representation. Perhaps the tiles could have been printed out or displayed as part of a back to school night PowerPoint slideshow. But instead, this project continued by importing these patterns into a 3D Computer Aided Design (CAD) software program and printing them out on a 3D printer. Pressed into firing clay and hand painted by students, these became a class project that could be shared with family and friends. This project represents a learning journey from culture, through geometry, into art, creating sharable artifacts that could not be created without programming.

COVERING CURRICULUM

Most teachers are responsible for "covering" a vast list of content that makes up every subject. Although teachers have more flexibility in how curriculum is covered than some

■ **Figure 3.1** Patterns in 3D art

like to admit, they are indeed responsible for students learning specific things. Learning to program can lead to greater understanding of traditional topics too.

For example, take fractions (please)! Fractions are taught to kids all over the world, over multiple years, and with great disparity in achievement. Fractions are one of the things we teach kids over and over again, yet they don't stay taught. Idit Harel-Caperton's American Educational Research Association award-winning research demonstrated that if you ask fourth graders to program a computer "game" to teach younger children fractions, the programmers gain a much deeper understanding of fractions, plus a host of other skills, than children who were taught fractions in a more traditional fashion (Harel, 1991).

Asking ten-year-olds to write a computer program that represents any fraction as a part of a circle leads to a greater understanding of fractions, as well as a working knowledge of variables, division, the geometry of a circle, and the knowledge that comes from design and debugging.

While some would claim that "we don't have time" to add programming to the curriculum, devoting several class periods to one programming project may be much more efficient than spending several years of instruction on the same topic.

A seventh grade girl completing an assignment to write a program to solve a linear equation will come to understand the math topic, perhaps better or quicker because she was able to add computer graphics, an animated story or a musical composition to her program. Programming supports a range of expression and learning styles. Therefore, a willingness to engage with someone else's assignment may become more palatable when you are motivated to do so in your own voice (Martinez & Stager, 2013).

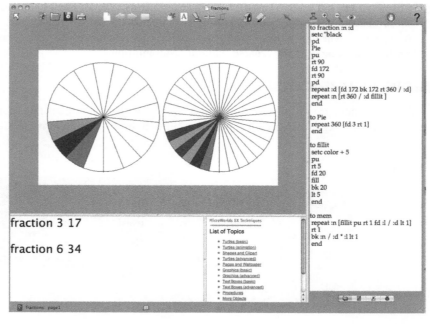

■ **Figure 3.2** Fraction program written by fourth graders in Logo using MicroWorlds (LCSI)

Why then should computers in schools be confined to computing the sum of the squares of the first twenty odd numbers and similar so-called 'problem-solving' uses? Why not use them to produce some action? There is no better reason than the intellectual timidity of the computers in education movement, which seems remarkably reluctant to use the computers for any purpose that fails to look very much like something that has been taught in schools for the past centuries. This is all the more remarkable since the computerists are custodians of a momentous intellectual and technological revolution.

(Papert & Solomon, 1971)

PHYSICAL COMPUTING IS A CRITICAL CONTEXT FOR LEARNING COMPUTER SCIENCE

In our book *Invent to Learn: Making, Tinkering, and Engineering in the Classroom,* we assert that we have entered a historical period of significant technological change. We identified three categories of game-changing technology; digital fabrication, physical computing, and computer programming. Physical computing may be thought of simply as robotics, but more broadly as adding interactivity and intelligence to a variety of materials. Microcontrollers, such as Arduino, the Hummingbird Robotics Kit, and even LEGO's WeDo or Mindstorms kits offer the ability to design things like interactive robots and prototype complex systems, and to build instruments capable of conducting scientific experiments. Coding supercharges a range of projects that can exist on and off the computer screen.

Most physical computing projects require careful sequencing, timing, logic, and sensory feedback. Regardless of the materials being used, all sensors return a range of values based on external stimuli. Your invention then behaves in a particular way based on that sensor data.

The first thing one needs to do when working with a sensor is to determine the kind and range of data it provides. This requires writing a simple program to continuously display data as you change the conditions impacting the sensor. (Some programming environments have a "watcher" built in for observing sensor behavior.) Once you can "read" the data, you need to determine its behavior as it responds to the world. For example, as the light sensor sees more light, do the numbers it reports increase or decrease? Inverse relationships are not uncommon (a nice context for more mathematical thinking). Once you get a sense of the data, you need to determine the threshold at which your program tells your machine to trigger a specific behavior. This almost always occurs when the data is within a particular range, relying on a working understanding of inequality more solid than trying to remember which way the crocodile's mouth is pointing on a worksheet.

The coding strategy just described is employed in countless scenarios, from making your cardboard robot dog bark at an intruder to turning on an air-conditioner when a room gets too warm. Despite the importance and ubiquity of this skill, it cannot be found in any of the K-12 "coding" standards we have surveyed.

INSTRUMENTAL CODING, ADDITIVE TEACHING

Two fifth grade boys in Vermont were inspired by the Blue Man Group to build a marimba out of PVC pipe. Since they wished to compose music for the marimba and play it, tempering the pitches was important. They found an equation for determining the length of the tube, based on its diameter and the frequency of the pitch they were trying to reproduce. Then they found tables of musical pitches and their frequencies on the Web, but now some mathematics was required. The boys explained that they were capable of performing the calculations, but they wanted all of their classmates to be able to participate as well. This display of empathy or hubris led to an ingenious plan. The boys wrote a Scratch program that asked users for the diameter of their tube and the frequency of the pitch they wished to reproduce. It then told you how long to cut the tube.

This is a quite elegant example of what one might call instrumental programming. The result of coding wasn't a computer program or app, as much as it was a marimba. Programming to solve problems en route to making something else, analyzing data, or conducting an experiment is a very powerful idea.

After the students shared their marimba with hundreds of adoring adults, it was suggested that since the program was about music, the user might wish to enter B Flat, instead of 466.16. Such a small intervention by a more experienced mentor is rooted in the knowledge that it is possible to modify the program in such a fashion and that *those* students were capable of doing so. It was well within their zone of proximal development.

Teaching coding like this, by scaffolding small but increasingly difficult additions to student projects, is quite different than just assigning standard problems of varying difficulty. Teachers learn to teach this way by watching and listening to students, not by following instructions in the teacher's manual. The confidence and competence to do this needs to be nurtured in teachers. Creating mentorships, critical friends networks, and ongoing professional development grounded in collaboration all create a space for teachers to gain these skills.

THERE'S MORE TO CS FOR KIDS THAN PROGRAMMING "VIDEO GAMES"

There are all sorts of possible programming projects, systems to invent, and problems to solve. Sometimes, educators fall into the trap of believing that all kids love video games and that programming video games will appeal to boys and girls equally. A similar fallacy is the idea that all kids want to create apps because after all, that's how you get rich. In our experience, some kids are motivated by these projects while other attempts feel like pandering and result in unsatisfying versions of things kids otherwise enjoy. We also know that kids enjoy writing programs to graph linear equations, collect and analyze polling data, answer the question, "Am I normal?," play a marimba, control a drone, generate random poetry, compose atonal music, bring a robot to life, or even do their homework. "This protean ability to take different forms and, if you use it right, to become a kind of mirror in which you can see reflections of yourself" (Papert, 1985) makes learning to code personally valuable and useful in other aspects of life.

SEEMINGLY SIMPLE PROJECTS CAN REVEAL AUTHENTIC OPPORTUNITIES TO GRAPPLE WITH BIG IDEAS

Connect a knob (potentiometer) to the Hummingbird Robotics controller, and, in Scratch or Snap!, ask students to write a program that turns the screen turtle as you adjust the knob.

The first thing you need to do is determine what sort of data you get from the knob sensor. The Hummingbird Kit has calibrated the sensor so that you get a lovely range of numbers between zero and 100. The next thing you need to do is write a program to set the turtle's heading to the sensor value times 3.6. Simple, right? But ask 100 students from third to twelfth grade how to solve this problem without programming and you will see the weakness even in basic algebraic reasoning.

Too often, adults seek to assess or judge student projects without understanding the creative and intellectual processes employed. This leads them to dismiss or disrespect the thinking of their students. Simple activities like programming the Logo turtle to draw your initials include more geometric reasoning than many students experience through high school. Creating a Scratch animation to illustrate a historical event can employ a laundry list of problem solving, mathematical, and computer science skills. The same goes for physical computing projects. Here is a seemingly simple problem using LEGO's early childhood robotics system, WeDo, and the Scratch programming language. It was observed in one of our recent "Invent to Learn" workshops for educators.

The student (in this case a teacher) connected a motor and a tilt sensor to his computer via the WeDo interface. He wanted to make the motor spin in the direction a user tilts the tilt sensor.

His first program looked like the one shown in Figure 3.3.

The problem was that while the motor spun rapidly, the sensor was not particularly responsive. It took a while for the motor to change direction when the sensor was tilted in the opposite direction.

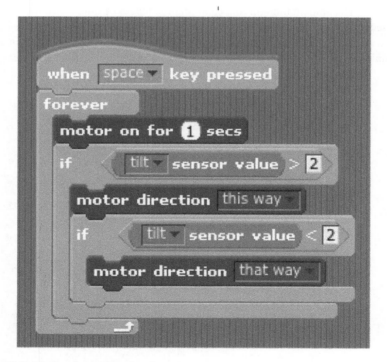

■ **Figure 3.3** Coding for motor direction

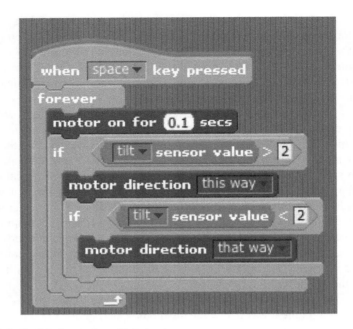

■ **Figure 3.4** Coding for motor without spin

The student thought that changing the length of time the motor was on for, from one second to 0.1 second, as shown in Figure 3.4, might improve performance.

Well, the sensor performance *was* a lot more responsive, but now the motor did not spin as smoothly or as quickly. Hmmm. . . Tradeoffs? That's a big idea!

Perhaps a slightly more elegant program might help? See Figure 3.5.

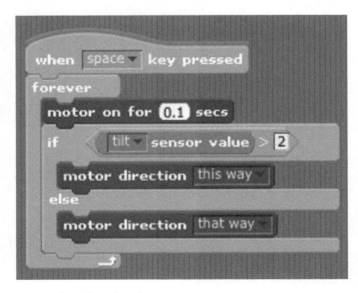

■ **Figure 3.5** Coding elegant motor

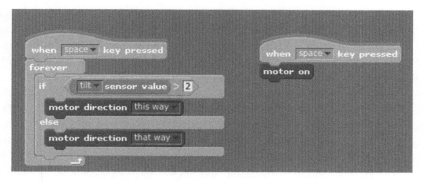

■ **Figure 3.6** Coding for speed and sensor response

Using If/Else rather than embedded Ifs must speed the program up a hair, but we still faced the tradeoff between sensor response and motor speed.

Just then, we remembered that Scratch is object-oriented and allows parallelism: the ability to execute multiple processes simultaneously. The program shown in Figure 3.6 allowed for speed and sensor response!

The superficially trivial problem born from a student's curiosity offered a context for using a number of engineering, computer science, and mathematical big ideas that might otherwise be inaccessible to students.

LogoWriter, MicroWorlds, Scratch, and Snap! offer students multiple turtles that can be animated with turtle geometry commands. Animation is turtle geometry with the turtle's pen up. Tickle's ability to program low-cost drones extends turtle geometry into three dimensions in ways Papert might never have imagined. Predicting the behavior of your drone before you execute your flying instructions may be more revolutionary than 3D printing.

THERE IS NO SUBSTITUTE FOR PERSONAL COMPUTING

Since learning to code, complete with the inevitable task of debugging, takes time, it follows that access to computers becomes critical. Coding, like writing, requires different motivation, venue, state-of-mind, and time of day for each programmer. Ideas don't stop when the school bell rings. That is why students need personal computers they may use 24/7 to store ideas, collaborate with others, and work on their projects continuously. You need a computer at your disposal whenever the coding muse strikes you.

To do this, we have to expand our vision beyond a low-level computer curriculum that focuses on digital citizenship, internet research, and basic workflow. We cannot paradoxically complain that students are "digital natives" (a dubious term at best) and simultaneously lower expectations about what they will do with the computer.

If a seventh grader doesn't know how to save a file, they have never created anything with a computer worth saving.

There is a complex relationship between what students want out of school and what school wants out of students. Learning to program a computer can level that playing field, but only if we expand what it means to learn to program the computer. If we rigidly define computer science and coding as only learning about algorithms, discrete mathematics, and correct syntax, we will create a generation of young people for whom computer science is boring and worthless. Of course a few will succeed: there are always people who are attuned to subjects the way school traditionally serves them. If we allow ourselves to be cheered by that limited success, nothing will change. The "CS for All" movement will be declared a failure and some "new new" education reform will take its place.

This does not have to happen. We need to champion coding as a liberal art, interesting because of what you can do with it, and connect it with student interests and passions. We need to teach teachers how to create challenges that provoke and inspire, and build teachers' confidence in themselves as creators of an ever-changing curriculum that can respond to individual student interests while at the same time tackling the big ideas of science, math, engineering, social studies, art, and all subject areas that society values.

NOTE

1 http://www.basised.com/achievements-and-results/advanced-placement.php

REFERENCES

Ackermann, E. (2001). Piaget's Constructivism, Papert's Constructionism: What's the Difference? Paper presented at the 2001 Summer Institute, Mexico City.

Beauty and Joy of Computing. (2016). Accessed from http://bjc.berkeley.edu.

Bell, T., Alexander, J., Freeman, I., and Grimley, M. (2009). Computer Science Unplugged: School Students Doing Real Computing Without Computers. *The New Zealand Journal of Applied Computing and Information Technology, 13*(1), 20–29.

Bell, T. C., Witten, I. H., and Fellows, M. (1998). *Computer Science Unplugged: Off-line Activities and Games for All Ages*. Accessed from http://csunplugged.org/wp-content/uploads/2015/01/unplugged-book-v1.pdf.

Berry, A. M., and Wintle, S. E. (2009). Using Laptops to Facilitate Middle School Science Learning: The Results of Hard Fun. Research Brief. Center for Education Policy, Applied Research, and Evaluation.

Cavallo, D. (2000). Technological Fluency and the Art of Motorcycle Maintenance: Emergent Design of Learning Environments. (Ph.D.). Cambridge, Mass.: Massachusetts Institute of Technology.

Cavallo, D., Papert, S., and Stager, G. (2004). Climbing to Understanding: Lessons from an Experimental Learning Environment for Adjudicated Youth. Proceedings of the International Conference on the Learning Sciences. Accessed from http://stager.org/articles/ICLS%20stager%20papert%20cavallo%20paper.pdf.Papert, S. (2000). What's the Big Idea? Toward a Pedagogical Theory of Idea Power. *IBM Systems Journal, 39*(3&4), 720–729.

CS Unplugged. (2016). Accessed from http://csunplugged.org.

Duckworth, E. R. (1996). *"The Having of Wonderful Ideas" & Other Essays on Teaching & Learning* (2nd ed.). New York: Teachers College Press, Teachers College, Columbia University.

Erickson, B. (2015). Is Computing Just for Men? American Association for University Women. Accessed from: http://www.aauw.org/2015/03/11/is-computing-just-for-men/.

Fellows, M., Bell, T., and Witten, I. (2002). Computer Science Unplugged. *Computer Science Unplugged.*

Goode, J., and Margolis, J. (2011). Exploring Computer Science: A Case Study of School Reform. *ACM Transactions on Computing Education (TOCE), 11*(2), 12.

Goode, J., Chapman, G., and Margolis, J. (2012). Beyond Curriculum: The Exploring Computer Science Program. *ACM Inroads, 3*(2), 47–53.

Grasso, I., and Fallshaw, M. (1993). *Reflections of a Learning Community: Views on the Introduction of Laptops at MLC*: Methodist Ladies' College, Kew, Victoria, Australia.

Greenberg, G. (1991). A Creative Arts Approach to Computer Programming. *Computers and the Humanities, 25*(5), 267–273.

Guzdial, M. (2014). NPR When Women Stopped Coding in 1980's: As We Repeat the Same Mistakes. Computing Education Blog. Accessed from: https://computinged.wordpress.com/2014/10/30/npr-when-women-stopped-coding-in-1980s-are-we-about-to-repeat-the-past/.

Harel, I. (1991). *Children Designers: Interdisciplinary Constructions for Learning and Knowing Mathematics in a Computer-rich School*. Norwood, N.J.: Ablex Pub. Corp.

Harel, I., and Papert, S. (1990). Software Design as a Learning Environment. *Interactive Learning Environments, 1*(1), 1–32.

Harvey, B. (1982). Why Logo? *Byte, 7*, 163–193.

Harvey, B. (2003). Logo. In *Encyclopedia of Computer Science*. Chichester, UK: John Wiley and Sons Ltd.

Henderson, P. (2008). Computer Science Unplugged. *Journal of Computing Sciences in Colleges, 23*(3), 168.

Herold, B. (2014). Big Race, Gender Gaps in Participation on AP Computer Science Exam. Education Week. Accessed from: http://blogs.edweek.org/edweek/DigitalEducation/2014/01/big_race_gender_disparities_discovered_on_ap_computer_science_exam.html.

Johnstone, B. (2003). *Never Mind the Laptops: Kids, Computers, and the Transformation of Learning*. Seattle: iUniverse.

Kafai, Y. B. (1995). *Minds in Play: Computer Game Design as a Context for Children's Learning*. Hillsdale, N.J.: Lawrence Erlbaum Associates.

Kafai, Y. B., and Resnick, M. (1996). *Constructionism in Practice: Designing, Thinking, and Learning in a Digital World*. Mahwah, N.J.: Lawrence Erlbaum Associates.

Kamii, C. (2000). *Young Children Reinvent Arithmetic: Implications of Piaget's Theory*. Early Childhood Education Series: ERIC. Williston, Vermont: Teachers College Press.

Kamii, C., and Joseph, L. L. (2004). *Young Children Continue to Reinvent Arithmetic – 2nd Grade: Implications of Piaget's Theory*. Williston, Vermont: Teachers College Press.

Kohl, H. R. (2012). *The Muses Go to School: Inspiring Stories about the Importance of Arts in Education*: New York: The New Press.

Luehrmann, A. (1980). Computer Literacy: The What, Why, and How. In R. Taylor (Ed.), *The Computer in the School: Tutor, Tutee, and Tool*. New York: Teacher College Press.

Martinez, S. L., and Stager, G. (2013). *Invent to Learn: Making, Tinkering, and Engineering in the Classroom*: Torrance, Calif.: Constructing Modern Knowledge Press.

Outlier Research and Evaluation. (2015). High School – Exploring Computer Science – Interviews. Accessed from: http://outlier.uchicago.edu/evaluation_codeorg/highschool-exploringCS-interviews/.

Papert, S. (1971). A Computer Laboratory for Elementary Schools. AI Memo 246. Cambridge, Mass: MIT Art. Intell. Lab.

Papert, S. (1972a). On Making a Theorem for a Child. Paper presented at the proceedings of the ACM annual conference – Volume 1, Boston, Mass.

Papert, S. (1972b). Teaching Children Thinking. *Programmed Learning and Educational Technology, 9*(5), 245–255.

Papert, S. (1972c). Teaching Children to be Mathematicians versus Teaching About Mathematics. *International Journal of Mathematical Education in Science and Technology, 3*(3), 249–262.

Papert, S. (1980a). Computer-Based MicroWorlds as Incubators for Powerful Ideas. In R. Taylor (Ed.), *The Computer in the School: Tutor, Tool, Tutee* (pp. 204–210). New York: Teacher's College Press.

Papert, S. (1980b). *Mindstorms: Children, Computers, and Powerful Ideas*. New York: Basic Books.

Papert, S. (1985). Different Visions of Logo. *Computers in the Schools, 2*(2–3), 3–8.

Papert, S. (1988). The Conservation of Piaget: The Computer as Grist. In G. Forman & P. B. Pufall (Eds.), *Constructivism in the Computer Age* (pp. 3–14). Hillsdale, N.J.: Lawrence Erlbaum Associates.

Papert, S. (Ed.) (1991). *Situating Constructionism*. Norwood, N.J.: Ablex Publishing Corporation.

Papert, S. (1993). *The Children's Machine: Rethinking School in the Age of the Computer*. New York: Basic Books.

Papert, S. (1997). Looking at Technology Through School Colored Spectacles. Accessed from http://papert.org/articles/LookingatTechnologyThroughSchool.html.

Papert, S. (1998). Technology in Schools: To Support the System or Render it Obsolete. Milken Exchange on Education Technology. Accessed from http://dailypapert.com/wp-content/uploads/2013/05/Papert-Milken-article.taf_.html.

Papert, S. (1999). Introduction: What is Logo and Who Needs It? In LCSI (Ed.), *Logo Philosophy and Implementation* (pp. v–xvi). Montreal, Quebec: LCSI.

Papert, S., and Solomon, C. (1971). Twenty Things to Do with a Computer. Accessed from ftp://publications.ai.mit.edu/ai-publications/pdf/AIM-248.pdf.

Papert, S., and Watt, D. H. (1977). Assessment and Documentation of a Children's Computer Laboratory. Accessed from https://dspace.mit.edu/handle/1721.1/6286.

Papert, S., Watt, D., diSessa, A., and Weir, S. (1979). Final Report of the Brookline Logo Project, An Assessment and Documentation of a Children's Computer Laboratory, Part III, Detailed Profiles of Each Student's Work. Accessed from https://dspace.mit.edu/handle/1721.1/6324.

Piaget, J., and Piaget, J. (1973). *To Understand Is to Invent: The Future of Education*. New York: Grossman Publishers.

Squires, D., and McDougall, A. (1994). *Choosing and Using Educational Software: A Teachers' Guide*. London: RoutledgeFalmer.

Squires, D., and Preece, J. (1996). Usability and Learning: Evaluating the Potential of Educational Software. *Computers & Education, 27*(1), 15–22.

Stager, G. (1998). Laptops and Learning: Can Laptop Computers put the "C" (for Constructivism) in Learning? *Curriculum Administrator*. Accessed from http://www.stager.org/articles/CAlaptoparticle.html.

Stager, G. (2003). The Case for Computing. In S. Armstrong (Ed.), *Snapshots! Educational Insights from the Thornburg Center*. Lake Barrington, Illinois: Thornburg Center.

Stager, G. (2006). Laptops: Growing Pains and Disappointments. *Teacher: The National Education Magazine* (August 2006), 44.

Stager, G. (2014). Progressive Education and the Maker Movement – Symbiosis Or Mutually Assured Destruction? Paper presented at the Fab Learn, Palo Alto, Calif., October 2014.

Stager, G. S. (1995). Laptop Schools Lead the Way in Professional Development. *Educational Leadership, 53*(2), 78–81.

Stager, G. S. (1997). Logo and Learning Mathematics – No Room for Squares. *Computers in the Schools, 14*(1–2).

United States Department of Education. (2010). A Blueprint for Reform: The Reauthorization of the Elementary and Secondary Education Act. Retrieved from: http://www2.ed.gov/policy/elsec/leg/blueprint/blueprint.pdf.

CHAPTER 4

CODING CLEVERNESS

A beginner's guide to artificial intelligence

Peter W. McOwan and Paul Curzon

NATURAL BORN COMPUTERS

It's a dark, wet winter's night, and you've just arrived home after a long day at work. The train was late, apparently a problem with the company's new signalling software you discover when they eventually announce the reason on the carriage intercom. The trip from the station, though, went more smoothly; your car satnav on the way back talked you through a route avoiding a new patch of roadworks. The car auto-park let you relax as the car slipped into that tight parking space near your front door, meaning you didn't get very wet from the torrential rain. As you approach the front door, a motion detector triggers the outside light to come on, and you are safely home.

It's a common enough story, but it shows how frequently we come across intelligent systems in our daily life. From the complex software that runs the signals based on where the trains are on the network, to the code being run on your car's computer to let it self-park or the simple on-off motion detection switch for the outside light, each of these is doing something that in its own way we would consider intelligent. The way they work is by following rules. Take the simplest, the outside light switch. Its rule base – the set of rules it uses to operate – is very simple. It normally takes as input the passive infrared (the heat energy we give off), and when it detects this it triggers the light switch to turn on. The basic code would be:

```
IF (detect heat) THEN (switch on outside light)
```

Just a simple rule, but a useful rule, as it gives us an effective smart switch. The manufacturers can add other tricks to improve the way it works. If the switch just detects heat, passing cats or other animals would mistakenly set it off. To avoid this, the detection can be given a threshold: an amount of infrared heat energy it has to detect before it triggers the switch. This works because cats, dogs and foxes all have much smaller bodies than humans, so give out less heat. The threshold can be set (i.e. a number, T, chosen) so that only when a human being comes into the sensor's view is there enough infrared to switch the switch. Our switch code, with just the simple introduction of a threshold, a number, got smarter. Above that value T, the detector's rule 'fires' and its signal is sent to the light to turn it on.

```
IF (heat > threshold T) THEN (switch on outside light)
```

If, instead, this 'human detecting' switch was operated by another human, we would most likely consider that person smart enough to do the job if they performed this way: clever enough to tell the difference between an animal and human. This is the basis of artificial intelligence: creating software and machines that mimic what we would identify as natural intelligence.

It's not just human level intelligence, though: we need to consider intelligence in animals and common insects like house flies and honey bees too. Flies can avoid being swatted. Bees have a strong social structure, and even the ability to communicate where distant nectar is through the waggle dance. Both creatures have many fewer nerve cells in their brains compared with a human, yet they can still be intelligent.

Human level intelligence comes from the complex networks of *billions* of specialist nerve cells, called neurons, which make up our brains. These neurons, in their simplest form, just add together the amount of signal that arrives at their inputs. In our brains, these signals are electrochemical pulses. If there is enough of a signal to pass a threshold, the pulses fire their own signal onward along long thin projections called axons. These connect to other neurons, and so on, forming a network. Connections can be positive or negative, depending on how the neuron is set. Positive excitatory signals add to the sum at the next neuron. Negative inhibitory signals are subtracted from the sum. Each axon also has a particular 'weighting', which determines how strong the signal passing through each axon is. It is the way these neurons are connected together, the values of the individual thresholds, and the strengths of the interconnections, that give our brains their individual characteristics. As your brain learns, these various values change, encoding new behaviours and knowledge. Networks of neurons give our brains their complexity, but, in their basic form, they are simply switches with simple rules, like our external light example. Their rules are only slightly more complicated:

```
X = SUM of Input Signals both excitatory (+) and inhibitory (-)

IF (X > Threshold) THEN (Fire weighted signal along axon to other connected
neurons)
```

REFLECTION ACTIVITY

Is simply following rules actually intelligent behaviour?

Is a single neuron in your brain intelligent? Does adding lots of neurons together make them intelligent?

Are there types of data we should prevent artificial intelligence from processing?

Can an artificial intelligence die? Should artificial intelligence have rights, similar to animal rights?

LEARNING THE UNPLUGGED WAY

What happens when we take these simple neural switches and start to put them together? The following 'unplugged classroom activity' explores this. Unplugged activities are ways to demonstrate computer science principles without the use of a computer. They are a good way to prepare a class, ensuring they understand the basic ideas before they start to write code. This activity is based on the book *Vehicles* by Valentino Braitenberg, which is an easy to read introduction to artificial intelligence and robotics. He describes theoretical creatures, simple robots he calls 'vehicles', with basic components that, when connected in different ways, give rise to different creature behaviours.

Classroom exploration: creature comforts

For this classroom activity you will need:

■ some clear space for the 'creatures' to move around in;
■ a torch;
■ some string to represent the axons; and
■ some small cardboard tubes to represent signals, with the tubes clearly labelled with marker pen as either + for excitatory signals or − for inhibitory signals.

Each pupil plays the part of one of two components: a light detector or a motor unit. These units (i.e. pupils) are connected together by short lengths of string, their axons, and on these strings the cardboard tubes represent the electrochemical signal as they run along the axon. When a rule is fired (activated), the signal, represented by the tube, is pushed along the string to the connected component. Neural networks can be easily built and modified by connecting pupils together with the string in more complex ways.

The light detector pupil has a simple job. They can't move themselves, but they do have a rule saying that when they see the torch is on they should 'fire' their signal along their axon. That is, they should push the cardboard tube along their string to the pupil the string connects to. The motor unit pupils have a different task: they can't detect whether the light is on or not (to reinforce this, they could be blindfolded), but they can move backwards or forwards. The direction is dependent on their personal rule and the sorts of input signal they get. For example, the rule could be that if they receive a positive, excitatory signal, they move forwards. If instead they receive an inhibitory signal, they move backwards. If the pupils' rules are written down for them to read, this helps them remember,. This also starts to form the elements of code they can develop later: programming either real robots or virtual ones in a programming environment like Scratch or Greenfoot.

Rules of the robot game

An example might be for the pupil playing the part of a motor unit called MOTOR UNIT, M1, to be given the rule:

```
IF (received signal is positive) THEN (move gently forwards)

IF (received signal is negative) THEN (move gently backwards)
```

The rule for the light detector pupil, let's call them LIGHT DETECTOR UNIT, L1, would be:

IF (torch on) THEN (fire positive signal)

assuming they are being an excitatory sensory neuron. On the other hand, if they are being an inhibitory sensory neuron, a light being present would instead mean that the neuron fires a signal that will inhibit other neurons. Their rule would then be:

IF (torch on) THEN (fire negative signal)

What happens if we link the sensory and motor units together? The two pupils should stand close together – facing the torch, linked by the string – to become a single combined 'creature'. The string here represents the axon link, which we will call W1, between the neurons. Our 'creature' now consists of the units L1, W1 and M1. When the torch is switched, on the 'sensor unit' detects this and, following its rule, fires a signal along (string) W1, to the motor unit, M1, by sliding the cardboard tube along the string, mimicking the electrochemical signal in a brain axon. Suppose the light detector used is an excitatory sensory neuron, so the signal it fires, following its rule, is positive: the cardboard tube is marked with a '+'. Then, when it reaches the motor unit at the end of the string axon, that motor unit in turn follows its rules, so moving the combined 'creature' gently forwards a few steps towards the light. The link resets, by sliding the tube back to the light detector pupil. If the light is still on, the signal fires again, the tube moves along the string and the 'creature' moves a few steps forwards again. We have built a creature that 'likes' bright light and will move towards it.

Now consider what happens if we replace the positive signal tube with the negative signal tube. This new 'creature' now moves gently backwards from the light. It 'dislikes' bright light. Through simply changing the type of connection we have changed the behaviour of the creature from light-seeking to light-avoiding. We could also change the rate at which the sensor fires, or its strength, so more signal is produced when the light is stronger (e.g. two torches). More signal might mean move forwards faster, for example. We could change the threshold for the light sensor, so that a half covered torch gives no detection, so no signal fires until the torch is at full brightness. These variations mirror the basic operations of a neural network: a series of interconnected, simple neurons that each have specific thresholds and strengths (often called weights) connected to other neurons. The trick is to know how to set the weights and the thresholds, and that's where learning comes into it.

REFLECTION ACTIVITY

Are there some jobs that robots and artificial intelligence should not be allowed to do?

Are robots a threat to humanity, and if so, why?

LEARNING ABOUT MACHINE LEARNING

There are two basic types of machine learning: supervised and unsupervised learning. All machine learning techniques have the goal of being able to take data and uncover important distinctions and patterns within that data.

Unsupervised learning uses statistical methods to automatically allocate the data to particular *clusters*. Clusters here are sets of data that share some common characteristic. Typically this is done by a method called 'K means clustering', where the computer starts by guessing some initial central values for the clusters. Then the data is introduced. Data that is close to these cluster central values is then added to that cluster, and the new centre recalculated based on the values in the cluster. In this way, over time, the various clusters build up to hold data that is alike in some way, and this happens without us needing to tell the computer what the cluster for any particular piece of data should be.

Supervised learning, by contrast, uses data we already know something about. As a simple example, consider a bank deciding on the credit rating to give a customer. Let's assume there are two credit rating categories: GOOD and POOR. The bank has decided that if a customer has a large amount of savings, or if they have had savings with the bank for a long time, their credit rating is GOOD. A POOR credit rating customer would have a small amount of savings or have only been saving for a short time with the bank.

In this example of supervised learning, the bank would take a set of its customers that it considered to have a good rating and label their data (their savings and time with the bank) as GOOD. Similarly, it would take a set of customers with a poor rating and label their data as POOR. The machine learning algorithm would now need to use this labelled data and work out what makes the difference between a GOOD and a POOR customer. How much savings do they need to be GOOD? How long do they need to have been with the bank? We can understand how it does this by thinking geometrically. Consider a standard two dimensional X, Y graph, where X along the horizontal is time with the bank, and Y vertically is the amount of savings. GOOD customers will tend to have both high X values (have been with the bank a long time) and high Y values (large amount of savings). POOR credit rating customers will correspondingly tend to have low X and Y values. To learn to tell the difference, we need to find some way to find the boundary between GOOD and POOR. We can then allocate any new customer into one of these two classes, or data clusters.

Separating the good from the bad

We can do this with a simple neural network. Consider one with two inputs, A and B, connected to a threshold unit that has threshold T. Input A is connected to the threshold unit with a weight, w1, and input B is connected to it with a different weight, w2. When two input values are applied at A and B, the amount of signal reaching the threshold unit will be the sum of the value input at A multiplied by the weight w1 plus the value input at B multiplied by w2. If this sum is greater than the threshold value T, the threshold unit fires (OUT=1); if not, the output is zero (OUT=0). The boundary where the threshold unit flips from giving output OUT=1 to output OUT=0 is the interesting bit. That's where the sum of the weighted signals from A and B equals the threshold, T.

A and B can be associated with the data we have for a particular customer. At A we will input the X value, the time with the bank, and B will be the Y value, the amount of the customer's savings. Using a dot (.) to denote multiplication, the boundary will be given by the equation w1.X + w2.Y = T, which just says that the sum of weighted values equals the threshold. With some rearrangement, this gives the straight line: Y = − (w1/w2)X + (T/w2). This is now in the familiar y = mx+c straight line form with gradient (i.e. slope) m = − (w1/w2) and y-axis intercept at the point c = T/w2. Any point above this line (the weighted sum is more than the threshold) is classified as a GOOD credit rating, so leads to the network firing (OUT=1). It will happen with large (X,Y) values. Low (X,Y) values typically won't beat the threshold (i.e. be below the line), so it won't fire and OUT=0. These are classified as POOR customers. The question is, though, what should the weights and the thresholds actually be, given our bank's data?

Changing the weights in the network changes the characteristics of the line, so the ability to learn to classify two different groups of input patterns corresponds to finding weights so that the line separates the groups, with those the bank labelled GOOD above the line and those it labelled POOR below. We don't know where the line should be, so we start by setting the weights and threshold randomly. We take each customer the bank has classified and check whether its corresponding point falls on the right side of the line: those marked POOR below the line, and those marked GOOD above it. If the weights and threshold values we currently have classify the customer correctly, nothing changes. However, as we go through all our labelled GOOD and POOR customers, there are going to be some mistakes − some customers misclassified by the random boundary line we drew by choosing random weights. When that happens, we need to adjust the weights and threshold to make the error as small as possible. We add some small value, e, to the old weight and old threshold to get their new values. That is, we do the calculations:

New threshold = Old threshold + e

New weighting = Old weighting + e . Input

For the weighting, we multiply the value by the input so that each weight is adjusted by the input's contribution towards the erroneous sum.

In its simplest form, e could just be the error for the customer being checked: the difference between the target output T for the customer (e.g. a GOOD rating so OUT=1 for a good customer) and the actual output OUT from the network at the current stage. As an assignment:

e = Target output − Actual Output

Changing values depending on this term (*Target output − Actual Output*) is often called 'delta rule learning'. It is positive if the output is too low and negative if the output is too high compared with the desired target. That means it will adjust the weighting and threshold in the right direction. However, rather than make big changes, it can be better to adjust the rating more slowly, nudging the line in the right direction. Therefore, a small positive constant R, called the 'learning rate', is used to scale the error. It determines the amount of change each weight undergoes in an iteration. The value of e is therefore set to:

e = R. (Target output − Actual Output)

This adjustment may help ensure this customer is rated the right way, but others that were right may become wrong as a result. To reduce this error, this simple network (called a perceptron) iterates through all the labelled data again and again. The full algorithm becomes:

```
Set the initial weights and the threshold to small random values.
Set the learning rate R to a small value.
REPEAT the following UNTIL there is no error for any data
{
      Enter labelled input training set of values and desired Target Output
      Calculate the Actual Output
      IF an error occurs (i.e. the Target Output and Actual Output differ)
      THEN adapt the weights and thresholds with:
      {
        e = R. (Target Output - Actual Output)

        New weighting of A = Old weighting of A + (e . Input of A)
        New weighting of B = Old weighting of B + (e . Input of B)
        New Threshold = Old Threshold + e
      }
}
```

Once this learning cycle is complete and the weights and thresholds are fixed, the network will have 'learned' the labelled training data. It will have drawn a line on the graph that can be used to label each customer. That means that when a new customer has to be rated, their (X,Y) values can be input into the network and the resulting output OUT=0 or OUT=1 for POOR/GOOD clarification can be made automatically.

For example, the line generated after the learning ends up being y=x, a straight line gradient 1 through the origin. This line boundary separates the classes based on customers with their savings equal to their time with the bank: y equals x. Therefore GOOD is when the (X,Y) value is above this line and POOR is below. The neural network that does this classification, remember $Y = -(w1/w2)X + (T/w2)$, is w1=−1, w2=1 and T=0. If the input is, say, (2,4) then 2.(−1)+4.1= 2; this is above the 0 threshold and so is classified as GOOD. Customer (2,1), however, is 2.(−1)+1.1= −1, which is less than the 0 threshold and so is classified as POOR.

Using the framework and methods described above, you can give pupils a simple exercise to code up and teach a simple perceptron, using a labelled set of data you provide. Their code can then be tested with a set of unseen data you provide at the end of the exercise.

Going in deep

There are, of course, limitations to this simple system: what if the GOOD and POOR customers can't be separated by a straight line? The error may not vanish, however long we cycle through. The best boundary line might be curved. What happens if we have more than the two values X and Y? For example, we may also want to include other factors like the customer's age, or whether they are a home owner. This is called multi-dimensional data. In fact, there are a whole load of problems with this simple perceptron system and the delta learning rule. To resolve them, computer scientists have worked out ways to build layers of these simple neurons, and developed the mathematics that allows errors in the output to be pushed back through the layers of the network, modifying the weights and thresholds as they go. These layers allow complex, arbitrarily shaped decision boundaries to be learned by combining sets of straight lines. It is the multi-dimensional training data sets that shape these boundaries as the data is processed. Complex neural networks like these, with many layers, are often referred to as 'deep neural networks'. At each layer, the network has learned to extract particular features and patterns in the training data, and it is the combinations of these different features that give these networks their overall power to classify.

These systems learn from their mistakes. For them, a mistake pointed out is just another piece of training data to be fed back into the layers, thereby generating new and better features to work with. Such multi-layer, deep systems can be used to mine genetic data looking for patterns that can give rise to diseases, or scan through financial transactions or internet communications looking for suspicious activity. As the computational power available to computers increases, so larger data sets can be processed and faster data learning can occur. The data sets input can be in the form of pixels in images or video footage. Even though these involve massive amounts of data, it's possible for neural networks to learn to recognise images such as faces or objects, spoken words as well as music, giving us new ways to provide useful services.

STANDING ON THE SHOULDERS OF EXPERTS

The rules that artificial intelligence systems use can be at a higher level than simply simulating the properties of switching neurons in a network. There are approaches to artificial intelligence that use far more detailed, natural and context specific rules. These are called *expert systems* or *production rule systems*. They are formed by having a series of rules, determined by human experts in particular topics or domains, and encoded into the systems rule base (its bank of knowledge). To build these systems requires special techniques to extract an expert's domain knowledge into an abstracted simplified world view, with rules that are simple to code. These rules normally exist in the form of complex sets of IF THEN ELSE type statements that can extract appropriate knowledge from the knowledge base to support decision making.

Existing examples include systems that help suggest a suitable diagnosis from a series of medical test results, or have the ability to optimise the performance of an oil drill, automatically tune the channels on a TV, play a game of chess or safely parallel park a car.

CLASSROOM EXPLORATION: MAKING THE RULES UP

Have the class select a simple task such as taking a good selfie, or making a cup of tea. In groups, they should work through and write down the series of IF THEN rules they feel capture the necessary knowledge and decisions involved in the task. The rules can then be swapped with another pupil group, who use them to perform the task. This will stress that differing experts may have differing approaches to the same domain, and that the activity of knowledge engineering is often very challenging: extracting the basics, blending these all together into an effective single rules set, and dealing with linguistic variances and vague terms. The different groups can evaluate the quality of the simple expert systems developed, perhaps giving a score for elements such as ease of use, effectiveness and so on. This is analogous to user group testing and feedback in a software engineering design cycle.

Pupils can improve the design and content of their own expert system in line with the feedback from the 'user group', then proceed to code it up on the computer. Once the code is implemented, they can test it with another group and see whether the scores have improved.

ROUND THE HOUSES NATURALLY

Brains, via expert systems and neural networks, aren't the only inspiration for artificial intelligence. Another popular form of supervised learning is called a 'genetic algorithm'. It is based on the evolutionary process of survival of the fittest. Here, the problem to be solved is represented by values on a 'digital chromosome'. One application is the classic travelling salesperson problem, where, given a collection of cities and the distance between them, you need to find the best route that visits all the cities only once and uses the minimum distance for the round trip. A series of possible solutions are first randomly created. This initial 'population' of individuals is simply a list of different random routes round the cities to visit. Each possible individual is then evaluated. That is, the distance that needs to be covered to go round the cities in the order given is calculated. This value is the individual solution's 'fitness': good, 'healthy' solutions have short distances, while poorer, less fit solutions have longer round trip distances.

Pairs of good solutions are then used to 'reproduce'. That is, a part of one good solution is swapped with a part of the other possible good solution. This is called 'crossover'. The fitness of these offspring individuals is then evaluated, and again the fittest survive into the next stage. The idea here is that concentrating on good solutions and swapping bits of them round may give even better solutions. Of course, it might be that an even better solution exists in patterns that haven't been tested, so to allow for this, in analogy to natural evolution, random mutations are allowed in the population. That means totally new solutions are created and evaluated. This cycle of breeding and mutation with survival of the fittest continues until a solution is found with the fitness level desired. Alternatively, a time limit is reached and the best solution then available is selected.

We now move on to look at an example, which allows pupils the opportunity to code this type of simulation.

CLASSROOM EXPLORATION: GAME OF ZONES

In a distant land, you are the Queen's messenger, fleet of foot and fast of tongue, but just ever so slightly lazy. The Queen needs a message to be taken around all the Clan Chiefs, warning of imminent invasion from the frozen North. The towns that sit in the middle of the zones controlled by the clans are connected by roads, safe from thieves and wolves. You know you should stick to using these. The five Clan stronghold towns are called Akalaban, Britanish, Covemear, Dela and Ewe, but the locals know them as A, B, C, D and E. You have an ancient chart that shows the towns and the road distances that connect them all to each other, so you can easily calculate the journey around the towns, visiting them all just once. For a particular journey, the total distance is the sum of all the distances between the cities visited. Now, all that remains is to find the shortest route, and that's done using the genetic algorithm introduced previously.

Enter the zombies: mutation

With 'swap mutation', two towns in the route are selected at random and then swapped. For example, a swap mutation to the journey [A, B, C, D, E] might end up with the journey [A, B, E, D, C]. Here, towns C and E were switched, creating a new possible journey, containing all the same towns as before. Now they are just in a different order and so have a different round trip distance. Because the swap mutation swaps pre-existing values, it can never create a journey with missing or duplicate towns – and that's exactly what we want.

It takes two to tango: crossover

We now need a 'crossover' breeding method that does the same: all towns present and no duplicates. One way to do this crossover is to select a subset at random from the first parent, and add that subset to the offspring being created. Any towns missing are then added to the offspring from the second parent, in the same order as in that second parent. It's clearer with an example. Suppose our two parents are Parent 1 = [B, D, A, C, E] and Parent 2 = [A, C, D, E, B]. We randomly select a subset of Parent 1, say A, C, E. These are the towns in positions 3, 4 and 5 of the route, so the offspring so far looks like [?, ?, A, C, E]; we then look at Parent 2 and add the missing towns in the order they are in the Parent 2 journey. The first town in Parent 2's journey is A, but that's in the offspring already; the next town is C, which is also already in the offspring, so we skip it. Town 3 in Parent 2 is D; that's not in the offspring, so in it goes in position 1, giving [D, ?, A, C, E]. Similarly, E in Parent 2 is skipped, as it is in the offspring already, leaving B. The final offspring values are [D, B, A, C, E]. Each of the towns is included only once, and the offspring carries both parents' journey traits.

The class can apply the ideas of a genetic algorithm to solve the problem for the Queen's messenger. Working it through first on paper, they can randomly generate a population of initial journeys by selecting the letters from a bag containing all five towns. For each journey, they score the total distance it covers. This is its fitness: shorter journeys are better or fitter than longer journeys. After selecting the good, fit, possible journeys, from those drawn, the pupils can perform the crossover and mutation operations as described on them. They then assess the fitness values of the resulting modified journeys. This series of steps – evaluation → crossover/mutation → evaluation – loops for a pre-set time. During this loop, pupils should see the fitness of the current best solution increase overall, giving at the end a route for the messenger to optimally use. Having trialled it, the pupils can then code up the problem. The outline of the code might look something like:

```
Create random initial population of possible solutions.
    REPEAT UNTIL stopping criteria met
    {
    Calculate fitness of each member of population
    Mutate random individuals and calculate fitness
    Crossover individuals with high fitness
    Delete individuals with low fitness
    }
```

As the number of towns increases, it become more difficult to find the shortest route. This type of problem, where the time taken to solve it grows significantly with the number of elements, is called an NP-complete problem. Very quickly, the straightforward solution of just checking every possible journey to determine the best becomes impractical. For example, if we have 16 cities, there are more than a trillion possible journeys round them! This is why we use techniques such as a genetic algorithm, which gets a good answer in a reasonable amount of time without checking all possibilities. It's called a 'heuristic method': a method of learning that works but may not be the very best possible.

CLASSROOM EXPLORATION: AIINGO – THE ARTIFICIAL INTELLIGENCE BINGO

The growth of the Internet has led to our homes and environments becoming permeated by connected, communicating intelligent devices. The ability of machine learning to win games in areas once considered to be areas of human supremacy such as chess, Go and the US TV quiz show *Jeopardy* starts also to give us an inkling of both the opportunities and the threats of artificial intelligence (AI).

This final activity is not about coding, but rather is about an equally important area: getting the class to consider many of the potential ethical and societal dilemmas that AI and robotics could pose, both now and in the future. The broad impact of AI based technology on society in terms of jobs being replaced, our feelings of trust towards AI as it drives our cars or flies our aeroplanes, the legal or medical consultation where AI is part of the picture, and philosophical questions on machine threats and computer creativity and consciousness should be part of an overall lesson. One way to accomplish this is by playing AI bingo.

First a set of bingo cards is prepared for the class. On the card grid, rather than a random bingo number, there are random keywords related to AI. Examples could be jobs, cars, safety, hospitals, children, space flight, military or the law. There are numerous themes around AI, and frequent media stories related to AI research and applications, allowing this activity to include topical discussions.

In addition to the class set of bingo cards, the keywords are all written on sheets of paper and crumpled into balls, which are held in a plastic bag or other container. The container is shaken and the paper balls removed at random; they are opened and the keyword read out. Pupils with that keyword on their bingo card score it out, the objective being to complete a line vertically, horizontally or diagonally as in a traditional bingo game. When each keyword is selected and called out, there is an opportunity for a wider ranging class discussion on the selected topics. By undertaking some background web research on these areas, teachers can gain sufficient basic knowledge to provoke the discussions about this wide ranging set of ethical dilemmas, but this class activity is more about the pupils' expressing their views on the issues, rather than deep technical knowledge, that are important. As an alternative, give the pupils different sets of the keywords to research themselves in advance, giving them the chance to share what they have found when the topics come up.

FINAL THOUGHTS

This chapter has given a brief introduction to some of the main techniques of artificial intelligence. We have seen how the natural world is used as inspiration and looked at a range of applications for the technology. Simple pseudo-code examples have been presented that can be used to develop simple AI programs, along with the discussions of the methods used. These principles are exactly those employed in current large scale AI applications.

The chapter concludes with an activity to engage pupils with the important issue of the ethical impacts of AI on our world and their future. Teachers may also find the questions for reflection that follow useful for discussion in class, alongside undertaking the unplugged and computer based exercises.

REFLECTION ACTIVITY

Would a robot make a better soldier than a human?

Would an artificial intelligence be a better politician than a human?

If a self-driving car crashes, who is responsible? Is it the occupant or the computer programmer who wrote the car's driving code?

Would you trust a computer to diagnose your illness and prescribe medicine?

Would you have a computer chip implanted in your brain to boost your intelligence?

Would you have a computer defend you in court?

Should a primary school child be sent to school alone in a self-driving car?

It's been argued that AI technology should not be used to replace people in positions that require respect and care; is that right?

REFERENCES

Braitenberg, V. (1984). *Vehicles: Experiments in Synthetic Psychology*. Cambridge, MA: MIT Press.

The machine learning and AI pages on our web pages, Computer Science for Fun (www.cs4fn.org) and Teaching London Computing (www.teachinglondoncomputing.org), give more information, stories on applications and unplugged activities to use in the classroom.

BITS AND BYTES IN BLUE, PROGRAMMING IN PINK

Gender bias or reality?

Kimberely Fletcher Nettleton and Michael W. Kessinger

I (Kimberely) have to admit that as a mother of boys, I have been known to beg, "Please, boys, let me just stand in the middle of the pink aisle for just a minute." While they looked on with disgust, a few minutes spent breathing in the atmosphere of pink and sparkle will fortify me for another half hour debate over which action figure has the most power. And I ask myself, "What is this strange power of pink?"

GENDER, GAMES, AND TOYS

Since early times, children have been playing with toys. Archeologists have found small toys nestled among the remains of children. From dolls to rattles, parents fashioned toys for their children. Children have sat on the floors of their homes and pushed everything from chariots to trucks. England has had an active toy industry since the early fourteenth century (Orme, 2001). When children died, favorite toys were lovingly placed alongside them in their graves. From pre-history to today, toys have been a part of childhood.

It is not known how much playtime children were given in the past. While children *had* toys, it is believed that many of these had an instructional value attached to them. A child-sized bow and arrow may have had more to do with learning to hunt than passing time, and many games may have been used to teach survival skills (Elkonin, 1999). Knowing how to find food or nurture may have been imparted through toys and games. Today's modern parents purchase survival-skill toys, which are cunningly labelled *educational*. Today's instructional toys are designed to increase memory, develop problem-solving skills, or improve understanding of science. Smith (2015) suggests socialization through toys has a strong correlation with the career choices that women and men make.

Until children are old enough to voice their preference, parents generally make the initial decisions on which toys to buy for them. Overwhelmingly, parents choose toys for children based on clearly defined gender roles (Rheingold & Cook, 1975). In case parents are confused about which toys are appropriate, advertisers and merchants helpfully steer them to the right toys by their use of color. Toy stores have pink and purple aisles for girls, black and red aisles for boys (Auster & Mansbach, 2012). Where to shop for the right toy cannot be made clearer. Surprisingly, while girls will choose to play with toys that have black or red packaging or any of the darker colors, boys will rarely play with a toy or game that has a girl color associated with it (Auster & Mansbach). Additionally, females are more likely to be attracted to bright colors than males (Cyr & Bonanni, 2005; Moss & Colman, 2001).

All of which begs the question: *Do I find the pink aisle energizing because I am a female or just because I have been socialized to like it? Or is it just a moment of calm in the dark world of superheroes and villains?*

Gender preferences in toys have been studied for many years. Several early studies showed a strong gender preference among children in their choices of toys. They found that gender stereotypes were very strong at an early age, with girls preferring dolls while boys consistently chose to play with toys that came with wheels or wings (Carter & Patterson, 1982; Connor & Serbin, 1977; Downs, 1983; Kahlenberg & Hein, 2010; Liss, 1981; Otnes et al., 1994).

Children develop their gender stereotypes early in life. Between the ages of 2 and 6, they develop a rigid understanding of male and female, which becomes more flexible between the ages of 6 and 11 (Trautner et al., 2005). Gender stereotyping in play is often strongly reinforced in schools, with teachers encouraging students to play only with gender appropriate toys (Lynch, 2015).

Based on gender, developing fetuses receive different hormones in the womb (Jordan-Young, 2010). Current brain research continues to suggest that there are differences in hormonal and activity variations in the brains of men and women that affect health, development, and growth. Disparities in male and female brains have been documented and are being closely studied (McCarthy et al., 2012). For example, the presence of a greater number of neuronal fibers in girls' brains is thought to be the reason why girls are better at reading the emotions of others. It may explain why girls process and collect information differently than boys (Patel et al., 1998). Additionally, a study of reading skills spanning forty countries found that girls consistently outperformed males in reading (Mullis et al., 2007).

Individuality should not be discounted, as it may be more determinative than gender (Honigsfeld & Dunn, 2003). Bluhm (2013) examined several brain research studies and suggests that they have been flawed by researchers allowing stereotype and bias to shape their data. There are many males and females whose skills and personalities are not closely identified with traditional gender stereotypes. The controversy of gender stereotyping continues.

Francis (2010) found that children between 3 and 5 years old identified strongly with toys and videos (or television shows) that were gender specific. Boys chose action and adventure toys and preferred watching films with male action heroes. Additionally, Francis claimed male toys supported building, science, and problem solving skills. These are skills that support a strong foundation in science, technology, engineering, and mathematics (STEM) curriculums.

In contrast, girls' choices: Dolls, stuffed animals, and videos supported communication and nurturing skills (Francis, 2010). The types of toys with which girls and boys choose to play provide support for early skill acquisition. A preponderance of toys that are sold and advertised primarily for boys have strong visual spatial, eye-hand coordination, and problem solving skills embedded within (Smith, 2015). While research suggests that males have stronger spatial abilities than females (Gurian et al., 2001), it may be that the experiences and type of toys that boys are exposed to at an early age contribute to what is considered an innate masculine trait.

In addition to playing with toys, children also play games. Weinberger and Stein (2008) found that the ways in which kindergarten girls and boys play games differed depending on with whom they were playing. When girls played with girls, they were not as competitive. Boys were competitive with each other and in mixed gender groups. Girls were found to be more competitive in mixed gender groups. It is interesting to note, however, that although the girls did not make as many *competitive* moves in games as boys, they did play as *strategically* as the boys did. Thus, while girls may not have played competitively, the use of analysis skills to strategize when playing was distributed evenly between boys and girls.

Many board games are thought to be gender neutral. Popular games such as *Clue* (also known as *Cluedo*) and *Monopoly* were not designed for only one gender. Children may interact with a game in very different ways. Based on current gender research, the storyline and puzzle involved in the game of *Clue* may be more appealing to girls, while the competition involved in solving the crime and reaching a goal first may be what appeals to boys (Gurian & Stevens, 2006).

VISUAL GAMES

One of the most popular visual games developed around 1987 was *Where's Wally?* or, as it is known in North America, *Where's Waldo?*. Martin Handford designed Wally/Waldo when asked to create a character with peculiar features that would be visible in the middle of a crowd (Slivers, 2010). The object of the game was to find Wally within an environment that contained anywhere from 100 to 4,000 tiny figures.

Handford created a number of children's books based upon Wally, and the first edition, *Where's Wally?*, was a big seller around Christmas time in 1987 (Slivers, 2010). Additional books published featuring Wally/Waldo were *Where's Wally Now?*; *Where's Waldo? The Fantastic Journey*; *Where's Wally in Hollywood?*; and *Where's Waldo? The Wonder Book*. Eventually *Where's Waldo?* (North American version) became a computer game in 1991, developed by Craig Jakubowski. Currently, *Where's Waldo?* is an online game devised for the enjoyment of his fans. As of 2013, the book was being printed in 19 different languages, with Wally's name changing according to the country: "Charlie" in France, "Walter" in Germany, "Ali" in Turkey, "Efi" in Israel, and "Willy" in Norway (Upton, 2013).

Why are visual games so attractive to young people? What are the benefits? According to Nettleton (2008), they can improve learning. With visual games, fast moving actions help develop the player's spatial abilities. For many young people, visual games provide a challenge of solving a problem that, in their minds, does not require "academic knowledge." Young people play games, focusing on developing skills, never realizing that the strategies they use are based upon the various academic experiences they have in school every day. Whether it's a puzzle, a maze, making words out of a series of letters, or a picture containing multiple images, the challenge is to make use of strategies to make it to the end – to win.

Gender differences in visual processing tend to focus on complexity and selectivity. Darley and Smith (1995) found that gender differences exist in visual processing skills. Women generally examine and analyze all data before making decisions. Thus, in *Where's Wally?*, females would be more apt to examine the whole picture, develop an understanding of the venue in which Wally is hiding, look at the activities taking place on the page, categorize the stories occurring within the picture, and search for Wally within small sections of where he would most likely be hidden. In contrast, males are generally considered goal orientated and are more selective when visually processing information (Meyers-Levy & Sternthal, 1991). When searching for Wally, most males would not look at the whole picture, but would look for any spots of red and white within the page. The focus would be on just finding Wally's red and white striped shirt within the picture.

"When I am old," I (Kimberely) have told my son, "Your one job will be to help me find my way out of the mall." Does this mean I am visually-spatially challenged because I have a hard time navigating my way out of a store? On the other hand, I can also call out to my husband, "Look in the closet, top shelf, left-hand side, in the red box." And know that whatever he is searching for will be there. Are these visualizing skills based on gender differences in abilities or individual survival skills?

VIDEO AND COMPUTER GAMES

Although gender research strongly suggests that males are more competitive when playing games (Gurian et al., 2001), Yang and Huesmann (2013) also found that boys do not just thrive on competition. They have a predilection towards violent media: whether playing video games or watching television. Many video games are demanding, and appear to be designed specifically for men's skills. Bonanno and Kommers (2005) noted, "Males prefer command structures that make them feel in control, especially by continually intervening through actions guided by their prominent visual spatial capabilities and manipulating information (guessing distances, calculating angles, deciding strength of action, and so on) in working memory" (p. 29).

While video console games are played by both males and females, this type of game is predominantly played by males (Entertainment Software Association (ESA), 2015). In 2014, two of the top ten video games sold were versions of *Call of Duty*. Also in the top ten were *Grand Theft Auto*, National Basketball Association (NBA) and National Football League (NFL) games, *Minecraft*, *Destiny*, *Super Smash Brothers*, *Watch Dogs*, and *FIFA 15*. These games were to be played on console devices. Of all the video games sold in 2014, 49.9 percent of the games were action or shooter games. Only 9.1 percent were role-playing games and 4.1 percent strategy games (ESA, 2015).

When examining how males and females played games, Hsieh et al. (2015) found that boys were more physically active when playing. When following movement, they moved. Boys leaned in towards the screen, matching body movement with their eye movement. Girls were more likely to remain focused and careful while they played, moving only their eyes to follow onscreen play. A fast-paced action game may be more suited to males, as they appear to need more positive emotional feedback than females do when performing tasks (Chia-Ju et al., 2015). This positive feedback may come in the form of earning extra lives, levels, points, or perks and should be given regularly and quickly (Kiili, 2005).

Many video console games are very structured, involving detailed character building and many levels of skill. The amount of time it takes to learn to play, create characters, and develop skill levels may be one reason why males play these types of games more often than females. Tenth grade boys (aged 15–16 years) allocate 38 percent of their time to video games, while girls spend only 6 percent (Canadian Teachers' Federation, 2003; Sanford & Madill, 2006). As young people enter college, the amount of time spent on video games falls dramatically. By their second year, men play video games approximately six hours a week and women play two hours a week (Bonanno & Kommers, 2005). The types of games that women and men each play may reflect the amount of time they are willing to invest in the game.

There was a great difference between the types of video games and the types of computer games sold in 2014. Although men are identified with being very competitive and action and goal oriented, both men and women enjoy games with a strategic element in them.

Eight of the top 20 computer games sold were versions of *The Sims*. Also in the top 20 were three games of *Elder Scrolls*, two versions of *Diablo*, two versions of *Warcraft*, and two games of *Civilization*. Of the computer games sold in 2014, only 7.5 percent of the games were action/adventure/shooter games. Instead, an amazing 37.7 percent were strategy games, 20.2 percent were role-playing games, and 24 percent were casual games (ESA, 2015).

CASUAL GAMES

The dearth of females playing video console games has been heavily researched, but casual gaming is an area that appears to be dominated by women. The casual game is considered to be a game that can be easily downloaded and played for a short period of time, usually eight to ten minutes. These games do not require strict attention to play, do not have complex instructions, and may have simple story narratives (Casual Games Association, 2010; Moltenbray, 2006). A surprising majority of players are women. In 2006, Moltenbray wrote, a "typical casual gamer is a 40-something woman. At Pop Cap, 72 percent of our seven million monthly visitors are female, and fully three-quarters are over the age of 35. This is reflective of the industry as a whole" (Moltenbray, 2006, p. 45). By 2010, the number of casual players on the internet had risen to over 200 million. The majority of players were women (Casual Games Association, 2010).

In the worldwide market, the percentage of men playing games on mobile devices is only slightly higher than that of women. While men may play more often, they tend to play popular console action games on their mobile devices. Women are far more interested in casual games. While the percentage of new men and women mobile game players is fairly even, the fastest growing population of new mobile game players are men and women over 51 years of age (Casual Games Association, 2013). And, in every demographic, women are leading in casual game play.

There are many reasons why casual games may appeal to females. Casual games do not require a great deal of time to learn or master. They can be played quickly, do not demand strict attention, and can easily be played as time fillers. Women either *have* less or *use* less leisure time than men. Women who work outside their homes still spend more time on domestic work and taking care of family business than their spouses: cooking, laundry, cleaning, shopping, etc. Women also typically keep the social calendar of the family (Sullivan, 2000; Wheatley, 2013). Perrone-McGovern et al. (2014) suggest that with advances in communication technology, many jobs ooze into evening or weekend time. Casual games can be squeezed into small time slots. Whether in a dentist's office or waiting for children after school, a casual game will easily fill small time slots. These types of games are compatible with a multi-tasking lifestyle.

The design of casual games seems to be more closely aligned to women's strengths. "Females prefer a more concrete, contextualized, and repetitive activity that does not demand risk taking. They prefer adopting a tinkering approach that requires rapid access and retrieval of information from memory involving comparisons and rhythmic movement." (Bonanno & Kommers, 2005, p. 29). On the whole, popular casual games are designed with these attributes.

When examining the characters in casual games, Wohn (2011) found they were primarily female. Additionally, as opposed to the video console game female characters, the casual game females primarily had normal body types and apparel that was not too revealing, and gender was "generally non-stereotypical" (p. 204). These characterizations may help make casual games more appealing to women.

CODING

According to Tom Cormen, a professor in the computer science department at Dartmouth College, there has been and continues to be a gender gap in the field of computer science (Sharp, 2015). He spends time recruiting female students to computer science and also provides mentoring to them. For example, a recent PhD graduate at MIT, Neha Narula, was one of Cormen's mentees, and this was a driving force behind her sticking with computer science (Sharp). Narula's area of study was distributed systems, one of the most male-dominated in computer science – and she "wants to be known for her work, not her gender" (Sharp, para. 1).

Females recognize that there is a gender gap when it comes to computer science and programming. Part of the problem is the culture of the business, and another is the culture of society (Galpin, 2002). According to James (2010), females are being discouraged from going after careers in STEM fields. Reported factors influencing female enrollment in computer science programs include "intimidating classroom climate, ineffective pedagogy, poor academic advising, and inadequate nurturing of students" (Varma, 2007, p. 362). The abilities and potential for success, not gender, should be the deciding factor in pursuing computer science degrees. The traits needed for success in the computing field – rationality, capability, and being goal driven – are shared by both males and females.

In the early years of computing, two women, Rear Admiral Grace Hopper and Augusta Ada Byron Lovelace, had a major impact on the initial development on computers. Women were involved in design, programming, and fund raising in the early years of computer development (Gürer, 1995). While computer science was dominated by males, females were also involved in the early direction computer science would take (Whitecar, 2010).

The history of computer programming has developed over a long period of time. "Although the history of computer science is well documented, one finds very few, if any, women mentioned in the standard texts on the history of this field" (Gürer, 1995, p. 45). If one would dig deep enough, one would find that during the period from 1942 to 1955, a number of young female college graduates were actually involved in the design, development, and operational usage of the first major computer system, the ENIAC (Fritz, 1996).

The fact of the matter is that modern programming languages had their beginning in the mid- and late 1940's. And because of the war efforts during World War II, most of the programmers during that time were women (Gürer, 1995). The languages at that time, "conditional control transfer," *Plankalkul*, and eventually *Short Code*, provided the operator with the ability to perform extremely elementary tasks (Ferguson, 2000; Haigh & Priestly, 2016). It wasn't until 1957 that the first major programming language appeared – *FORTRAN*, a shortened version of the term "FORmula TRANslating" (Ferguson, 2000; Haigh & Priestly, 2016). This language was primarily used for scientific computing and for dealing with numerical data.

One of the restrictions of FORTRAN was its limited ability for handling input and output, which was an essential skill needed in business and industry. Thus, the programming language *COBOL* came to the business and data processing world in 1959. COBOL, whose name is an acronym for "COmmon Business-Oriented Language," was used to handle data processing in the business, financial, and administrative systems for various companies and government (Sammet, 1981).

Behind the scenes, the US Department of Defense was a great influence on COBOL's development. COBOL not only served the business community, but was also used by major universities and various governmental agencies (Bemer, 1971). FLOW-MATIC, a predecessor to COBOL, was invented by Dr. Grace Hopper, a female US Navy Reserve officer and computer programmer (Orlando, 2002). Hopper was a guiding force behind computer engineering principles (Whitecar, 2010).

FLOW-MATIC was developed by Hopper along with a team of programmers to remove the challenges of programmers to be symbol oriented and mathematically trained. Common English was used to provide the instructions for computers to execute (Whitecar, 2010). An example of FLOW-MATIC code would be:

```
(0)  INPUT INVENTORY FILE-A PRICE FILE-B ; OUTPUT PRICED-INV FILE-C
     UNPRICED-INV FILE-D ; HSP D .
(1)  COMPARE PRODUCT-NO (A) WITH PRODUCT-NO (B) IF GREATER GO
     TO OPERATION 10 ; IF EQUAL GO TO OPERATION 5 ; OTHERWISE GO TO
     OPERATION 2 .
(2)  TRANSFER A TO D .
(3)  WRITE-ITEM D .
(4)  JUMP TO OPERATION 8 .
(5)  TRANSFER A TO C .
(6)  MOVE UNIT-PRICE (B) TO UNIT-PRICE (C) .
(7)  WRITE-ITEM C .
(8)  READ-ITEM A ; IF END OF DATA GO TO OPERATION 14 .
(9)  JUMP TO OPERATION 1 .
(10) READ-ITEM B ; IF END OF DATA GO TO OPERATION 12 .
(11) JUMP TO OPERATION 1 .
(12) SET OPERATION 9 TO GO TO OPERATION 2 .
```

```
(13)  JUMP TO OPERATION 2 .
(14)  TEST PRODUCT-NO (B) AGAINST ZZZZZZZZZZZZ ; IF EQUAL GO TO
      OPERATION 16 ; OTHERWISE GO TO OPERATION 15 .
(15)  REWIND B .
(16)  CLOSE-OUT FILES C ; D .
(17)  STOP . (END)
```
(Sammet, 1981, p. 323).

From that point on, various programming languages began popping up around the world almost on a regular schedule: *LISP*, *Algol*, *BASIC*, *Pascal*, *C*, *C++*, and *Java* are all languages that have been used not only in schools, but also in the development of computer applications (Ferguson, 2000).

As the internet became popular and the cost of computers became more affordable for homeowners and business operators, more adaptable computer languages were needed to support new applications. Webpages, created as portals to business, government, and education sites, became commonplace. The ability to create webpages that would eventually be hosted on a webserver for millions to access required writing instructions using a new set of codes. *HyperText Markup Language* (HTML) became a popular computer language for individuals to learn in order to make their mark on the World Wide Web (Raggett, Lam, Alexander, & Kmiec, 1998).

HTML makes use of tags, such as "<p>" and "</p>", to mark the beginning and end of an instruction. The line "<p>Example paragraph</p>" tells the internet browser to display the text: "Example paragraph." Currently, anyone interested in learning to create code with HTML can find a free, complete course online, at Khan Academy. Anyone taking the online course is given an opportunity to learn how to use HTML to create webpages or use it in other applications (Khan Academy, 2016).

Beginning in 2013, the term "coding" began to be used. Is there a difference between programming and coding? Many old-time programmers would say that they provided the code needed for computers to perform a particular task and insist the two words, "programming" and "coding", are synonymous. However, according to Prottsman (2015), there is a distinct and real difference between programming and coding. Programming concerns writing code to be entered into a computer for a specific purpose. Coding, on the other hand, is more about a "playful and non-intimidating description of programming for beginners".

Over the last few years, there has been a push for young people to explore the world of coding. The Hour of Code is a global, web-based movement consisting of a "one-hour introduction to computer science, designed to demystify code and show that anybody can learn the basics" (Hour of Code, 2016a, para 1). Code.org is a non-profit organization started in 2013 (Code.org, 2016a), which created the concept of "The Hour of Code" with a vision that states "every student in every school should have the opportunity to learn computer science. . . computer science could be part of a core curriculum, alongside other courses such as biology, chemistry or algebra". The overall purpose of the Hour of Code program is to afford anyone the opportunity to explore the world of coding. Various organizations such as Khan Academy, Apple, Microsoft, Facebook, Amazon, and Google are currently involved with partnering and supporting Hour of Code. To hold the attention of those participating, themes for the modules used to teach the coding aspects within the

Hour of Code program have included children's favorites such as *Minecraft, Star Wars, Angry Birds*, and *Frozen.*

The curriculum within many of the modules for learning coding in the Hour of Code program is relatively consistent. There is a sequence of basic steps that the student follows, each building on the previous step. Coding consists of blocks of instructions that perform a single function or task. Once these blocks are combined together, the instructions that will allow the performance of a particular action are created. Videos help guide the young learner, and lesson plans for instructors are provided so that the information could be used as part of a classroom group activity. The modules have online assessments that allow the learner to receive immediate feedback on questions related to tasks being learned. A nice set of examples of the process used to teach coding at various age levels can be found at https://studio.code.org.

The drive behind the Hour of Code is to prepare people for positions involving computing. According to Code.org (2016a), 71 percent of all new jobs in STEM in the US will be in computing, but currently only 8 percent of STEM graduates are in the computer sciences. Jobs in computer science will be available, but there will not be enough applicants to fill the positions (Bureau of Labor Statistics Employment Projections, 2014). According to Hour of Code, only one in four US schools are teaching computer science although 90 percent of parents want their child to study it. The need is there, but schools do not appear to be addressing future demands.

According to Code.org (2016b), male enrollment in computer science courses in the US outnumbers female enrollment four to one. But in comparison, the male/female ratio is 1:1 in advanced math courses. In the first year of the online program (2013), 20 million students tried the computer science module in a single week (Code.org, 2016b). Of those 20 million students, half were female. No gender gap was found in the people who initiated the coding learning module. Girls, as well as boys, have access to the opportunity to learn about coding, and both genders are pursuing coding skills. All it takes is someone to serve as a guide and let the students learn little steps at a time.

Larson (2014) noted "computer science is the only field in science, engineering and mathematics in which the number of women receiving bachelors degrees has decreased since 2002" (para. 7). According to Larson, only 18 percent of the undergraduate degrees in computer science are awarded to women. "In 1985, women earned 37% of computer-science undergraduate degrees" (Larson, para. 5). Despite the opportunities for high-paying jobs now available in computer science and to "influence the software-driven future of society" (Larson, para. 6), many more men are pursuing computer science degrees than women.

As men and women contribute to the software we use on our machines, a question that might be asked is which are better coders: males or females? One avenue for software developers is the writing of open source code. Programs such as OpenOffice, Apache HTTP Server, Moodle, Firefox, and MySQL are available at no cost for users to install on their computers. In like manner, there are "free" apps for the iPhone, the iPad, and Android devices. For these open source programs, individuals make suggestions to help improve the program or to address bugs in the software.

An investigation conducted by Terrell, Kofink, Middleton, Rainear, Murphy-Hill, and Parnin (2016) sought to learn whether gender had an impact upon the acceptance rate of suggested corrections. Their findings revealed an interesting conclusion. Women's suggestions were "more likely to have pull requests accepted than men" (Terrell et al., p. 16).

Another conclusion of the study was that "women have lower acceptance rates as outsiders when they are identifiable as women" (Terrell et al., p. 16). A clear gender bias existed, as women were found to be better coders as long as they remained incognito and no link to the individual's gender was available.

CLOSING

My (Kimberely's) *four sons all love to play games with their dad. I join in only when they assure me it is "one even you'll like, Mom." Meaning it is going to be over within an hour (30 minutes if I am lucky), it moves quickly, and I don't have to concentrate on remembering if my powers are sputtering and if my life levels are* (finally!) *flat lining. Are my feelings towards these games my sons love because of my gender or just because of who I am as an individual?*

Honigsfeld and Dunn (2003) researched the traits of adolescents from eight cultures. They concluded that gender-based differences are cross-cultural and to some extent innate. Other research suggests that it is social conditioning which decides traditional gender traits. While the debate continues between genetic and social conditioning, the real measure of differences between the genders is in proportion to the unique characteristics that are part of each person.

Computer programming, aka coding, is being revived, with opportunities for learning for both male and female students. The industry is growing and there is a sufficient need for individuals to enter the computing field. During the early 1940's, when the world was in a middle of a war, it was the vision of females to develop what is today a common device found in almost every home, on every desk, and in part, in our pockets. To have individuals ready to write the code needed is not dependent on the gender of the individual. Who can write the code needed for our future? Anyone!

REFLECTION ACTIVITY

What differences are there between casual and most video console type games?

How do perceived gender stereotypes affect the development of games?

What are the perceived differences between males and females in game and toy preference?

Are there sociological forces that support gender preferences for violent games?

How can bias toward females, with regard to their involvement in the computer industry, be eliminated?

REFERENCES

Auster, C., and Mansbach, C. (2012). The gender marketing of toys: An analysis of color and type of toy on the Disney Store Website. *Sex Roles*, *67*(7–8), 375–388.

Bemer, R. W. (1971). A view of the history of COBOL. *Honeywell Computer Journal*, *5*(3), 130–135.

Bluhm, R. (2013). Self-fulfilling prophecies: The influence of gender stereotypes on functional neuroimaging research on emotion. *Hypatia, 28*(4), 870–886.

Bonanno, P., and Kommers, P. A. M. (2005). Gender differences and styles in the use of digital games. *Educational Psychology, 25*(1), 13–41.

Bureau of Labor Statistics Employment Projections. (2014). Accessed from: https://docs. google.com/document/d/1gySkItxiJn_vwb8HIIKNXqen184mRtzDX12cux0ZgZk/pub.

Canadian Teachers' Federation. (2003). Kids take on media: Summary of finding. Accessed from https://www.ctf-fce.ca/Research-Library/KidsEnglish.pdf.

Carter, D. B., and Patterson, C. J. (1982). Sex roles as social conventions: The development of children's conceptions of sex-role stereotypes. *Developmental Psychology, 18*, 812–824.

Casual Games Association. (2010). Who plays casual games? Accessed from http://www.cga. global.

Casual Games Association. (2013). Smartphone & tablet gaming 2013. Games market sector report. Accessed from http://www.cga.global.

Chia-Ju, Chin-Fei, Ming-Chi, Yu-Cheng, Chia-Hung, and Yueh-Min. (2015). Does gender influence emotions resulting from positive applause feedback in self-assessment testing? Evidence from neuroscience. *Journal of Educational Technology & Society, 18*(1), 337–350.

Code.org. (2016a). About us. Accessed from: https://code.org/about.

Code.org. (2016b). Every student in every school should have the opportunity to learn computer science. Accessed from: https://code.org/files/Code.orgOverview.pdf.

Connor, J. M., and Serbin, L. A. (1977). Behaviorally based masculine- and feminine-activity-preference scales for preschoolers correlates with other classroom behaviors and cognitive tests. *Child Development, 48*, 1411–1416.

Cyr, D., and Bonanni, C. (2005). Gender and website design in e-business. *International Journal of Electronic Business, 3*(6), 565–582.

Darley, W. K., and Smith, R. E. (1995). Gender differences in information processing strategies: An empirical test of the selectivity model in advertising response. *Journal of Advertising, 24*, 41–56.

Downs, A. C. (1983). Letters to Santa Claus: Elementary school-age children's sex-typed toy preferences in a natural setting. *Sex Roles, 9*, 159–163.

Elkonin, D. B. (1999). On the historical origins of role-play. *Journal of Russian and East European Psychology, 43*(1), 49–89.

Entertainment Software Association (ESA). (2015). Essential facts about the computer and video gaming industry. Accessed from Entertainment Software Association: http:// www.theesa.com/wp-content/uploads/2015/04/ESA-Essential-Facts-2015.pdf.

Ferguson, A. (2000). A history of computer programming languages. Accessed from: cs.brown. edu/~adf/programming_languages.html.

Francis, B. (2010). Gender, toys and learning. *Oxford Review of Education, 36*(3), 325–344.

Fritz, W. B. (1996). The women of ENIAC. *IEEE Annals of the History of Computing, 18*(3), 13–28.

Galpin, V. (2002). Women in computing around the world. *SIGCSE Bulletin, 34*(2), 94–100.

Gürer, D. W. (1995). Pioneering women in computer science. *Communications of the ACM, 38*(1), 45–54.

Gurian, M., Henley, P., and Trueman, T. (2001). *Boys and girls learn differently!* San Francisco, CA: Jossey-Bass.

Gurian, M., and Stevens, K. (2006). How boys learn. *Educational Horizons, 84*(2), 87–93.

Haigh, T., and Priestly, M. (2016). Where code comes from: Architectures of automatic control from Babbage to Algol. *Communications of the ACM, 59*(1), 39–44.

Honigsfeld, A., and Dunn, R. (2003). High school male and female learning-style similarities and differences in diverse nations. *The Journal of Educational Research, 96*(4), 195–206.

Hour of Code. (2016a). Hour of Code. Accessed from: https://hourofcode.com/us.

Hsieh, Y.-H., Lin, Y.-C., and Hou, H.-T. (2015). Exploring elementary-school students' engagement patterns in a game-based learning environment. *Educational Technology & Society, 18*(2), 336–348.

James, J. (2010). IT gender gap: Where are the female programmers? Accessed from: www.techrepublic.com/blog/sofware-engineer/it-gender-gap-where-are-the-female-programmers.

Jordan-Young, R. M. (2010). *Brain storm: The flaws in the science of sex differences.* Cambridge, MA: Harvard University Press.

Kahlenberg, S. G., and Hein, M. M. (2010). Progression on Nickelodeon? Gender-role stereotypes in toy commercials. *Sex Roles, 62,* 830–847.

Kahn Academy. (2016). Intro to HTML/CSS: Making webpages. Accessed from: www.khanacademy.org/computing/computer-programming/html-css.

Kiili, K. (2005). Digital game-based learning: Towards an experiential gaming model. *The Internet and Higher Education, 8,* 1, 13–24.

Liss, M. B. (1981). Patterns of toy play: an analysis of sex differences. *Sex Roles, 7,* 1143–1150.

Larson, S. (2014). Why so few women are studying computer science. Accessed from: readwrite.com/2014/09/02/women-in-computer-science-why-so-few.

Lynch, M. (2015). Guys and dolls: A qualitative study of teachers' views of gendered play in kindergarten. *Early Child Development & Care, 185*(5), 679–693.

McCarthy, M. M., Arnold, A. P., Ball, G. F., Blaustein, J. D., and Vries, G. D. (2012). Sex differences in the brain: The not so inconvenient truth. *Journal of Neuroscience, 32*(7), 2241–2247.

Meyers-Levy, J., and Sternthal, B. (1991). Gender differences in the use of message cues and judgments. *Journal of Marketing Research, 28,* 84–96.

Moltenbray, K. (2006). Casual approach. *Computer Graphics World, 29*(4).

Moss, G., and Colman, A. M. (2001). Choices and preferences: Experiments on gender differences. *Journal of Brand Management, 9,* 89–98.

Mullis, I. V. S., Martin, M. O., Kennedy, A. M., and Foy, P. (2007). *PIRLS 2006 international report: IEA's progress in international reading literacy study in primary schools in 40 countries.* Chestnut Hill, MA: Boston College.

Nettleton, K. F. (2008). Fair game: Gender differences in educational games. In C. T. Miller (Ed.), *Games: Purpose and potential in education* (pp. 55–71). New York: Springer.

Orlando, M. (2002). Amazing Grace. *Poptronics, 3*(7), 26.

Orme, N. (2001). Child's play in medieval England. *History Today, 51*(10), 49–55.

Otnes, C., Kim, K., and Kim, Y. C. (1994). Yes, Virginia, there is a gender difference: Analyzing children's requests to Santa Claus. *The Journal of Popular Culture, 28*(1), 17–29.

Patel, S. C., Drury, C. C., and Shalin, V. L. (1998). Effectiveness of expert semantic knowledge as a navigational aid within hypertext. *Behaviour & Information Technology, 17*(6), 313–324.

Perrone-McGovern, K. M., Wright, S. L., Howell, D. S., and Barnum, E. L. (2014). Contextual influences on work and family roles: Gender, culture, and socioeconomic factors. *Career Development Quarterly, 62*(1), 21–28.

Prottsman, K. (2015). Coding vs. programming – battle of the terms! Accessed from: http://www.huffingtonpost.com/kiki-prottsman/coding-vs-programming-bat_b_7042816.html.

Raggett, D., Lam, J., Alexander, I., and Kmiec, M. (1998). *Raggett on HTML 4.* London, England: Addison-Wesley Professional Publishing.

Rheingold, H., and Cook, K. (1975). The contents of boys' and girls' rooms as an index of parents' behavior. *Child Development, 46,* 459–463.

Sammet, J. E. (1981). The early history of COBOL. In R. L. Wexelblat (Ed.), *History of programming languages.* New York, NY: Association for Computing Machinery, Inc.

Sanford, K. and Madill, L. (2006). Resistance through video games: It's a boy thing. *Canadian Journal of Education, 29*(1), 287–306.

Sharp, J. (2015). For women in computer science, a little mentoring goes a long way. Accessed from: www.pri.org/stories/2015-06-15/women-computer-science-little-mentoring-goes-long-way.

Slivers, C. (2010). Where's Waldo? *Entertainment Weekly.* Accessed from: www.ew.com/article/1990/12/14/wheres-waldo.

Smith, N. L. (2015). Built for boyhood? A proposal for reducing the amount of gender bias in the advertising of children's toys on television. *Vanderbilt Journal of Entertainment & Technology Law, 17*(4), 991–1049.

Sullivan, O. (2000). The division of domestic labour: Twenty years of change? S*ociology, 34*(3), 437–456.

Terrell, J., Kofink, A., Middleton, J., Rainear, C., Murphy-Hill, E., and Parnin, C. (2016). Gender bias in open source: Pull request acceptance of women versus men. *PeerJ PrePrints*, 4:e1733v1. Accessed from: https://doi.org/10.7287/peerj.preprints.1733v1.

Trautner, H.M., Ruble, D.N., Cyphers, L., Kirsten, B., Behrendt, R., and Hartmann, P. (2005). Rigidity and flexibility of gender stereotypes in childhood: Developmental or differential? *Infant and Child Development, 14*, 365–381.

Upton, E. (2013). The origin of "Where's Waldo". Accessed from: www.todayifoundout.com/index.php/2013/08/the-history-of-wheres-waldo/.

Varma, R. (2007). Women in computing: The role of geek culture. *Science as Culture, 16*(4), 359–376.

Weinberger, N., and Stein, K. (2008). Early competitive game playing in same- and mixed-gender peer groups. *Merrill-Palmer Quarterly, 54*(4), 499–514.

Wheatley, D. (2013). Location, vocation, location? Spatial entrapment among women in dual career households. *Gender, Work & Organization, 20*(6), 720–736.

Whitecar, M. (2010). Prelude: The capture and challenge of discovery and innovation, celebrating 50 years of the information age. *Journal of Research Administration, 41*(3), 13–19.

Wohn, D. (2011). Gender and race representation in casual games. *Sex Roles, 65*(3/4), 198–207.

Yang, G. S., and Huesmann, L. R. (2013). Correlations of media habits across time, generations, and media modalities. *Journal of Broadcasting & Electronic Media, 57*(3), 356–373.

PART II
THE SUBJECT OF CODING

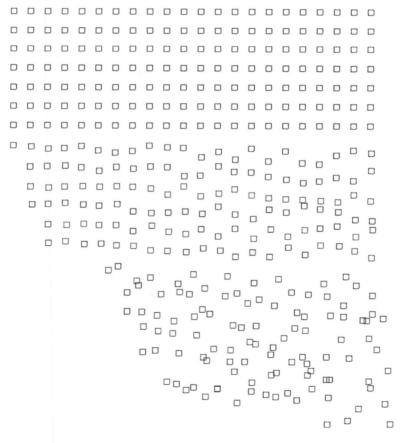

Figure II.1 Order to tumbling disorder

PART II

THE SUBJECT OF CODING

DIY ZONES FOR SCRATCH DESIGN IN CLASS AND CLUB

Quinn Burke

INTRODUCTION

Channeling the potential of Web 2.0 technologies to make children not only followers but also creators of digital media, the DIY moniker (meaning "do-it-yourself") invokes a sense of individualism and autonomy, a call not only to make youth more attentive to the usage of digital media, but also to become more creative and entrepreneurial in nature. Yet despite the DIY name, to what extent does the scrappy, "can-do" autonomy associated with Web 2.0 media actually mesh with the nature of schools? Institutions that historically have been "top-down" and largely conformist in both design and practice. For the past twenty years, researchers and theorists (Holloway & Valentine, 2003; Jones, 1996; Papert, 1993) have been heralding the arrival of the Information Age while also decrying schooling systems' seeming inability to integrate such technology into school curricula and wider culture. To what extent is it realistic to expect that DIY media, the concrete technology itself, can not only thrive within schools but also affect a fundamental change in the way schooling itself is conceived and practiced?

This question serves as the starting point for a recent exchange entitled "Is New Media Incompatible with Schooling?" between media theorist Henry Jenkins and Richard Halverson, co-author of *Rethinking Education in the Age of Technology* (Collins & Halverson, 2009). The future of technology in K-12 schools (kindergarten, primary, secondary, and twelfth grade (for 17-to-19-year-olds)), Halverson points out, is not so much dependent upon the devices themselves but more broadly reliant upon one's perspective of how people best learn. One strand of thought, he points out, continues to perceive learning largely through the traditional "institutional channel" in which (i) learning happens in schools and (ii) schools are strictly considered accredited "brick-and-mortar" spaces. Another strand, however, has veered away from these firm strictures of time and geography, asserting Web 2.0's potential to open ideal learning opportunities through peer and interest-driven activities. Referring to the latter as the "digital media channel", Halverson remarks that while learning in this manner is far less standardized and often entirely unpredictable, it does "highlight three critically important aspects of learning missing from many school learning activities: *motivation*, *production* and *legitimate audience*" (as quoted in Jenkins, 2010).

Halverson's three-part focus of motivation, production, and legitimate audiences offers an excellent lens through which to explore DIY media's potential to foster learning within two distinct school-based settings: an afterschool technology club and a language arts core curricula classroom. As Halverson suggests, K-12 schooling is currently at a "threshold" in terms of its incorporation of DIY media: while schools have long been comfortable relegating such digitally based activity to clubs and afterschool programs, there is increasingly a push to challenge the dominant institutional model and integrate such digital media into core curricular coursework. What are the benefits of such integration in terms of making core subjects more multi-disciplinary in scope and more relevant to students? Conversely, what may be lost with the increased standardization of digital learning—does the "can do" autonomy associated with DIY media dissipate in the classroom?

This chapter reports on research with two sets of middle school participants, introducing children to what has been referred to as "the original DIY media" of computer programming. How did students learn with Scratch in the language arts classroom versus an afterschool fan-fiction club? How did the structure of each environment affect children's motivation, production, and wider exposure using this particular DIY media application, and what are the larger implications for DIY media in schools, in general? While children's use of Scratch has been documented both in the classroom (Crook, 2009; Kafai, Fields, & Burke, 2010) and in afterschool and out-of-school technology clubs (Burke & Kafai, 2010; Peppler & Kafai, 2007), there is increasingly the need to focus not simply upon the DIY media applications in certain settings but also upon how these various settings likewise inform how children use DIY media.

DIY MEDIA: MOTIVATION, PRODUCTION, AND LEGITIMATE AUDIENCES

As stated, the question of how to best motivate students with real-world, project-based learning has been a struggle endemic to U.S. schooling since its inception. The incorporation of digital technology into schools may very well be just the latest iteration of educators addressing these longstanding issues seemingly endemic to K-12 schooling. Yet for the purposes of this study, rather than attempt to track these weighty issues of motivation, production, and authenticity across all school-based learning, this section provides an overview of the trio as they specifically relate to the growth of DIY media in and around schools over the past decade, and in particular to the DIY medium of computer programming.

Computer programming—long considered to be the erudite pastime of techies—is increasingly being recognized by educators as a potential pathway by which to get youth more engaged in the workings of the web-based media that surrounds them and more motivated to produce web-based products for wider audiences (Resnick et al., 2009; Wing, 2006). In his recent *Program or be Programmed*, media theorist Douglas Rushkoff (2010) goes so far as to name programming as the "new literacy for the 21st Century". By introducing young users to the underlying code upon which countless applications run, programming helps demystify the media-production process and ultimately gives children the opportunity to be not only consumers but also producers of such media (Gee, 2003; Kafai, 2006). The goal is not to make all children future computer scientists but to give them a basic understanding of computational concepts, making them more discerning end users and potentially innovative creators themselves (Scaffidi, Shaw, & Myers, 2005). Of course, actually getting programming into K-12 classrooms presents an entirely new challenge.

Historically this DIY medium has struggled to find a foothold in school culture precisely because of its failure to engage a diversity of students with project-based learning intended for wider audiences. While the work of Seymour Papert (1980) with the Logo programming language was an inspired first step in introducing coding as a means for creative personal expression, its lack of integration into K-12 core subject content eventually undermined Logo's popularity in the classroom (Pea, 1987a; Pea 1987b). Whatever initial excitement children may have experienced with the technical components of the hardware itself, the lack of connection to wider subject matter left them without the necessary motivation to persist with the software after this early enthrallment had expired.

Motivation

Now, over thirty years later, advocates of DIY media (Gaston, 2006; McHale, 2005; Prensky, 2006) name motivation as one of the primary reasons why such technology is so powerful as a learning tool and a key reason to move beyond afterschool use into core curricula classrooms. Has the technology itself evolved in these past three decades to the point where it singularly has the capacity to motivate children to learn? A brief article by DiSalvo and Bruckman (2011) in the *Communications of the ACM* suggests the answer is not so easy. In "From Interest to Values" they report on "Glitch-Testers", an ongoing program at Georgia Tech which utilizes video game debugging activities to specifically motivate interest in computer science (CS) among low-income African-American teenage boys. "Computer science is not that difficult", the authors write, "but wanting to learn it is" (p. 27). Exposing children to innovative—even fun—technologies through the Glitch-Testers, they argue, does spark temporary interest in such DIY media. But it alone is not sufficient motivation for children to persist in CS-based problem solving and creative reasoning—to do this, DiSalvo and Bruckman point to the need to create clear pathways from DIY media activities to careers in computer science and engineering. The primary success of the Glitch-Tester program has been to steer computer programming away from being the object of such learning and rather treat it as the means to learn another discipline or trade, echoing Holloway and Valentine's (2003) conclusion that technologies only become motivating "cool tools" when they directly relate to the social context of children's everyday and off-line lives. This same point is supported by Kelleher and Pausch's (2005) taxonomy of introductory programming environments, which finds that while improved technology has made the mechanics of computer science much more manageable for young users, the underlying social and cultural stigmas surrounding programming can stifle motivation altogether (Margolis & Fisher, 2002). These sociological barriers (e.g., "programming is for nerds"; "programming is isolating"; "only boys like programming"), Kelleher and Pausch conclude, are "harder to address than mechanical ones because they are harder to identify and some cannot be addressed through programming systems" (p. 132). Yet recognizing their existence is a crucial step in designing learning environments that attract a greater number and greater range of K-12 children to computer programming.

Production

Kelleher and Pausch's development of Storytelling Alice was their attempt to mitigate some of these underlying sociological issues associated with programming. Storytelling Alice is a programming environment that allows the user to build interactive narratives, create animations, and develop simple games. It is designed to motivate learning through creative exploration – teaching the fundamentals of coding through computational thinking skills. Building off the success of the introductory programming language Alice,[1] which was developed at Carnegie Mellon University in the late 1990s, Kelleher and Pausch (2007) created an alternative version of the software, which adjusted the original program to specifically target children interested in telling their own digital stories. By accentuating a certain *product*, Kelleher and Pausch found that 200 middle school children using Storytelling Alice learned programming concepts just as well as children who had used traditional Alice, but that Storytelling Alice participants spent forty-two percent more time using the program on their own time. Based on the Constructionist model, in which students simultaneously learn new information and design a product that reflects such learning (Harel & Papert, 1990; Kafai, 2006), Kelleher and Pausch's study is joined by other CS-based initiatives which specifically couch the learning of coding in a distinct product, be it video games (Kafai, 1995; Maloney et al., 2008), interactive art displays (Peppler & Kafai, 2007), music (see Georgia Tech's EarSketch prototype[2]), or once again stories (Burke & Kafai, 2010; Wolz et al., 2011). By focusing on a specific product, children not only have a tangible item to call their own but also a goal, a discernible end to which programming is the means.

Legitimate audiences

These socio-cultural connections are of paramount importance to the nature of DIY media, as they represent the "authenticity" of more than just self-generated products but also the audiences with which one creates and shares one's work. As Knobel and Lankshear (2010) point out in their analysis of DIY media, "DIY existed as an *ethic* long before Web 2.0 technology existed, manifestly evident in England's late nineteenth century Arts and Crafts movement as a reaction against the Industrial Revolution's technologies of mass production" (p. 6). These homespun communities continue today, still aligned against the decided inauthenticity of mass consumerism as they share their homemade creations and solicit feedback online. Numerous DIY communities have sprung up over the past decade using programming as a central tool for their productions, including sites like makezine. com and instructables.com where members have posted hundreds of thousands of videos on virtually any topic (Torrey, McDonald, Schilit, & Bly, 2007). Other communities follow the open source movement and have networks develop around the Processing programming language, particularly popular with the design media arts community (Reas, 2006a/b). Among children, the introductory programming languages Scratch and Alice both have established online sites for youth to post projects, share ideas, and remix one another's work. Yet connecting school-based learning to these wider, external audiences proves to be a persistent challenge. While the need for legitimate communities of learning within schools is one of the central tenets of the Progressive model— tracing all the way back to Dewey's seminal *Democracy and Education* (1916)—many schools persist in treating web-based interactions entirely in defensive and prohibitive terms, developing steeper firewalls and hosting workshops around the dangers of the Internet.

METHODOLOGY: SETTING AND PARTICIPANTS

The study here involved two different groups of middle school students, all of whom attended an urban public school located on the west side of a large U.S. city (over one million population). Serving grades kindergarten through 8th grade (aged 14–15 years), the school has an enrollment of approximately 600 children from a wide range of social and racial/ethnic backgrounds. Located within a transitional neighborhood in the city, the school is one of the more economically diverse within the district, serving both students from an upper-middle class background and a significant number of children who qualify for a free or reduced lunch based on the federal Title I Act. Both class and club met twice a week at separate times in the same third-floor classroom. Furnished with laptops and a semi-circle of wooden tables, the classroom serves as one of the school's two "computer rooms", the other being the more "official" computer lab located in the school's library.

Setting 1: Classroom—Choice writing workshop

For seven weeks, a total of ten middle school students participated in the "Storytelling with Scratch" Choice elective course, which ran every Tuesday and Thursday for one hour. Ranging from ages 11 to 14, participants were representative of the schools' diverse population of African-American, Caucasian, and Latino children. Gender-wise, however, there was far less diversity, as all ten participants were boys, having learned about the elective course through their middle school language arts instructor, Mrs. Steinberg (a pseudonym, as are all names hereon). The course itself consisted of a total of eleven writing workshops based upon the model developed by Calkins (1986) in her book *The Art of Teaching Writing* and utilized by Mrs. Steinberg with all middle school writing instruction. The goal was for every student in the class to generate their own digital story in Scratch by the last workshop. Mrs. Steinberg was instrumental in reviewing the proposed Scratch workshop curriculum with me as well as providing me with examples of how she used Calkins' text within her own classroom writing instruction.

Over the course of the seven weeks, every class would open with what Calkins refers to as a "mini-lesson" emphasizing a particular element of effective composition (such as characterization, foreshadowing, setting a scene), which would also be tied to learning a particular coding procedure in Scratch (e.g., using the broadcast feature to establish dialog, importing external images, using loops to standardize behavior). Every mini-lesson was supported by anywhere from one to three sample digital stories selected from the Scratch website, which exemplified a particular storytelling element or genre of storytelling (e.g., mystery, action/adventure) featured within the lesson. This not only grounded the lessons in practical application but also offered an excellent segue to examining the actual coding scripts of the projects, exploring exactly how the sample story creators achieved a particular effect with the Scratch code. All lesson plans were aligned to Pennsylvania state standards Reading, Writing, Listening, and Speaking on the 8th grade level and supported by Mrs. Steinberg's rubrics and pre-writing activities.

In total, we collected eleven projects (one participant created multiple stories) that were presented in class on the last day.

Setting 2: Afterschool Fan-fiction Scratch Club

For eight weeks, also that fall, the "Fan-fiction Scratch Club" occupied the third-floor classroom for one hour every Tuesday and Thursday. A total of seventeen students, aged 10 to 13, participated in the club and were again representative of the schools' population of African-American, Caucasian, and Latino children as well as their Asian and Middle-Eastern population. Unlike the Choice elective, the club had more gender diversity—four of the participants were female (all of whom were in the 5th grade).

The club environment was far less structured and prescriptive than that of the class. Based on popular middle school stories and games including anime, manga, Harry Potter, and *Twilight*, the club advertised itself as open to any middle school students interested in these themes or other fandoms that they themselves would like to introduce to the club. Within the afterschool club, students were free to move about the classroom and no sessions were tied to any specific curricular lesson plans. Students sampled the Scratch software and explored the accompanying Scratch website at their own pace; unlike in the classroom, they never had to commit to any single project over the course of the two months. While there were no mini-lessons demonstrating sample projects and their underlying coding scripts, there were a series of planned "nuts & bolts" information sessions, including (a) an opening discussion about stories and being a "fan", (b) a basic introduction to the Scratch software and the accompanying website during the first week, and (c) a designated "gallery walk" midway through the club in which all members viewed and played their peers' ongoing project and offered off-hand feedback. Like in the class, all participants in the club also presented select projects to their peers on the last day.

In total, we collected thirty-one projects by the end of the club.

DIY PROGRAMMING: SCRATCH

Since its public launch in 2007, Scratch has helped introduce basic programming concepts to children (primarily ages 8 to 16) while also allowing them to create and share their own digital media. Scratch was designed as a coding tool for personal expression with the capacity to share one's work with the wider community, It was intended to achieve "programming for everyone" by both making coding personal and individualistic and also linking to a wider social network of mutual interest—two of the distinct elements of the DIY ethos. Designed to be highly intuitive in its operation, Scratch allows users to manipulate media through a process of "dragging-and-dropping" command blocks of code, then stacking these blocks together to form coding scripts (Resnick et al., 2009). These scripts are then activated by various inputs, be it a keystroke or the click of a mouse, bringing to life the various Scratch character "sprites" and backgrounds. Simply knowing how to use a mouse is enough to get started, though the program's wide variety of textual coding bricks ensures that users can create projects of significant complexity as they progress.

DATA COLLECTION AND ANALYSES

Over the course of both class and club, there were a variety of data sources, each of which was separately collected and maintained depending upon the class/club setting.

■ **Scratch project (artifact) analysis**: With a removable flash drive, projects were periodically collected over the duration of each program (a minimum of three times per project, regardless of class or club) and subsequently examined in terms of their staged storylines and underlying coding scripts. All projects were also analyzed using Scrape technology, a tool developed by RiverSound Media[3] specifically to identify the "underlying DNA" of Scratch projects.

■ **CS attitudes pre-surveys**: Adapted from a Georgia Tech computer science attitudes survey developed by Lijun Ni and Mark Guzdial,[4] the same pre-surveys were given to all participants in each environment, gauging their familiarity with and attitudes to digital media, their sense of their capacity to use DIY media, and their own attitudes toward working collaboratively and creatively.

■ **Field note observations**: Collected daily and transcribed within a twenty-four-hour period, these were subsequently coded thematically (Strauss & Corbin, 1998) capturing particular usage trends across the class and, to a lesser degree, online.

■ **Post-interviews**: At the program's end, all students participated in five- to ten-minute interviews gauging their experience in the classroom. As with the field note observations, these interviews were subsequently coded thematically based on students' attitudes toward programming and storytelling, the overall structure of each program, and the projects that they had recently completed.

FORMULATIONS AND FINDINGS

In terms of presenting formulations and findings, the data here addresses the three purported affordances of DIY media as evident in the classroom and the club setting:

■ What motivated students to initially partake in either the class or the club? What served as their motivation(s) throughout the duration of each program?

■ What products did students create using Scratch in the classroom's digital storytelling workshop and within the less-structured environment of the afterschool club? What elements of computer programming did projects entail and in what frequency?

■ With whom did students share their work, and did these audiences (or projected audiences) affect the way students created in Scratch? If so, how?

MOTIVATION

Pre-survey data

With the administration of the pre-surveys, one of the first questions addressed was exactly why children opted to join either the class or the club. In addition to this question, the pre-surveys gauged students' prior experiences using technology in school and at home, their confidence in their own computing abilities, and whether they had any future aspirations in computing as a career. The overall goal was to try to gain further understanding about the students entering the classroom and club—what were their similarities and differences in terms of their attitudes toward, experiences with, and plans for DIY media?

In terms of commonalities, one hundred percent of the Choice class as well as the Club "Agreed" or "Strongly Agreed" with the following statements:

- "Computing is fun"
- "I can become good at computing"
- "I like computing"
- "I think computing is useful"
- "I can become good at computing"

This is not altogether surprising given that in both class and club, students had deliberately chosen to be part of the program, suggesting they had an interest in computing as well as a solid degree of confidence in their own abilities. However, while fifty-seven percent of entering club members either "Agreed" or "Strongly Agreed" that they were interested in a career in computing, only thirty percent within the class likewise expressed similar interest career-wise. This did not mean, however, that class members were less engaged with technology—significantly more (forty percent) of the class respondents (versus sixteen percent of club respondents) indicated they spent 3+ hours using a computer every day; the majority (2+ hours) was outside of school. Yet while classroom participants used computers more on a daily basis, club members reported to be much more inclined toward gaming with technology—forty-five percent of club respondents spent 3+ hours playing games with computers on a weekly basis, versus only thirty percent of class respondents.

Perhaps the most glaring contrast between the class and club on the pre-survey was in response to the open-ended question "What are you hoping to learn from this experience?" Sixty-five percent of club respondents identified a particular topic in their responses (e.g., "create games", "make comics", "make stories", "do funny slideshows"). Within the class, however, only one of the ten respondents indicated an interest in a particular topic ("making better stories/games"). The other nine either replied in terms of the technology itself (e.g., "here to learn Scratch", "do Scratch") or simply left the answer blank, despite having sufficient time to complete the short survey. This suggests that club participants were more "product driven" from the outset, whereas class members saw the course as "learning Scratch" despite the deliberate focus on storytelling.

This lack of a professed focus is especially surprising given that a large number (seventy percent) of the entering class participants had actually used Scratch before and had some understanding of the software and its capacity to generate specific media content, be it stories, games, or interactive art pieces. Meanwhile, within the club, only twenty-nine percent of the participants had ever used Scratch before, yet their responses were considerably more focused on creating a particular type of media product.

Considering the two distinct flyers advertising Scratch that fall, perhaps some of this lack of specificity on the part of the class may simply be due to the fact that the product—namely, storytelling—was already a given, whereas within the club, participants had a greater freedom to create a variety of different projects and may therefore have felt a greater need to identify exactly what products they intended to create. On the other hand, a degree of club participants' specificity may also be attributed to the entirely voluntary nature of the club setting. That is, while both class and club participants had the option to choose Scratch, class members *had* to choose a fall elective regardless (be it "Storytelling with Scratch" or one of three other Choice options). Meanwhile, club members' choice was between going to the "Fan-fiction Scratch Club" after school and simply going home. Clearly club members were making a higher stakes commitment, and their expressed interest in particular types of media products may very well be reflective of their greater overall enthusiasm for the DIY media.

Motivation throughout the program

Certainly afterschool participants' excitement for Scratch was much more palpable than that of class members on Day #1 of each program. While some of the club members' excitement that first day may simply stem back to the fact that the school day had ended, four of the children were particularly enthused on the first day, high-fiving each other and patting each other on the back, setting an almost celebratory tone. All four were 7th graders, and three of them had used Scratch before. All were self-professed "gamers", which, through the first half of the program, gave them an air of superiority when using the software, though two other participants in the club had equal, if not more, experience using Scratch than this foursome.

In an effort to make the club more personal and interest-driven, circling up that initial day, the conversation was not about Scratch or computing, but about the particular stories (be it movie, TV, games) of which we are a fan. "*Halo!*" called out one of the experienced gamers, named Corey, followed by calls of "*Modern Warfare*" and "*Call of Duty*" by two of his compatriots, one of whom then proceeded to carefully elaborate on exactly why *Modern Warfare* was superior to the others. For a moment, it appeared that the club was destined to turn into a "members only" experience entirely centered on shooting games, but then the next speaker, a 5th grade girl named Kaja, volunteered an entirely new topic of which she was a fan. "Justin Bieber," she said, blushing but also laughing as the majority of boys let out feigned or genuine groans. But Kaja's response set an excellent precedent that first day, opening the potential for fandom to extend beyond the commercial shooter video games that had previously dominated the discussion. "I like Michael Jackson," a popular 7th grader named Brock subsequently volunteered, while 6th grader Michael offered, "I read manga and draw Naruto," referring to the popular Japanese animations. Sixth grader Ben nervously fiddled with his fingers a moment before proudly announcing, "I am a fan of Captain America!" adding a moment later a bit of trivia: "And a fact to know about . . . who was the first super-hero?" After allowing for a brief pause, Ben revealed the (somewhat expected) answer to good-natured laughter: "Captain America, who initially appeared after World War I!" The club was on its way.

"The Storytelling with Scratch" class also opened with a roundtable discussion, though it was positively subdued compared with the club's roundabout discussion. Based around the question of where one finds good stories and what makes for a good story, the group went one-by-one, speaking briefly about storytelling and writing alike. While the initial two participants were reluctant to say much other than their names and grades and that writing was "okay, I guess", the third speaker, Carlos, was more forthcoming. Clearly one of the higher-status members of the class, Carlos was an 8th grader who had only recently come to the school during 7th grade, but he exuded a certain confidence that his peers seemed to appreciate. After explaining that he had lived in New York City and still considered himself a New Yorker, he moved on to the subject of writing. In a matter-of-fact voice, he stated, "I love writing—and I think I am pretty good at it." This set a tone for the remainder of that first session; whereas the previous two students barely touched upon the subject of writing in their self-introductions, the next three speakers all led with their attitudes toward writing—all of which were positive, though not as effusive as Carlos' initial statement. It was only on one of the last introductions—Daryl's—when some of the enthusiasm for writing waned. "Truthfully, I hate writing with all my soul, all my heart, and all my mind." This, though, brought the day's first laughter as the group returned to their laptops and begin to access the Scratch software to begin their own digital compositions.

Regardless of their attitudes toward writing, all ten students in the class clearly were familiar with the writing workshop process and Calkins' book through Mrs. Steinberg's class. Within the first week of the workshop, students were already generating ideas within or consulting ideas from their "writer's notebook". Given by Mrs. Steinberg to every 7th and 8th grader at the start of the academic year, the thin black-and-white speck-led pad is the mandated starting point for any student composition (regardless of the medium). According to Mrs. Steinberg, students need to generate at least three potential ideas in their writer's notebook before they opt for any single one—a requirement that was maintained for the Choice class as well. In addition to the writer's notebook, all students mapped out their stories in Scratch using a basic storyboard template that outlined the narrative sequence frame-by-frame through rough sketches and accompanying descriptors. Capturing *the who?* (character/programmable objects), *the what?* (actions/scripts), and *the where?* (settings/stages) of each progressing scene, the storyboards subsequently served as an effective "roadmap" and motivator when students "hit a wall" in their programming. While students may not have known exactly how to phrase what was not working with their projects in terms of the underlying coding scripts, the "external" script of the storyboard served as the reliable indicator of where the narrative was supposed to go and offered me, as the supporting instructor, a clear indication of what the student wanted to happen, even when the student himself could not verbally express it.

Despite some initial resistance to using the storyboard—"Do I really have to do this?" lamented Daryl, at one point—in the post-interviews seven out of ten students identified the storyboard as a particularly helpful tool in helping them complete their project (see Figure 6.1 for examples of students' storyboards).

In addition to the writer's notebook and the storyboard, grades played the role of an additional, if tacit, motivator in ensuring students worked on their projects. While Choice does not have letter grades assigned to it, the elective coursework is evaluated in terms of "Pass/Fail", and if a student fails a Choice course, he or she is no longer eligible to take any elective the following trimester, regardless of grade point average eligibility. While the "Pass/Fail" was never mentioned explicitly in the class, it was a leverage point, particularly in terms of ensuring participants completed their story-boards in a timely fashion and had draft projects uploaded online for feedback midway through the workshop.

No such deadlines existed in the "Fan-fiction Scratch Club," nor did participants use writers' notebooks or storyboards as external support throughout the process. All partici-pants did receive encouragement from me as the club facilitator, as well as from their own peers during the formal gallery walk midway through the club. Yet the near lack of delib-erate scaffolds on my part as club facilitator was in part to see whether participants would increasingly rely on their fellow club members as well as leverage the website and the wider Scratch community (800,000 registered members) as the primary sources to spark ideas and solicit feedback. Having learned how to upload and share projects at the Scratch

■ **Figure 6.1** Sample storyboards

website within the first two weeks of the club, participants were regularly encouraged to "search it at the site" or to "check projects out online" when they had questions about code or were trying to generate new ideas.

This approach had decidedly mixed results in terms of motivating the club participants. The casual nature of the club was much more conducive to easy interactions between the middle school participants, and there were two pairs of students who opted to collaborate with each other over the course of the eight weeks. There was also far more laughter in the club than in the class, with participants sharing particularly interesting and funny Scratch projects they had found online and occasionally tinkering with each other's uploaded sprites. However, despite the apparent sociability, there was also a discernible insularity among some club members both in person and online at the Scratch website. In the club, two distinct cliques formed within the first week of the program. The four "gamer boys" maintained a spot along the south wall, regularly trading quips and testing each other's knowledge of video games with quick-fire trivia questions; meanwhile, three out of the four girls formed their own group along the east wall, chatting about friends and school as they tinkered with the website and their own projects. While the remaining thirteen participants were part of neither group, the fact that these two polarized groups existed created a barrier in establishing a total-group cohesiveness. Club members may reach out to certain peers but not to others and certainly not to the entire group. In fact, despite my professed role in the club strictly as "facilitator", multiple students—including a member of the "gamer boys"—repeatedly turned to me over weeks #3 and #4, asking me to take the helm and "teach for everybody" how to use less-intuitive coding bricks such as variables to keep score and track player lives in games. Though at least two members of the club (both "gamer boys") already were well versed in using variables and despite my repeated encouragement, others apparently felt uncomfortable asking them for their assistance, leaving me to work with them instead.

PRODUCTION: PROGRAMMING CONCEPTS UTILIZED

In terms of production, in the "Storytelling with Scratch" class, nine out of ten students generated a complete digital story, and one class member actually composed two stories, making for a total of ten. All of the ten digital stories submitted used multiple characters, settings, and plot stages, as well as entailing a number of key coding concepts that are not simply characteristic of Scratch but of all programming languages—from Java to C++. These fundamental programming concepts were also present in the projects generated in the afterschool "Fan-fiction Scratch Club", though less consistently so.

Within the club, only seventy-one percent of participants (twelve of seventeen) submitted at least one project; however, a number of members generated multiple projects, making the total number of projects submitted thirty-one. Unlike the class setting, projects within the club were not all narrative stories—some were interactive art pieces while others were video games, making for a much wider spectrum in not only project type but also the frequency of coding concepts utilized.

Table 6.1 highlights the key programming concepts class and club members used in the creation of their projects, along with the frequency of such use.

This comparison of class and club based upon the type and the frequency of project code indicates that students in the class were more consistent in the range of programming concepts they used, even though they used certain coding elements (threads, event-handling) with far less frequency than club members. In terms of the percentage of class members consistently using certain coding concepts, the numbers suggest that the mini-lessons' deliberate introduction of specific coding bricks served as an effective means to encourage middle schoolers to sample and utilize a variety of Scratch programming scripts. In fact, the least used coding bricks in the class—namely Boolean logic, conditionals, and variables—were also the coding bricks never explicitly introduced in the class's mini-lessons, as these types of coding scripts are characteristic of games in which there are no fixed outcomes and that are not integral to linear narratives. In the club, this trio of Boolean logic, conditionals, and variables were also the least utilized concepts, but when club members *did* utilize the three (largely in the creation of video games), they were used with significantly greater frequency. This also explains the significantly higher number of threads, a programming technique more characteristic of the variable nature of games.

Table 6.1 Type and frequency of programming concepts utilized across class and club

PROGRAMMING CONCEPT	*% of CLASS vs. CLUB Projects Utilizing the Concept*	*Frequency per Project CLASS vs. CLUB*
Coordination & Synchronization	100% (class) 77% (club)	8.8 (class) 3.5 (club)
Threads (Parallel Execution)	100% (class) 87% (club)	1.6 (class) 11.5 (club)
Loops	90% (class) 68% (club)	2.5 (class) 2.6 (club)
Event-Handling	100% (class) 94% (club)	1.5 (class) 7.6 (club)
Boolean Logic	20% (class) 26% (club)	1.6 (class) 2.7 (club)
Conditional Statements	30% (class) 26% (club)	1.7 (class) 2.4 (club)
Variables	10% (class) 23% (club)	.3 (class) .6 (club

Less intuitive to understand and far more difficult to implement into one's projects, both Boolean logic and particularly variables figured more prominently in the club because of members' capacity to create video games and not simply stories; however, their increased presence was also the result of club members' greater inclination to remix others' work. Of the club's thirty-one total projects, four were remixes of projects that had been discovered online; another four were partial remixes utilizing a sprite or multiple sprites imported from another's work; and one project, while ostensibly a "remix", in fact had made no changes to the code or imagery, so was essentially a copy of another's work. Of the class's ten total projects, only a single one was a partial remix, using a basketball figure sprite that had been discovered within another project online.

Part of the class's greater reluctance to remix may stem from the school-based nature of the writing workshops. While both class and club participants were encouraged to remix from the Scratch website as well as from each other, in the class the notion of "remix" seemed to often be synonymous with "copying" or even "cheating". "He's trying to copy me," exclaimed 7th grader Amadu during the third Choice class, while Daryl retorted, "Well, all you've done is copy off of the website anyway." Working almost entirely independently, students within the class talked with each other but there seemed to be a tacit rule against sampling others' work either in person or online.

Meanwhile, in the club, although remixing offered participants exposure to a greater number and variation of coding scripts, searching the website for projects to remix could also be a barrier in and of itself. "I'm just trying to find something to work off of," Brock exclaimed in exasperation during the third week of the club, seemingly unable to find the "perfect" project to remix. In some cases, searching the Scratch site for the ideal project became its own motivation, usurping actual production in the software itself. Two club participants, 6th grader Tyree and 7th grader James, spent the entire first half of the club searching the site but never downloaded another project to actually repurpose. Both, while dazzled by the complexity of projects they discovered online, lacked the intricate coding skills to actually remix such projects. Yet despite my advice, neither seemed to want to "start small" and develop a project from the "bottom up", and neither had projects to demo by the end of the club.

CASE STUDY PROJECTS

In terms of the projects themselves, similar to their coding sequences, the digital stories from the "Storytelling with Scratch" class had a general uniformity to them, while those projects from the club exhibited a much wider range of styles.

Within the class, students' projects fell into one of two categories: (a) personal stories based on real-life experiences that they usually gleaned from their writers' notebooks, and (b) participatory stories, in which the protagonist and antagonist were based upon pop culture figures from movies, television, or comic books, among other media sources. Eighth grader Greg's "Skateboard" digital story (Figure 6.2) exemplifies the personal. Based upon an actual occurrence, in which he and his friends had nearly been ticketed by the police for riding their skateboards illegally in a park, Greg turned to his writer's notebook for the idea. Initially he had planned to write about the incident for his English class, but wanting a project with "real action" he instead opted to turn the idea into a Scratch digital story.

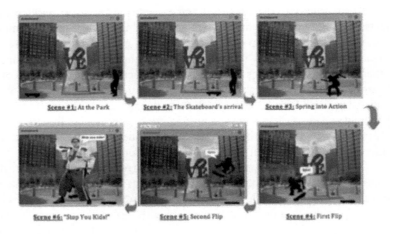

Scene #1: At the Park   Scene #2: The Skateboard's arrival   Scene #3: Spring into Action

Scene #6: "Stop You Kids!"   Scene #5: Second Flip   Scene #4: First Flip

■ **Figure 6.2** Scene-by-scene depiction of Greg's "Skateboard" story

Though Greg's digital story is brief (just over a minute in length), it took over ten hours to program, as he worked hard at coordinating the skateboarder's moves with a beat-box song he had imported into the project. The majority of the class's Scratch stories (seven of the ten) were like Greg's, based directly or indirectly on a personal experience.

Within the club, projects were largely participatory in nature. Ungrounded in the storytelling motif, they varied considerably in both length and purpose, with the most minimalistic club project consisting only of a mere three coding scripts while the most intricate used a total of 103. Some of these minimalistic projects were participants' initial creations over the first two weeks of the club as they acquainted themselves with the Scratch software. This includes Brock's project "Thriller" and Kaja's "Justin B.", which were both simply music simulations, featuring a looped animation moving back and forth to a pop song (Figure 6.3).

LEGITIMATE AUDIENCES

Central to this element of legitimate audiences was the role of the Scratch website as a place to share one's work with fellow Scratch users.

■ **Figure 6.3** Sample project music simulations and video games from the club

In the class, the website played a limited role. Students viewed sample projects from the website, but this was largely through the brief mini-lessons that opened each class session. While they were then encouraged to download and tinker with these sample projects after the close of each mini-lesson, there was never an explicitly designated time to explore the website on their own. Class members, particularly two returning members, seemed comfortable accessing the website and trying out projects posted on the front page, but no one in the class shared their own ongoing digital stories on the website by their own volition. Students in the class only uploaded their ongoing projects to the website midway through the course, which was a requirement for the course as this initial upload represented their rough draft. These drafts were subsequently reviewed using the "Comments" feature. A mix of encouragement, observations, and occasional questions, these comments were intended to make classroom participants more reflective about the narrative arc of their digital stories and to ensure they were technically sound (e.g., addressing glitches). Given the 600-word character limit of the Comments box along with the non-academic nature of the website, comments were succinct and casual—the goal was not to exhaust the students with a "to do" list but rather to engage them with the potential of sharing their work with wider audiences online. Each student reviewed their comments over the following class, and they took many of the suggestions, be it adding a new character, clarifying dialog, or adjusting timing in a looped interaction. Only five students reposted, however, and only two responded directly to the comments and queries they received. Classroom students' lack of posts on the website likely stems in part from the formal way in which the site was utilized as a "place to submit your rough drafts" but, as a whole, the group also seemed reluctant to share what was still an ongoing project, though all did post (i.e., "publish") their final projects at the end of the program. In his post interview, 7th grader Amadu names the website as a "good testing place for sprites and scripts", but, like his peers, he never posted comments or solicited feedback, seemingly willing to experiment with what others had shared but less willing to let his own work be tested upon and sampled.

Club members, on the other hand, were introduced to the website during the first week of the program and relied heavily on sampling others' work online over the course of the eight weeks. Yet while the club members enjoyed searching the site and sampling others' work, like class participants, they too were generally reluctant to post comments on others' work and upload their own work. "It's not ready yet," remarked Daryl and others multiple times at my own encouragement to upload. Such hesitancy persisted until the seventh and eighth weeks of the club, with members wanting to make it "just right" before they decided to upload. Within the club, there was no designated upload date. While participants were encouraged to post their projects on an ongoing basis and after final presentations on the last day, such postings were never mandated, and six members of the club never shared any project online at all. Yet the "go to the website" mantra that club members had heard from me throughout the program appeared to make them more comfortable sharing online than their peers in the classroom. Of the thirty-one projects that class members had created, twenty were uploaded to the website, and these twenty uploads received a total of twenty-five comments from the community. Only eight of these comments came from me as club facilitator, while the other seventeen came from other, random Scratch users. Some of these comments were simply observations—even reflections—while others were follow-up questions. Happily, in fourteen of the twenty-five comments posted,

Scratch club members replied to the initial post, further explaining their work, answering a question, or simply thanking the other user for the comment itself. A selection of these user comments follows (each comment is from a different Scratch user):

■ About 5th grader Lizzie's "Run from the Dragon" video game:

- *"this strange when the dragon gets you, nothing happens"* –
- *"this is clever but does the timer work? Or is it meant to be the way it is . . . ?"*

■ About Brock's Michael Jackson "Thriller" music simulation:

- *"add more! I want to look at the video singer assassination!!!!!"* (sic)
- *"ah, first project . . . I remember it as if it was yesterday"*

■ About Tyree's "Person-Planet Game Remix":

- *"hey, I don't see what has been changed here"*

As evident in the selection above, not all comments were effusive praise—the comment Tyree received on his "Person-Planet Game Remix" came from the original creator of the project, who aptly noted that Tyree never actually changed anything about his project but simply changed the title and reposted as a "remix". Yet even when comments may be slightly critical or questioning (as with Lizzie's draft video game), club participants were always unequivocally excited to see that others from the Scratch community were viewing their work. "I got a comment," members would cry out, to which others would come over to look at the screen. Three of the girls even spent half of a session examining other users' profiles, trying to figure out from where on the globe their feedback was coming.

WRAPPING UP AND NEXT STEPS

In summarizing the results across these three measures of (1) motivation, (2) production, and (3) legitimate audiences, it is beneficial to return to the research questions identified in the introduction of this chapter. In terms of integrating DIY media into a core curricula language arts course, it is clear that the workshop model (Calkins, 1986) was an effective and utilitarian means to get the middle school students composing their own stories within the Scratch medium. The class was heavily scripted and set very deliberate "bars" for the students throughout the process. In terms of product, this measured approach appears highly effective—ninety percent of the classroom participants completed a full digital story, posted it online, and presented it to their peers at the close of the workshop. And in terms of code, the students employed a wide range of fundamental concepts characteristic of all programming languages. This is important, as computer science is not yet one of the K-12 core media topics (Cooper, Pérez, & Rainey, 2010) utilized in classrooms, particularly within middle schools. By integrating CS concepts into traditional classrooms, programming, the original DIY activity with computers, reaches a broader and more diverse group of students.

In terms of production, the class was very much a success, but in terms of the other two measures, motivation and legitimate audiences, the class fared less well in its capacity to leverage the intended affordances of DIY media. In terms of motivation, while the classroom's participants were clearly enthusiastic about computers and computing, it is also telling that ninety percent reported they were in the class "to do Scratch" as opposed to describing the particular story they planned to create with Scratch. While motivation peaked at certain moments for different class members, there were also periods when the entire class seemed to drag, particularly in the submission of storyboards and the initial draft upload, which appeared to be nothing short of a chore for some class members. In terms of legitimate audiences, while all students posted their initial drafts online, only fifty percent reposted their final story, none replied to external comments from the Scratch community, and only ten percent of the final stories were remixed from others' creations online—altogether underlining the fact that the group neither utilized, nor had much time to utilize, the Scratch website over the course of the regimented curriculum.

Conversely, in the club, while only seventy-one percent of the participants produced completed projects, those who did engage, engaged with gusto. Club members produced nearly two (1.8) projects for every one produced by class members. In terms of motivation, sixty-five percent of members reported a specific genre of project (e.g., "making comics", "making funny slideshows") as the reason why they were in the club, which was generally buoyed by an atmosphere of playfulness and socializing over the course of the eight weeks. In terms of reaching and utilizing legitimate audiences beyond the instructor, of the twenty projects posted online, twenty-five received external comments and twenty-six percent of these final projects were remixes—altogether underlining club participants' greater propensity to use the Scratch website as a community in which to explore, socialize, and sample projects.

Despite these numerical differences, this is not to suggest that learning occurred less in the classroom than in the club. On the contrary, students in the class very much experienced the effectiveness of the writing workshop as a means to translate a new medium into a series of manageable steps. It is also worthwhile to reiterate that the differences between class and club members were not limited to externalities such as age and gender—while club members elected to stay after school, class members, while selecting the Scratch elective, nonetheless were bound by the school day requirements. This certainly affected the overall motivation. And even among those who elected to stay after school, nearly thirty percent of club participants never submitted any final project, and the majority of these participants also never attended the last week of the club, when the group made their final presentations. Altogether, results suggest that by regimenting children's use of DIY media by means of particular lessons and due dates, a program will be successful in ensuring the completion of a *certain type of product*—here, digital stories—though children's incentive for completing such a product is likely to be more closely linked to these same lessons and due dates. This is not necessarily a bad thing—after all, if DIY media is to reach more children at younger ages, it needs to enter classrooms, and to do this, it needs to align to academic objectives and assessments.

What is more is that while the club has promising results, it is also much harder to gauge a particular pathway to successfully stir individual motivation among participants, enhance their production, and have them reach authentic audiences. Cultural theorists and researchers Gregory, Long, and Volk (2004) almost reverentially refer to the plethora of "invisible literacies" children enact daily, but is it not schools' responsibility to make these nascent literacies not only visible but to some degree measurable?

Reviewing club data from the teacher's perspective, results seem to suggest that in terms of student motivation and particularly in terms of legitimate audiences, the "less is more" maxim may apply when it comes to incorporating DIY media into classrooms. Much of the club participants' success in utilizing the Scratch website as a source of personal motivation and a gateway to legitimate audiences derives from the simple fact that there was very little direct instruction in the afterschool environment. Besides them utilizing their in-person peers for support, and going online to sample, to remix, and/or to explore the "How To" sections of Forums, it was significant how the majority of the club participants acquainted themselves with Scratch. This is certainly encouraging in terms of children taking the initiative to educate themselves and reach out online, but such enthusiasm must be tempered by the statistic that nearly thirty percent of the club members completed no project, and for all purposes, effectively dropped out of the program by the end of December.

"Never let your education interfere with your learning," is the often-quoted phrase attributed to Mark Twain, and it is a sentiment that both Rich Halverson and Henry Jenkins (Jenkins, 2010) consider in their discussion of the future prospects of DIY media in classrooms. For such media to really take hold, can it only exist "in the wild" far from brick-and-mortar school walls? No—in terms of this study investigating children's use of Scratch in class and club environments, the sentiment represents something of a false dichotomy. It ought not to be an *either/or* scenario of picking one environment over the other, as each setting not only has its own affordances, but in terms of (a) motivation, (b) production, and (c) legitimate audiences, can potentially be used in conjunction with the other to offset the limitations of its counterpart. Of course, if only every K-12 school had the time, room, and financial resources to sponsor both a class and club around DIY media, which is not likely the case. Moving forward, though, it would be interesting to explore children's use of Scratch through a series of workshops that amalgamate elements of both class and club to arrive at some hybrid that incorporates assessment and direct instruction while also maintaining significant periods of free play among participants. Of course, such a hybrid may prove to be a greater challenge to incorporate, particularly among middle schools, where the division between class and club often means the difference between total instructional regimen and utter free play. But utilizing external challenges and competitions—such as the annual Scratch-sponsored "Collab Challenges" or the National STEM Video Game Challenge—may very well serve as an effective means to align the inherently "school-like" requirements of due dates and assessments with the legitimate audiences characteristic of extracurricular activities as a dual motivator for children's DIY learning.

NOTES

1 http://www.alice.org/
2 http://www.gvu.gatech.edu/node/5470
3 http://happyanalyzing.com
4 http://coweb.cc.gatech.edu/mediaComp-teach/16

REFERENCES

Burke, Q., and Kafai, Y.B. (2010). Programming & storytelling: Opportunities for learning about coding and composition. In *Proceedings of the 9th International Conference on Interaction Design and Children*, Barcelona, Spain: Universitat Pompeu Fabra.

Calkins, L. (1986). *The art of teaching writing*. Portsmouth, NH: Heinemann.

Collins, A., and Halverson, R. (2009). *Rethinking education in the age of technology: The digital revolution and the schools*. New York: Teachers College Press.

Cooper, S., Pérez, L.C., and Rainey, D. (2010). K-12 computational learning. *Communications of the ACM, 53*(11), 27–29.

Crook, S. (2009). Embedding Scratch in the classroom. *International Journal of Learning and Media, 1*(4), 17–21.

Dewey, J. (1916). *Democracy and education.* New York: Simon & Schuster.

DiSalvo, B., and Bruckman, A. (2011). From interest to values. *Communications of the ACM, 54*(8), 27–29.

Gaston, J. (2006). Reaching and teaching the digital natives. *Library Hi Tech News, 23*(3), 12–13.

Gee, J. (2003). *What video games have to teach us about learning and literacy.* New York: Palgrave.

Gregory, E., Long, S., and Volk, D. (2004). A socio-cultural approach to learning. In E. Gregory, S. Long, and D. Volk (Eds.), *Many pathways to literacy: Young children learning with siblings, grandparents, peers and communities,* pp. 6–20. New York & London: Routledge Falmer.

Harel, I., and Papert, S. (1990). Software design as a learning environment. *Interactive Learning Environments, 1,* 1–32.

Holloway, S., and Valentine, G. (2003). *Cyberkids: Children in the information age.* London: Routledge Falmer.

Jenkins, H. (2010). Is new media incompatible with schooling?: An interview with Rich Halverson. Accessed from http://henryjenkins.org/2010/03/is_new_media_incompat able_with.html.

Jones, B.L. (1996). *Schools for an information age: Reconstructing foundations for teaching and learning.* Westport, CT: Greenwood Publishing Group, Inc.

Kafai, Y.B. (1995). *Minds in play: Computer game design as a context for children's learning.* Hillsdale, NJ: Lawrence Erlbaum Associates.

Kafai, Y.B. (2006). Playing and making games for learning: Instructionist and constructionist perspectives for game studies. *Games and Culture, 1*(1), 36–40.

Kafai, Y.B., Fields, D.A., and Burke, W.Q. (2010). Entering the clubhouse: Case studies of young programmers joining the Scratch community. *Journal of Organizational and End User Computing, 22*(2), 21–35.

Kelleher, C., and Pausch, R. (2005). Lowering the barriers to programming: A taxonomy of programming environments and languages for novice programmers. *ACM Computing Surveys, 37*(2), 83–137.

Kelleher, C., and Pausch, R. (2007). Using storytelling to motivate programming. *Communications of the ACM, 50*(7), 59–64.

Knobel, M., and Lankshear, C. (Eds.). (2010). *DIY media: Creating, sharing, and learning with new technologies.* New York: Peter Lang.

Maloney, J., Peppler, K., Kafai, Y., Resnick, M., and Rusk, N. (2008). Programming by choice: Urban youth learning and programming with Scratch. Paper presented at the SIGCSE 2008 Conference, Portland, OR.

Margolis, J., & Fisher, A. (2002). *Unlocking the clubhouse: Women in computing.* Cambridge, MA: MIT Press.

McHale, T. (2005). Portrait of a digital native. *Technology and Learning, 26*(2), 33–34.

Papert, S. (1980). *Mindstorms: Children, computers, and powerful ideas.* New York: Basic Books.

Papert, S. (1993). *The children's machine: Rethinking school in the age of the computer.* New York: Basic Books.

Pea, R.D. (1987a). The aims of software criticism: Reply to Professor Papert. *Educational Researcher, 16*(5), 4–8.

Pea, R.D. (1987b). Programming and problem-solving: Children's experiences with Logo. In T. O'Shea & E. Scanlon (Eds.), *Educational computing* (An Open University Reader). London: John Wiley & Sons.

Peppler, K. & Kafai, Y.B. (2007). From SuperGoo to Scratch: Exploring creative digital media production in informal learning. *Learning, Media, and Technology, 32*(2), 149–166.

Prensky, M. (2006). *Don't bother me, Mom, I'm learning! How computer and video games are preparing your kids for 21st century success and how you can help*. St. Paul, MN: Paragon House.

Reas, C. (2006a). Media literacy: Twenty-first century arts education. *AI & Society, 20*(4), 444–445.

Reas, C. (2006b). Processing: Programming for the media arts. *AI & Society, 20*(4), 526–538.

Resnick, M., Maloney, J., Hernandez, A.M., Rusk, N., Eastmond, E., Brennan, K., Millner, A., Roenbaum, E., Silver, J., Silverman, B., and Kafai, Y.B. (2009). Scratch: Programming for everyone. *Communications of the ACM, 52*(11), 60–67.

Rushkoff, D. (2010). *Program or be programmed: Ten commands for a digital age*. New York: O/R Books.

Scaffidi, C., Shaw, M., and Myers, B. (2005). Estimating the numbers of end users and end user programmers. *IEEE Symposium on Visual Languages and Human-Centric Computing*, 207–214.

Strauss, A., and J. Corbin. (1998). *Basics of qualitative research: Techniques and procedures for developing grounded theory*. Thousand Oaks, CA: Sage.

Torrey, C., McDonald, D.W., Schilit, B.N., and Bly, S. (2007). How-To pages: Informal systems of expertise sharing. In *Proceedings of the Tenth European Conference on Computer Supported Cooperative Work. ECSCW '07*, 391–410.

Wing, J.M. (2006). Computational thinking. *Communications of the ACM, 49*(3), 33–35.

Wolz, U., Pearson, K., Pulimood, S.M., Stone, M., and Switzer, M. (2011). Computational thinking and expository writing in the middle school: A novel approach to broadening participation in computing. *Transactions on Computing Education, 11*(2). Accessed from: http://dl.acm.org/citation.cfm?id=1993073.

CHAPTER 7

A JOURNEY FROM ORDER TO DISORDER

Coding snippets in mathematics

Steve Humble

INTRODUCTION

Today, computers are commonly used in mathematical research in areas that require complex calculations. This is relatively new, however, and has altered the way mathematicians think about proof. One of the most famous examples of mathematicians using a computer to help to prove that something is always true is the 'Four Colour' theorem. The problem states that when constructing a map so that no two adjacent countries are represented by the same colour, only four colours or fewer are required to allow this to be true. In 1976, Kenneth Appel and Wolfgang Haken (Wilson, 2003) used coding to show that this was always true for any map you could ever create.

Computers have also been used to find contradictions. In the eighteenth century, after an extraordinary number of calculations, Leonhard Euler (Calinger, 2015), one of the greatest mathematicians of all time, came to the conjecture that a total of at least n positive nth powers of integers are required to produce an nth power. The calculations required to investigate this number theory prediction turned out to be difficult. Leon Lander and Thomas Parkin's (1967) computer counter-example showed that Euler's postulate was, in fact, not true. They found from their coding an example, which gave a 5th power with only four positive integers:

$$27^5 + 84^5 + 110^5 + 133^5 = 144^5.$$

But it's not only mathematicians wanting to create 'new' mathematics who can benefit from coding. In recent years, there have been a number of key mathematical reforms focusing on the development of children's conceptual understanding and problem solving ability (Cai and Howson, 2013; Conway and Sloane, 2005). In conjunction with these reforms, research has suggested that the use of technology in mathematics lessons can make the subject more meaningful and engaging (Ainley et al., 2011; Drijvers et al., 2010; Hoyles and Lagrange, 2010; Olive et al., 2010). The research suggests that coding could be used to support the pupil's learning journey in mathematics. Through coding, time is given for the pupil to build conceptual models and construct mathematical structures for themselves. This kind of scaffolding enables pupils to consolidate their learning and lay down solid foundations on which they can build. To this end, coding can help pupils to explore mathematical concepts in a directed and meaningful way, thereby giving time for pupils to experiment with the subject.

What are the benefits of coding? Mathematical activity involves creating algorithms, experimenting, writing algebraic generalisations and establishing proofs. Coding can support and allow time for children to develop these skills in the classroom. It is generally agreed in educational research that ideas are easier to understand when they are made more concrete and less abstract (Ball, 1992; Boaler, 2015; Borich, 1996; Humble, 2002, 2017; McDonough, 2016; Papert, 1972a, 1972b, 1980, 1993, 1999; Papert and Solomon, 1971; Papert, et al., 1979; Piaget and Piaget, 1973).

When an abstract idea is approached in a lesson using coding, a child's mind sees the concept in a more concrete way. This allows for greater ownership in the development of concepts. The activity of coding can be used to help develop processes represented by abstract ideas. The act of coding also allows children to develop individual journeys of discovery. When a child formulates ideas in this way, a corresponding construction is made in their mind. This in turn stimulates both short and long term memory. It is therefore possible, using this abstract-to-concrete concept, to organise coding tasks to enhance the pupil's mathematical knowledge and understanding. In terms of teaching pedagogy, once these various constructs have been created and used in the classroom, it can be useful to reflect on what they are and how children can be engaged through these processes.

In this chapter we will look at a series of number patterns in mathematics and think about ways children can construct algorithms and code to help them understand the processes involved. The simplicity of the code considered in this chapter demonstrates that one can exploit the computer mathematically without being an expert programmer. My interested reader may feel that they can write more elegant versions of the code than those suggested in this chapter. However, my intention is to offer a version that is simple to understand and widely acceptable no matter which package is being used. Again, in order to keep the code simple and short, no attempt has been made to include checking procedures that ensure that sensible values are entered from the keyboard. For example, if the code asks for integer values, it expects the user to use only integers!

There are four parts to this chapter. The aim is to stimulate, through coding, experimentation that provides access and empowerment around the concepts of number. The first part discusses what is meant by pattern and order. The next section investigates well-known number patterns through coding. Historical contexts and number facts are included, to allow more in-depth further exploration. The third part discussed the means to determine the level of order existing in finite number patterns. This allows more comprehensive discovery around number patterns and the use of coding. Finally the chapter ends with thoughts on the future of coding in mathematics education.

THE MEANING OF ORDER

There is a great richness existing in the basic number line of integer values. A variety of patterns can be found in what may seem to be a random collection of numbers. An analogy in everyday life is the complexity of trying to observe order when faced with a large collection of choices. Everyone has experience of seemingly random events, such as the shuffling of cards, or the tossing a coin at the start of a game of football. Most of us encounter chance daily, and misconceptions abound. The psychologists Daniel Kahneman and Amos Tversky (1982) suggest that people make decisions based on small sample sets. They tend to reject randomness in the appearances of long runs in short samples, feeling it seems too purposeful to be random. For example, what comes next in this sequence?

HTHTHHHHHHHHHHH......

After a long run of heads, most would predict either a tail is due, or possibly another head owing to its popularity. At its heart, this gambler's fallacy lies in a misconception about fairness of the laws of chance. Chance is regarded as a self-correcting process in which deviations in one direction will soon be countered with deviations in the other direction. In fact, probability shows that these deviations in the short run are not corrected. They are merely diluted over the long run. The philosophical questions around randomness were raised as far back as the time of the ancient Greeks. In 450 BC, Leucippus purportedly said, "Nothing happens at random; everything happens out of reason and by necessity."[1]

The challenge is how we transfer some understanding of order and disorder to children. A good place to start this journey is with whole numbers. These are the first numbers we come across as a child: counting the stairs as we walk up them, or counting toy bricks. They have a strange property in the mind of a child, as they go on forever – very different from the alphabet, which stops at 26 with 'z'. It's not until we get older that these ubiquitous numbers start to take on a new meaning, when we discover that they can be categorised into ordered groups such as even, odd, square, triangular, prime, 'happy numbers' and 'sad numbers' (Humble, 2013; Stewart, 2010). The world of numbers comes out of the shadows and offers a crazy, chaotic glimpse at the rich world of mathematics. Welcome to the world of patterns. The next section provides three examples of how to experiment through coding to allow children to explore patterns with whole numbers.

CODING FOR NUMBER PATTERNS

As a starting point, it is valuable for children to see how they can create outputs of whole number values through coding. This basic number pattern starts at 1, and the simple rule is to add 1 each time. Visually, children can see this on a number line, or by using counters or blocks for a more concrete visualisation. Code can be written using what is known as a 'FOR, NEXT' loop to visually output integers and show how they stretch on forever. The code set out below starts at 1 and gives an output of the first 12 whole numbers.

```
REM **The first 12 whole numbers**
FOR A = 1 TO 12
PRINT A; " ";
NEXT A
```

Output:

```
1 2 3 4 5 6 7 8 9 10 11 12
```

REFLECTION ACTIVITY

Try changing the code to print out other groups of whole numbers. By changing the FOR line of code, you can output any group of whole numbers; for example, for the group 50 to 60, this would require editing the above to FOR A = 50 TO 60.

Odd and even numbers

The hidden secrets of our number system can often reveal the magical quality of mathematics. Through the process of discovery and discussion with fellow classmates, the hidden depths of mathematics takes on new appeal. Such discussions might focus the children to investigate even and odd number sequences. Even and odd numbers are used in everyday life in the case of house numbers, with one side of the street being even numbers and the opposite side odd, for example. Children can explore even and odd numbers through coding. Using the expression 2*A for even numbers, code can be written to print out numbers in the two times table. The expression for the numbers not in the two times table, odd numbers, can be written as 2*A-1 (as shown below).

```
REM **Even numbers to 10**
FOR A = 1 TO 5
PRINT 2*A; " ";
NEXT A
REM **Odd numbers to 10**
FOR A = 1 TO 5
PRINT 2*A-1; " ";
NEXT A
```

Output:

```
2 4 6 8 10 1 3 5 7 9
```

REFLECTION ACTIVITY

What changes to the code would be required to output all the odd numbers from 20 to 30, or 300 to 350?

Once the children understand how to write code expressions for even and odd numbers, they can then start to explore what happens when you add groups of even and odd numbers. The code below sets out how to add consecutive odd numbers. If the first number is written as 2*A−1, the next consecutive odd number is then two on from this, and can be written as (2*A−1)+2, simplified to 2*A+1.

```
REM **Sum of two consecutive odd numbers**
FOR A = 1 TO 20
PRINT 2*A-1; " + ";2*A+1; " = ";(2*A-1)+(2*A+1)
NEXT A
```

Output:

```
1 + 3 = 4
3 + 5 = 8
5 + 7 = 12
7 + 9 = 16
9 + 11 = 20
11 + 13 = 24
13 + 15 = 28
15 + 17 = 32
```

REFLECTION ACTIVITY

Children can now explore pattern.

■ What is the pattern when you add two consecutive odd numbers? The answer is always even and divisible by 4.
■ What happens if two consecutive even numbers are added? What is the pattern?
■ What if you add three or more consecutive numbers? (For three consecutive odd numbers, you can use the expression 2*A−1 + 2*A+1 + 2*A+3.)
■ Explore other groups of consecutive numbers, writing code to look for patterns when adding different combinations of odd and even numbers.

Square and triangular numbers

Children can appreciate through using multiple representations that there are many ways to explore numbers. The visual representations of numbers can help children to see them from a new perspective rather than thinking of them as symbols. Figure 7.1 shows such a representation for square numbers.

In order to code square numbers, the expression A*A is used.

```
REM **Square numbers to 4**
FOR A = 1 TO 4
PRINT A*A; " ";
NEXT A
```

Output:

```
1 4 9 16
```

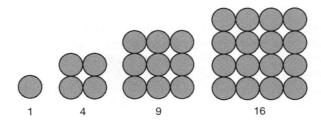

■ **Figure 7.1** Visual representation of square numbers

Throughout history, a great variety of patterns has been discovered by mathematicians. The ancient Greeks named one such pattern 'triangular numbers'. As with square numbers, this number sequence can be represented visually using shapes, as seen in Figure 7.2. Each subsequent number in the triangular number sequence is created by adding a row to the bottom of the triangle. This informs us of a way to write the code for this sequence. The next three triangular numbers in this sequence are 15 (10+5), 21 (15+6) and 28 (21+7).

```
REM **Triangular numbers to 7**
B=0
FOR A = 1 TO 7
B=B+A
PRINT B; " ";
NEXT A
```

Output:
```
1 3 6 10 15 21 28
```

The code shown above is one way to generate triangular numbers. Starting with B equal to 0, we increase A by 1 using the loop. This value is added to B and then printed. The counter then increases A to 2, and this value is then added to B to give the next triangular number (1+2), and so on. But there are other ways to write code to generate this pattern. One way would be to use an expression as shown below for square numbers. Using this technique, the code expression for triangular numbers is $A*(A+1)/2$.

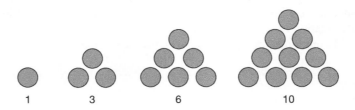

■ **Figure 7.2** Visual representation of triangular numbers

```
REM **Triangular numbers to 7**
FOR A = 1 TO 7
PRINT A*(A+1)/2; " ";
NEXT A
```

Output:

```
1 3 6 10 15 21 28
```

REFLECTION ACTIVITY

It is interesting for children to add consecutive square numbers and find that these always give odd numbers. When you add consecutive triangular numbers, you always get square numbers; the expression for this is:

```
A*(A+1)/2 + (A+1)*(A+2)/2
```

Taking further the concept of triangular numbers and introducing the great mathematician Carl Friedrich Gauss provides a historical story linking the abstract to the concrete. On 10 July 1796, when he was 19 years old, Gauss wrote in his diary with great excitement: "I have just proved this *wonderful* result that any whole number is the sum of three or fewer triangular numbers" (Humble, 2002, p. 42).

By looking at some whole numbers, it can be seen how they can be generated by adding three or fewer triangular numbers. Here is a selection of whole numbers (4, 5, 9 and 25) so you can start to see how Gauss's idea works.

$4 = 3+1$
$5 = 3+1+1$
$9 = 3+3+3$
$25 = 21+3+1$

REFLECTION ACTIVITY

Write code to test Gauss's idea for some large whole numbers.

Prime Numbers

Prime numbers have always intrigued mathematicians. The definition of a prime number is that it can only be divided by itself and 1, without a remainder. They follow no predictable pattern; therefore a coding expression cannot be applied as with square and triangular numbers.

To construct the code to find primes, we can use a fact that was first discovered by Eratosthenes of Cyrene around 200 BC. If a number (N) is not a prime, it can be written as the product of at least two of its factors (N=A*B). This implies that A and B cannot both exceed the square root of N. Therefore any composite integer N is divisible by a prime that does not exceed the square root of N. It follows that to find prime numbers it is only necessary to divide each number by whole numbers less than or equal to its square root. If the answer for any of these calculations is a whole number, the number being investigated is not a prime number. In the following code, this information is synthesised in the IF THEN statement: IF A*A <= N THEN GOTO 30.

```
10 FOR N = 3 TO 30 STEP 2
20 A = 2
30 IF N/A = INT(N/A) THEN GOTO 70
40 A = A+1
50 IF A*A <= N THEN GOTO 30
60 PRINT N;" ";
70 NEXT N
```

Output:
```
3 5 7 11 13 17 19 23 29
```

No one has found a general expression to generate all primes, yet it has been known since 300 BC that there are infinitely many. Euclid, a Greek mathematician, published the proof of this fact in his classic book *The Elements*. Although no general expression has yet been found for *all* primes, there are many simple expressions that allow the generation of small sets of primes. For example, the expression A*A+A+17 gives 15 prime numbers.

```
10 FOR A = 1 TO 17
20 PRINT A*A+A+17;" ";
30 NEXT A
```

Output:
```
19 23 29 37 47 59 73 89 107 127 149 173 199 227 257 289 323
```

Note that this expression fails, as we said, to find any more than 15 primes. In this output, the last two numbers are not prime, with 289 and 323 both being divisible by 17. This highlights that an important part of coding activities is to check the output and discover the range for which the expression is valid.

REFLECTION ACTIVITY

Other expressions pupils can try are:

- A*A – A + 41, giving primes for values of A between 0 and 40
- A*A – 79*A + 1601, giving primes for values of A between 0 and 79
- 6*A*A + 6*A + 31, giving primes for values of A between 0 and 28

There are many strange and wonderfully curious facts that have been discovered over the years about prime numbers. This is by no means an exhaustive list of prime curiosities. Classroom web investigations will discover more results on primes and create opportunities for more prime number coding projects.

REFLECTION ACTIVITY

■ There are no primes between 370,261 and 370,373, or between 20,821,533 and 20,831,323. Ask pupils to search to find the largest gap they can find between sets of primes.

■ The primes 13,331, 15,551, 16,661, 19,991, 72,227 and 1,777,771 are all examples of palindromic numbers. These are numbers that remain the same when the digits are reversed. Ask your pupils to find other examples of palindromic prime numbers.

■ If two consecutive odd numbers are both primes, they are called 'twin primes'. The ancient Greeks were the first to state that there are infinitely many primes, but, to this day, it is not known whether there are infinitely many 'twin primes'. Here are some examples of twin primes: 3 and 5, 5 and 7, 11 and 13, 17 and 19. Ask your pupils to write code to find other twin primes. What are the biggest twin primes they can find?

■ In 1850, the Russian mathematician Chebyshev conjectured and proved that there is at least one prime number between N and 2*N for every value of N greater than 5. More recently, the Polish mathematician Sierpinski improved on Chebyshev's result, proving that there are at least two prime numbers between N and 2*N, for N greater than 5. Children can test these results by editing the code that was initially used to find primes. One example would be to discover how many primes are between 9 (N=9) and 18 (2*N=18). The code below demonstrates this:

```
10 FOR N = 9 TO 18 STEP 2
20 A = 2
30 IF N/A = INT(N/A) THEN GOTO 70
40 A = A+1
50 IF A*A <= N THEN GOTO 30
60 PRINT N;" ";
70 NEXT N
```

Output:
```
11 13 17
```

WHEN IS THERE PATTERN?

So far, the chapter has considered different kinds of order that exist in the set of whole numbers, using short pieces of code to investigate their patterns. The previous section initially explored clear patterns (even, odd, square and triangular numbers) and moved to prime numbers, which are more difficult to generate through coding. This lack of order within primes could be due to an incomplete understanding of primes.[2] In this part of the chapter, an investigation is carried out on how to test for levels of order. To start, random numbers are explored, looking at how computers attempt to generate numbers with no apparent pattern.

Computers and calculators have the facility to produce pseudo-random numbers, so called because the code that generates such numbers uses a predetermined routine – a random function (RND). The following code produces 20 random whole single-digit numbers:

```
FOR A = 1 TO 20
PRINT RND(10);" ";
NEXT A
```

Output:
```
3 2 6 2 7 7 4 2 1 0 1 9 2 8 1 3 6 1 8 1
```

The random number function is one of the standard expressions that can be used to perform specific tasks in coding. In order to see behind the function and give an understanding of how it generates its output, the following provides a simple example. The 147 random number generator is the simplest way to produce pseudo-random numbers. So how does it work? First a decimal between 0 and 1 is randomly selected. Then it is multiplied by 147. (Historically, the '147' random number generator has been used as a simple way to produce pseudo-random numbers.) The generator then takes the fractional part of this result $(147*X - INT(147*X))$ and multiplies it by 10, to produce the random whole number. The following code will generate a set of 30 pseudo-random whole numbers from 0 to 9, prompted by decimals input by the user.

```
FOR A = 1 TO 30
INPUT "Input a decimal between 0 and 1"; X
B = 147*X - INT(147*X)
PRINT INT(10*B);" ";
NEXT A
```

A possible output for the user's range of random decimal inputs between zero and one is as follows:
```
0 7 8 1 4 6 4 7 5 4 4 4 7 5 7 3 6 3 2 1 4 2 7 7 2 7 0 0 7 7
```

Two- and three-digit pseudo-random numbers can be obtained using similar code, by multiplying B by 100 or 1,000 respectively in the PRINT statement. This type of generator is very simple, and much more complex versions are used when using the RND function. As with the above code, after a large set of pseudo-random numbers have been produced, repeating sequences are visible in the output. Thus these generators produce pseudo-random numbers and not pure randomness.

REFLECTION ACTIVITY

Use the 147 code to generate pseudo-random numbers, and then search for sequences within the output.

Reflecting back to the start of the chapter, a question was posed around the meaning of randomness. The simplest definition of a random event is one whose outcomes are all 'equally likely' or 'fair'. This definition implies, for example, when tossing a coin, getting equal numbers of 'heads' and 'tails'. Throwing a dice repeatedly reveals an equal chance of returning any number from 1 to 6. It is this definition of randomness that is used in this section of the chapter to define when a pattern (or lack of it) is seen in a finite sequence of whole numbers. John Venn, the English statistician after whom the Venn diagram was named, stated this definition of randomness in the nineteenth century, saying "random sequences are often ones whose elements are equally likely" (Venn, 1876, p. 109).

Typically, children are asked to find a 'pattern' within a finite sequence, often through a 'what comes next' question, and are rarely asked to uncover the *lack* of pattern. An understanding of randomness is a skill that can help to prepare children for their future mathematical journey, as it links to working with large data sets and real-life patterns. Kendall and Babington-Smith (1938) suggest, in their landmark work, tests to assess for local randomness, of which two are investigated[3] in the remaining part of the chapter:

■ The *frequency test* is a test of the uniform occurrence of each of the ten digits 0 through to 9. The expectation is that each of the digits will occur an approximately equal number of times.

■ The *serial test* is a test of the uniform occurrence of two-digit pairs, with the expectation that each possible two-digit pair will occur an approximately equal number of times.

This next part provides a series of examples of how to apply these two tests to look for the degree of order in sets of finite digits.

Let's begin by taking a sequence of numbers. First we need to think about the random case and what we would expect to find in the sequence of digits using the numbers 1, 2 and 3 only. Using John Venn's definition of randomness, we would expect, if all things were equally likely, to find two cases of 1's followed by a 1 in the sequence. There would be two cases of 1's followed by a 2. Finally, there would be two cases of 1's followed by a 3. This would similarly be true for the numbers following the six 2's and the six 3's. The number sequence below shows one possibility of this case:

331122131133221232

The representation of this sequence is shown in Table 7.1, which shows how many times the number 1 is followed in the sequence by the numbers 1, 2 and 3. Similarly for 2 and 3, we can look at the next number in the sequence in the same way.

▓ Table 7.1 Expected pattern for John Venn's random case

First number	No. of times followed by a 1	No. of times followed by a 2	No. of times followed by a 3
1	2	2	2
2	2	2	2
3	2	2	2

The above sets out the expected case for a random sequence using the numbers 1, 2 and 3 only. This can be used as a baseline case to compare all observed sequences created subsequently.

REFLECTION ACTIVITY

Create a number sequence using only the digits 1, 2 and 3 six times each.

Look for different patterns and see how they compare with the base random case above.

For younger children, sequences can be generated using three different coloured pieces of card with six of each colour (red, blue, yellow) rather than digits. Children will be able to explore the different patterns they can make.

Let's look at two other examples, which could be observed sequences. First, an 18-number sequence, with each of the numbers 1, 2 and 3 occurring six times, could result in this ordered sequence: 123123123123123123. When John Venn's method is used to analyse this pattern, a table can be constructed as illustrated in Table 7.2.

Table 7.3 provides the 'difference' between Tables 7.1 and 7.2 for each of the cells providing the absolute value. Therefore this shows the difference between what you would 'expect' if the sequence were random in agreement with John Venn's 'rule' and the observed case constructed in the first example.

The total of all the deviations can be found by adding together all of the values in the above table. This gives 2+4+2+2+2+4+4+2+2 = 24. As the observed sequence has an

▓ Table 7.2 Observed pattern for 123123123123123123

First number	No. of times followed by a 1	No. of times followed by a 2	No. of times followed by a 3
1	0	6	0
2	0	0	6
3	6	0	0

■ **Table 7.3** The deviation of the pattern in Table 7.2 from the random expected case

First number	No. of times followed by a 1	No. of times followed by a 2	No. of times followed by a 3
1	2 (2−0=2)	4 (6−2=4)	2(2−0=2)
2	2	2	4
3	4	2	2

obvious repeating pattern, the test reveals the deviation value is high. The smaller the total (deviation score), the more random the observed pattern. If the observed sequence were completely random, the deviation score would be zero.

The second example considers a sequence with less structure to show how the method differentiates, and gives a measure of disorder in finite sequences. The second sequence is 122312231313123122. Table 7.4 shows the observed pattern.

Table 7.5 provides the 'difference' between tables 7.1 and 7.4 for each of the cells providing the absolute value, again showing the difference between the 'expected' value and the 'observed' value.

The total of all the deviations can be found by adding together all of the values in Table 7.5. This gives 2+0+2+3+2+2+2+1+2 = 16. As this sequence has less of a pattern than the first sequence, the value of the deviation score (16) is less than that found in the first example (24). As this sequence still has some semblance of order, the total deviation score is still quite high.

■ **Table 7.4** Observed pattern for 122312231313123122

First number	No. of times followed by a 1	No. of times followed by a 2	No. of times followed by a 3
1	0	2	4
2	5	0	0
3	0	3	4

■ **Table 7.5** The deviation of the pattern in Table 7.4 from the random expected case

First number	No. of times followed by a 1	No. of times followed by a 2	No. of times followed by a 3
1	2 (2−0=2)	0 (6−2=4)	2(2−0=2)
2	3	2	2
3	2	1	2

> ## REFLECTION ACTIVITY
>
> Try to find a sequence that has a smaller value and so is less ordered.

The above examples have provided ideas around the generation of number sequences and given a method to determine the randomness of such sequences. These two processes can be carried out using coding to support learning around order, randomness and pattern.

It is possible to code random sequences using strings. In the example below, the strings A$ and B$ are used to store sequences of digits. B$ stores the randomly generated single digits 1, 2 and 3; and A$ builds an 18-digit string using a random selection of these three digits.

```
FOR N = 1 TO 18
B$ = RND(3)+1
A$ = A$+B$
NEXT N
PRINT A$;" ";
```

Output:

```
1 2 3 2 2 3 2 1 3 1 2 2 1 1 3 3 1 2
```

Notice that in the output produced from the above code, each digit does not appear an equal number of times. If, as in the observed sequence examples above, each digit is required to appear a certain number of times, a decision statement should be used to check on the frequency or appearance. Alternatively, the data command (DATA) could be used to store the digits required in the sequence, and accessed from the READ command.

```
DATA "1","2","3","1","2","3"
DATA "1","2","3","1","2","3"
DATA "1","2","3","1","2","3"
DIM A$(20)
FOR N = 1 TO 18
READ A$(n)
B$ = B$+A$(n)
NEXT N
PRINT B$
```

Output:

```
1 2 3 1 2 3 1 2 3 1 2 3 1 2 3 1 2 3
```

This time, the output produces each digit an equal number of times, but in a very ordered structure – in fact, the same structure that exists in our DATA set.

In the code below, once the DATA has been taken into the A$ array, the first loop randomly swaps the positions of the digits. The second loop assembles this into a randomised full string (C$) and then prints this out.

```
FOR M = 1 TO 18
B$ = A$(M)
C = RND(18)+1
A$(M) = A$(C)
A$(C) = B$
NEXT M
FOR P = 1 TO 18
C$ = C$+A$(P)
NEXT P
PRINT C$
```

Outputs:
```
131131213222233132
>RUN
213312123312231231
>RUN
312123212312112333
>RUN
112123231232231133
```

Moving on to test for local randomness, an IF THEN statement would be required with 'counters' to record the number of occasions when two digits are paired with each other (e.g. when a 1 is followed by a 1, 1 followed by a 2, and so on for all possible cases). The MID$ command is useful in this case, as it gives a way of 'slicing up' your randomised string C$ and checking the next digit. For example, the following code checks for a 1 followed by 1 or 2 and records these cases as 'countone' and 'counttwo' respectively.

```
IF MID$(C$,r,1) = "1" AND MID$(C$,r+1,1) = "1" THEN countone = countone+1
IF MID$(C$,r,1) = "1" AND MID$(C$,r+1,1) = "2" THEN counttwo = counttwo+1
```

REFLECTION ACTIVITY

■ Ask pupils to check the relative randomness of strings generated by this method. Does it make any difference if you increase the length of the string or the range of possible digits?

■ Sequences appear in the world around us and offer the opportunity to test for pattern order and disorder. Use patterns from the classroom environment as starting points to explore sequences. (Hint: for example, you could analyse your pupils' birthdays or their house numbers. Examples in the wider world could include the FTSE 100 stock prices, biodiversity in animal species in certain regions around the world, coloured patterns in art (red = number 1, blue = 2, etc), varying architectural structure patterns (triangle = 1, square = 2, etc), to name but a few. Our mathematical world is full of pattern: we need only to open our eyes to see its rich beauty (Humble, 2015).)

THE FUTURE

Coding is already proving to be a powerful tool to help advance mathematical thinking, both in mathematical research and in mathematics education at all levels. The empirical evidence shows greater success is achieved in the educational process when coding is used to enhance meaning (Aydın, 2005; Calao, et al., 2015; Resnick, 2012; Zavala et al., 2013). This can be through either understanding mathematical processes or the use of computer environments for exploration and construction of concepts.

Yet mathematics is not a spectator sport. It is a subject that needs to be experimented with (Behrends and Humble, 2013; Humble, 1991a, 1991b, 1992, 1994, 1995, 2001, 2007, 2011). The chapter has shown how this is possible by using very short pieces of code. The advancement of mathematical thinking will continue to thrive through human curiosity. Coding is just one tool that can help children explore the rich and beautiful world of mathematics (Humble, 2002).

NOTES

1 Leucippus, Fragment 569 – from Fr. 2 Actius I, 25, 4
2 http://www-groups.dcs.st-and.ac.uk/history/HistTopics/Prime_numbers.html
3 If the reader is interested, Knuth (1981) discusses the development of Kendall and Babington-Smith's work and some further tests.

REFERENCES

Ainley, J., Button, T., Clark-Wilson, A., Hewson, S., Johnston-Wilder, S., Martin, D., and Sutherland, R. (2011). Digital technologies and mathematics education. University of Warwick. Accessed from http://wrap.warwick.ac.uk/51564/.

Aydın, E. (2005). The use of computers in mathematics education: A paradigm shift from "computer assisted instruction" towards "student programming". *Journal of Educational Technology* 4(2).

Ball, D. (1992). Magical hopes: Manipulatives and the reform of math education. *American Educator,* 16(2), pp. 14–18 & pp. 46–47.

Behrends, E, and Humble, S. (2013). Triangle mysteries. *The Mathematical Intelligencer,* 35(2), 10–15.

Boaler, J. (2015). *The elephant in the classroom: Helping children learn and love maths.* London: Souvenir Press.

Borich, G. (1996). *Effective teaching methods.* New York: Macmillan.

Cai, J., and Howson, G. (2013). Toward an international mathematics curriculum. In M. A. K. Clements, A. J. Bishop, C. Keitel, J. Kilpatrick, and F. K. S. Leung (Eds.), *Third international handbook of mathematics education* (pp. 949–974). New York: Springer.

Calao, L. A., Moreno-León, J., Correa, H. E., and Robles, G. (2015). Developing mathematical thinking with Scratch: An experiment with 6th grade students. G. Conole, T. Klobučar, C. Rensing, J. Konert, and E. Lavoue (Eds.), *Design for Teaching and Learning in a Networked World.* pp. 17–27. New York: Springer International Publishing.

Calinger, R. S. (2015). *Leonhard Euler: Mathematical genius in the Enlightenment.* Oxford: Princeton University Press.

Conway, P. F., and Sloane, F. C. (2005). *International trends in post-primary mathematics education.* Dublin: National Council for Curriculum and Assessment. Accessed from http://www.ncca.ie/uploadedfiles/Publications/MathsResearch.pdf.

Drijvers, P., Mariotti, M. A., Olive, J., and Sacristán, A. I. (2010). Introduction to section 2. In C. Hoyles and J. B. Lagrange (Eds.), *Mathematics education and technology – rethinking the terrain: The 17th ICMI Study* (pp. 81–88). New York: Springer.

Hoyles, C., and Lagrange, J. B. (Eds.). (2010). *Mathematics education and technology – rethinking the terrain: The 17th ICMI study*. New York: Springer.

Humble, S. (1991a). Classroom chaos: Mathematical discovery in the A level classroom. *Mathematics Teaching*, 137, 20–23.

Humble, S. (1991b). Spirals – number patterns in geometry. *Mathematics Teaching*.

Humble, S. (1992). Graphical calculators and investigations. Lissajous Curves. *Mathematics Teaching*, 16–17.

Humble, S. (1994). Anyone for tennis? Classroom experiments to find drag, lift and spin. *Teaching Mathematics and its Applications*, 13(3), 120–123.

Humble, S. (1995). *Graphical calculators and investigations: Lissajous Curves. Mathematics Teaching*, 141, 56–60.

Humble, S. (2001). Rolling and spinning coin: a level gyroscopic processional motion. *Teaching Mathematics and its Applications*, 20(1), 18–24.

Humble, S. (2002). *The experimenter's A–Z of mathematics: Maths activities with computer support.* London: David Fulton.

Humble, S. (2007). Skimming and skipping stones. *Teaching Mathematics and its Applications*, 26(2), 95–102.

Humble, S. (2011). Create your own mathematical mysteries. *Plus* magazine. Accessed from http://plus.maths.org/content/surprising-maths-make-your-own-conjecture&src=fpii.

Humble, S. (2013). *Maths for every day! 366 primary maths activities linked to every day of the year.* Kirkby-in-Ashfield, Nottinghamshire, UK: TTS.

Humble, S. (2015). *How to be inventive when teaching primary mathematics: Developing outstanding learners.* Oxon, UK: Routledge.

Kahneman, D, and Tversky, A. (1982). *Judgement under uncertainty: Heuristics and bias.* New York: Cambridge University Press.

Kendall, M. G., and Babington-Smith, B. (1938). Randomness and random sampling numbers. *Journal of the Royal Statistical Society*, 101, 147–166.

Knuth, D. E. (1981). Random numbers. Ch. 3 in *Seminumerical algorithms*, Vol. 2 in *The art of computer programming.* 2nd ed. Reading, Massachusetts: Addison Wesley.

Lander, L. J., and Parkin, T. R. (1967). A counterexample to Euler's Sum of Powers Conjecture. *Mathematics of Computation*, Vol. 21, January 1967, 101–103.

McDonough, A. (2016). Good concrete activity is good mental activity. *Australian Primary Mathematics Classroom.* 21(1), 3–7.

Olive, J., Makar, K., Hoyos, V., Kor, L. K., Kosheleva, O., and Sträßer, R. (2010). Mathematical knowledge and practices resulting from access to digital technologies. In C. Hoyles and J. B. Lagrange (Eds.), *Mathematics education and technology – rethinking the terrain: The 17th ICMI Study* (pp. 133–177). New York: Springer.

Papert, S. (1972a). On making a theorem for a child. Paper presented at the Proceedings of the ACM annual conference – Vol. 1, Boston, Massachusetts.

Papert, S. (1972b). Teaching children to be mathematicians versus teaching about mathematics. *International Journal of Mathematical Education in Science and Technology*, 3(3), 249–262.

Papert, S. (1980). *Mindstorms: Children, computers, and powerful ideas.* New York: Basic Books.

Papert, S. (1993). *The children's machine: Rethinking school in the age of the computer.* New York: Basic Books.

Papert, S. (1999). Introduction: What is Logo and who needs it? In LCSI (Ed.), *Logo philosophy and implementation* (pp. v–xvi). Montreal, Quebec: LCSI.

Papert, S., and Solomon, C. (1971). *Twenty things to do with a computer*. Accessed from ftp:// publications.ai.mit.edu/ai-publications/pdf/AIM-248.pdf.

Papert, S., Watt, D., diSessa, A., and Weir, S. (1979). *Final Report of the Brookline Logo Project, an assessment and documentation of a children's computer laboratory, Part III: Detailed profiles of each student's work*. Accessed from https://dspace.mit.edu/ handle/1721.1/6324.

Piaget, J., and Piaget, J. (1973). *To understand is to invent: The future of education*. New York: Grossman Publishers.

Resnick, M. (2012). Point of view: Reviving Papert's dream. *Educational Technology* 52(4), 42–46.

Stewart, I. (2010). *Professor Stewart's cabinet of mathematical curiosities*. London: Profile Books Ltd.

Venn, J. (1876). *The logic of chance: An essay on the foundations and province of the theory of probability, with especial reference to its application to moral and social science*. London: Macmillan.

Wilson, R. J. (2003). *Four colours suffice: How the map problem was solved*. London: Penguin.

Zavala, L. A., Gallardo, S. C. H., and García-Ruíz, M. A. (2013). Designing interactive activities within Scratch 2.0 for improving abilities to identify numerical sequences. In: *Proceedings of the 12th International Conference on Interaction Design and Children*, pp. 423–426. ACM.

CHAPTER 8

COMPUTER SCIENCE

The silent 'C' in 'STEM'

Yasemin Allsop

INTRODUCTION

There is no doubt that recent technological advances have influenced not only the way we communicate but also the way we think and learn. There has been a shift in the anatomy of thinking and learning from a ready static to an interactive-dynamic experience, where learners have transformed how they conceptualise their learning. Nonetheless schools find it very challenging to change their set ways to accommodate this shift in their curricula. Papert (1993) also criticised the schooling environment for treating children as passive learners – with knowledge about numbers and grammar being valued more than knowledge about learning – rather than adopting a learner-centred approach. He described learning as a reconstruction rather than as a transmission of knowledge, and suggested that learning happens when learners actually engage in the act of producing an artefact by working in micro-worlds that they can control. This may be seen as contrary to the traditional approach to education, where the teacher's role in the classroom was seen as the sole giver of knowledge and the pupil's role was that of a passive receiver. It is evident that our learners are no longer passive learners waiting to be taught; they want to be in control of their own learning process, therefore the traditional way of teaching subjects in isolation is not the best way of teaching them. In order to learn, the learner has to be at the centre of the learning experience and also have opportunities to learn the same material in different contextual settings.

This innovation in thinking and learning might be one of the reasons why in recent years both STEM learning and teaching children coding have gained considerable momentum. Although technology is included in the definition of STEM education, it is often said that computer science is the silent 'C' in 'STEM', as it has very strong links with mathematics and science as well as design and technology; therefore it can be used to support children's learning in these disciplines. This provides educators with a unique opportunity to integrate activities that will support learners in developing their skills and knowledge in many disciplines. According to Huber, Hutchings and Gale (2005), making connections between different curricula, disciplines, knowledge and practice can provide learners with a more authentic understanding. Nevertheless, this is not an easy task, as one needs to have sound knowledge of STEM learning and how it relates to computer science in order to facilitate meaningful learning. In the following section, we will discuss STEM learning, computer science and how they are related. We will also share example projects that can be used for integrative learning to support learners in developing both STEM and computer science skills.

WHAT IS STEM LEARNING?

'STEM' stands for 'science, technology, engineering and mathematics'. The terms 'STEM', 'STEM education' and 'STEM learning' have been used in an interchangeable manner. The term 'STEM' was introduced in 2001 by Judith A. Ramaley, the former director of the National Science Foundation's Education and Human Resources Division in the U.S. STEM education aims to blend scientific inquiry and technological design processes through project based learning that focuses on developing pupils' critical thinking, problem solving, logical reasoning, technical, communication, collaboration, self-directing and creativity skills. Although the subjects included under the umbrella of STEM can vary in different countries, mathematics, biology, chemistry, computer science, and electronic, communications and mechanical engineering are mainly identified as the STEM disciplines.

STEM learning gives children opportunities to investigate an idea in different contexts and connect the learning across disciplines. For example, by creating a wearable technology such as 'a felt bracelet with LEDs', children learn about Boolean Logic and practical use of binary data. They investigate how electrical circuits work and how this information can be used to create a functional product. They practice working with different materials such as felt, a sewable battery holder and conductive threads, and plan the main stages of making. Learning in this way becomes more relevant to pupils, as they can draw learning points from their activities in different disciplines to construct meaning. This purposeful integration of learning cannot be merely seen as cross-curricular learning, as it requires learners to use higher-order strategies to facilitate their creative and critical thinking for solving real-life problems. They need to be able to deploy their cognitive resources to organise, transfer, apply and evaluate their knowledge and skills in different disciplines through integrated activities. Additionally, they need to have the ability to direct their self-learning process, which can be seen as metacognitive awareness. Having skills is not enough, and it is important that pupils can transfer and apply these skills when solving different problems. Foremost, the pupil needs to understand the concepts and become expert in the skills, then know how and when to apply the skills to new situations. Although these steps look very straightforward, they are only viable when one develops the ability to understand and reflect one's own thoughts – in other words, metacognitive skills (Flavell, 1979; Fisher, 2005).

As mentioned before, developing STEM skills has recently received much attention; however, this has not been mainly from educators – it has also been from the industries that have been focusing on skill shortages. Focusing on accelerating economic growth worldwide, a report published by the Intel Corporation (2015) suggests that science, technology, engineering, and maths (STEM) disciplines play an increasingly important role in employability. This report also emphasises that 'the STEM skills gap in European EMEA countries is widening compared to other regions across the globe' (2015, p.4).

According to a recent study done for the EU Committee on Employment and Social Affairs by Caprile et al. (2015), there is evidence of skill shortages in STEM fields despite high unemployment rates in many member states. The study also suggests that 'a sufficient labour supply equipped with STEM skills is essential to implement the European Agenda for Growth and Jobs,' and that by 2025, 7 million jobs will be available that will require STEM skills (2015, p.8). This report concluded that, in order to promote a positive image of science and transform learners' attitudes towards science, more should be done to improve school based STEM learning, and there should be a systematic evaluation of different mediums.

COMPUTER SCIENCE IN STEM

Computer science (CS) is the study of how computers and computational processes work and how they are designed. Computer scientists create algorithms to transform information and abstractions into complex model systems. The most important skill for a computer scientist is problem solving – this involves formulating problems, thinking creatively about solutions and designing a clear solution. They also use processes such as debugging, and forming generalisations, and approaches such as tinkering, persevering and collaboration, when creating programs and solving problems. The combination of these skills and approaches forms another higher-level skill, namely computational thinking.

Seymour Papert (1980, 1996) was the first person to use the term 'computational thinking' and described it as the skill that is necessary for working with computers, especially in a Logo environment. He created Logo – the turtle that can be programmed by young children to move and rotate on a computer. Papert (1993) suggested that young children develop problem-solving skills by working in micro-worlds that they can control. He saw 'Turtle'[1] as a simple way of introducing children to complex systems and argued that although most of the micro-worlds are difficult to understand, they still engage learners in a way that schools can't. In his book *Mindstorms: Children, Computers, and Powerful Ideas*, he clearly explained how programming relates to STEM disciplines.

> In many schools today, the phrase 'computer-aided instruction' means making the computer teach the child. One might say the computer is being used to program the child. In my vision, the child programs the computer and, in doing so, both acquires a sense of mastery over a piece of the most modern and powerful technology and establishes an intimate contact with some of the deepest ideas from science, from mathematics, and from the art of intellectual model building.
>
> (Papert, 1980)

Wing defined computational thinking as: 'Designing systems for more effective problem solving with computers' (2006, cited Kafai & Burke 2015, p.316). Based on the ability to think logically, algorithmically and recursively, computational thinking involves knowledge of the fundamentals of computing such as algorithm, abstraction, iteration and generalisation. It also includes logical reasoning, problem decomposition, testing, debugging and visualisation skills. Developing these skills enables pupils to represent and solve problems computationally, in any discipline and in daily life. When supported with a constructionist teaching approach, children's interaction with digital tools provides a context for them to develop computational thinking, as it offers a space to practice and develop metacognitive, problem-solving and reasoning skills (Allsop, 2015; Clements & Meredith, 1992).

By comparing computational thinking and STEM skills, it is clear that they both contribute to the development of similar competencies. We defined logical reasoning, critical thinking, self-directing, creativity, communication, collaboration and problem solving as STEM skills. These skills are also fundamental to the computational thinking process.

Logic (logical thinking)

Logical thinking is an important element of computational thinking. It is all about using rules to solve problems. When we think about logic in computing, we are actually talking about logical thinking and reasoning. If we give the same problem to two children with the same input, they will probably solve it in two different ways. They will understand the problem differently, ask different questions and use different strategies to come up with their solutions. Their prior knowledge of the problem and skills will also impact on this. We could not program them to behave in the same way – therefore it would be very difficult for us to predict either their solution or the methods that they might choose! But this is different with computers. If you give two computers the same problem with the same input, their solution (the output) will be the same. It is possible to predict what a computer will do and how it will behave. Of course, we must not forget that we need to program computers to think logically – they can't think for themselves, not yet anyway!

Problem solving

When coding, children continually solve problems. They test their code regularly to identify errors and then design solutions to solve the problems. They learn to break down the complex problems into small manageable parts, so that they can solve them more easily. They recognise the common patterns across a problem and design common solutions for similar problems. This saves time and effort!

Creativity

When programming, children use their design, making, imagination and visualisation skills to create solutions for real-word problems. They begin with designing, then making and finally evaluating both their and their friends' work. Creativity involves experimenting with original ideas, rather than merely copying codes and instructions. For example, when creating a game using a Scratch program, children design their sprites, create their backgrounds and give a role to their character (actions).

Collaborating

According to Vygotsky (1978), social interaction is central to learning and development. Working together with others to solve problems can be very useful, especially when working with complex problems, as children can have discussions about possible solutions. 'Pair programming' is widely used by many schools, where children work together to write code using a shared computer. Collaborating also provides opportunities for children to share and celebrate their work.

Communicating

It is a very important skill to be able to articulate your thoughts and communicate them effectively and clearly with others. When coding, children have opportunities to talk about what they are doing; they make suggestions to others, ask questions, have discussions and talk about what they liked and so forth!

Computer science can contribute to the development of the STEM skills, as the learning in both fields follows a similar path. For example, problem-solving skills are vital for STEM learning, and are equally integral to computer science. In mathematics, students start solving a problem by understanding the problem; they design a means of solution and apply this to achieve a solution, sometimes using technology such as computers or calculators. Finally, they evaluate their solution within the context of the original problem. Similarly, in science, children start by setting up the problem; they think about ways of solving it and investigate different solutions by testing their ideas. Lastly, when they have completed their investigations, they share what they have done, discuss it and come up with conclusions. In programming, learners start by understanding the task and what they need to accomplish – in other words, the problem. They design an algorithm to achieve the specific task and then write code for the computer to carry out the solution. They test their code to make sure that it works, and debug errors as they occur. They share their program with their friends and discuss the effectiveness of their solution. In many ways, coding can be seen as applied mathematics and science, as it provides a context for learners to solve problems using the iterative approach; thus computer science can be seen as a STEM discipline.

According to a recent worldwide survey undertaken by European Schoolnet (2015), 16 countries had already included some elements of computer science in their curriculum: Austria, Bulgaria, the Czech Republic, Denmark, England, Estonia, France, Hungary, Ireland, Israel, Lithuania, Malta, Spain, Poland, Portugal and Slovakia. Finland and Flanders (in Belgium) were also planning to integrate programming into their curriculum in 2016. In the U.S., many districts have also agreed to have coding classes. At the same time, there has been a steep increase in running informal learning spaces for teaching coding across the globe. Initiatives such as CoderDojo, Hour of Code, Code Clubs and Code Week EU have helped volunteers to reach people within their local communities to promote learning to code. These developments pose a question in the mind of educators: what is the best way of teaching computer science, both at school and outside, combined with STEM learning in an integrated approach? Below we share some of the projects that can be used as part of both formal and informal learning to support people developing STEM and computer science skills.

PROJECT NAME: WHAT SHAPE AM I?

Description: There are many coding programs that enable users to draw shapes, letters and patterns, such as Logo, Scratch and Hopscotch. This provides a great opportunity to teach mathematics and computer science concepts at the same time through cross-curricular tasks. The Scratch 'Pen' function works very similarly to a pencil. If you keep it down, it leaves a trail line behind it; if you keep it up, it doesn't. Children can be taught to use the Scratch 'Pen' function to draw two-dimensional shapes. For this, they need to know about the properties of the shapes but also the sequence of the script that will draw specific shapes. Figure 8.1 shows example code for drawing a square using the Scratch 'Pen' function.[2]

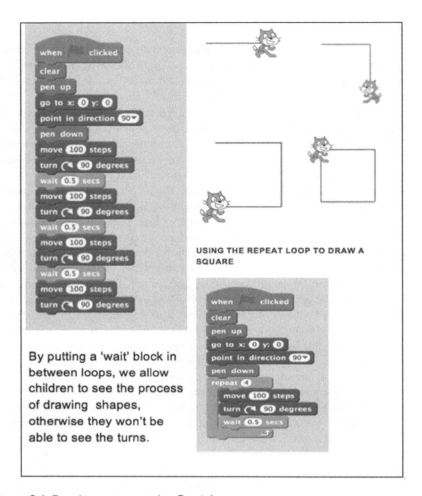

USING THE REPEAT LOOP TO DRAW A SQUARE

By putting a 'wait' block in between loops, we allow children to see the process of drawing shapes, otherwise they won't be able to see the turns.

■ **Figure 8.1** Drawing a square using Scratch

PROJECT NAME: CREATE A WEARABLE TECH FELT BRACELET WITH LEDS

Description: Wearable technology is becoming very popular amongst young people. In many cases, tasks to create wearable technology are seen as an effective way of engaging girls with programming activities. Children learn about electric circuits through making a felt bracelet with LEDs, which is a wearable technology. They create a bracelet using some felt fabric and then decorate it using conductive thread and LED lights. They learn about Boolean Logic, and work with different materials such as felt, a sewable battery holder and conductive threads. They plan the main stages of making, and critically evaluate the quality of the design for the purpose it was planned for when designing and making.

REFLECTION ACTIVITY

What is wearable technology?

What wearable technology would your class want to design?

Some examples of wearable technology and instructions for sewing circuits are available on various websites[3] to help you think about this question.

PROJECT NAME: MAKE A LIGHTHOUSE WITH AN LED LIGHT AT THE TOP

Description: For this task, the children could design, make and evaluate a lighthouse with an LED light at the top. The design process would have two stages. In the first stage, the children design a lighthouse. For this, they can use a wide range of materials such as paper cups, LEGO bricks or a roll of kitchen paper. In the second stage, they can construct a circuit to enable the program to switch on the LED at the top of the lighthouse. An example can be seen in Figure 8.2. They can use a physical computing tool such as Raspberry Pi or Arduino to create their electric circuit and program the LED to behave in a specific way. They would need to have some experience of using either Scratch or the Python language, depending upon their choice. They would also need to have an understanding of how circuits work.

◼ **Figure 8.2** A lighthouse with an LED light at the top

Making a lighthouse with a LED at the top will help children to develop design, evaluation, computational thinking and coding skills. At the same time, this project will provide a space for them to apply and improve their knowledge about electrical circuits, allowing for cross-curricular learning.

REFLECTION ACTIVITY

How can you support children through the coding and design process?

There are many websites[4] that offer support when using the Raspberry Pi in the classroom.

PROJECT NAME: CREATE A BIRTHDAY CARD WITH A CIRCUIT

Description: In this project, children learn about electric circuits through making a card with LEDs for an occasion, such as Christmas, a birthday or Mother's Day. They investigate how a circuit works and use this information to create a basic electric circuit and turn on an LED light on either cardstock paper or felt. They first create their card and then decorate it using different materials and LED lights. They will learn about Boolean Logic.

Making allows children to tinker with ideas. They can express their unique ideas by developing their designs over and over again. In order to transform their design on a paper into a 3D model, they need to plan and evaluate their work, which would involve continual problem solving.

REFLECTION ACTIVITY

What occasions would you use in the classroom as a means of learning about electric circuits[5]?

PROJECT NAME: SPINNING PLANETS

Description: This activity is inspired by the 'Spinning flower' activity devised by the Raspberry Pi learning resources team. You can find many other fabulous tasks on their website.[6]

Ask children to create a model of the planets using a paper cup, motor and Raspberry Pi. They can write a simple program using the Python language to control the behaviour of the motor. This would allow them to work with procedures and variables. They would learn about the characteristics of the planets and use this information to create a 3D model of the solar system.

CONCLUSION

The time children have at school to learn their vast amount of knowledge and develop skills that are essential for learning is very limited. The challenge of delivering a packed curriculum also places pressure on teachers, resulting in too much teaching and not enough learning. Learning in this way sets a barrier against pupils gaining a deeper understanding of either subjects or the skills that are vital for life, such as critical and creative thinking, problem solving, communication and collaboration.

Computer science, as the fastest growing STEM field, provides opportunities for teachers to unpack the curriculum and create a platform for pupils to construct their own understanding through hands-on projects. Although it seems like an easy task, this requires a shift in approach to teaching and learning as a whole. The school curriculum needs to be flexible enough to accommodate interdisciplinary learning through integrated activities. The teachers also need to have a good knowledge and understanding of pedagogical and content knowledge for designing such learning experiences. They need to understand both their role and that of their pupils in this learning cycle, and involve pupils in the process of designing the curriculum. Carefully designed tasks should offer not only the learning of subject knowledge in different disciplines, but also a space for learners to link concepts to achieve deeper learning.

NOTES

1 https://www.turtle.ox.ac.uk
2 Useful links:
   http://scratch.mit.edu; http://www.j2e.com/j2code/
   http://www.ictinpractice.com/a-big-list-of-apps-programs-and-websites-for-teaching-coding-and-game-design/
3 http://www.techgirlsproject.com/curriculum.html; and step-by-step instructions for sewing circuits: http://www.atxdiy.com/2010/07/05/tutorial-sew-a-simple-circuit/
4 https://www.raspberrypi.org/learning/physical-computing-with-scratch/worksheet/
   https://www.arduino.cc/en/Tutorial/Blink
5 http://makerprojects.wikispaces.com/papercircuits and http://www.learningcircuits.co.uk
6 https://www.raspberrypi.org/resources/.

REFERENCES

Allsop, Y. (2015). Computing. In: Caldwell, H., and Bird, J. *Teaching with tablets*. (pp.104–123). London: Sage.

Caprile, M., Palmen, R., Sanz, P., and Dente, G. (2015). Encouraging STEM studies for the labour market. Study for the EMPL Committee, The European Union.

Clements, D. H., and Meredith, J. S. (1992). Research on Logo: Effects and efficacy. Accessed from: http://el.media.mit.edu/logo-foundation/resources/papers/pdf/research_logo.pdf.

European Schoolnet. (2015). Computing our future: Computer programming and coding: Priorities, school curricula and initiatives across Europe. Accessed from: http://fcl.eun.org/documents/10180/14689/Computing+our+future_final.pdf/746e36b1-e1a6-4bf1-8105-ea27c0d2bbe0.

Fisher, R. (2005). *Teaching children to think*, Cheltenham, UK: Nelson Thornes.

Flavell, J. H. (1979). Metacognition and cognitive monitoring: A new area of cognitive-developmental inquiry. *American Psychologist, 34,* 906–911.

Huber, M. T., Hutchings, P., and Gale, R. (2005). Integrative learning for liberal education. *Peer Review.* Association of American Colleges and Schools, Washington, DC. Accessed from: http://www.aacu.org/publications-research/periodicals/integrative-learning-liberal-education.

Intel Corporation. (2015). Increasing employability and accelerating economic growth worldwide. Accessed from: http://www.intel.com/content/dam/www/public/us/en/documents/brief/innovation-for-employability-brief.pdf.

Kafai, Y., and Burke, Q. (2015). Constructionist gaming: Understanding the benefits of making games for learning, *Educational Psychologist, 50*(4), 313–334.

Papert, S. (1980). *Mindstorms: Children, computers, and powerful ideas.* New York: Basic Books.

Papert, S. (1993). *The children's machine: Rethinking school in the age of the computer.* New York: Basic Books.

Papert, S. (1996). An exploration in the space of mathematics educations. *International Journal of Computers for Mathematical Learning.* Accessed from: http://www.papert.org/articles/AnExplorationintheSpaceofMathematicsEducations.html.

Vygotsky, L. (1978). *Mind in society.* Cambridge, Massachusetts: Harvard University Press.

CHAPTER 9

SONIC PI

Live coding in education – engaging a new generation of coders

Sam Aaron

The education landscape is continually in flux, with changes in approach, focus, priority and direction. However, one trend that's becoming increasingly clear is the growing importance of teaching coding to learners of all ages. The motivation is clear – coding is affecting an ever larger subset of our society, both at home and in the workplace. Those individuals who have no knowledge of programming/coding will therefore likely be increasingly marginalised and unable to fully participate in tomorrow's world.

This has led a number of countries, including the UK, to introduce coding and the broader context of computing into their curricula. Unfortunately, this is only the first step towards a true society of digital natives. The next challenge is to discover effective mechanisms with which to engage this new generation of learners with the core aspects of coding. This is not proving to be a straightforward task. One approach has been to ask today's expert programmers what excited them and engaged them with coding when they first started. This has yielded a range of schemes of work and resources that are not necessarily engaging and meaningful to pupils who are not intrinsically interested in coding as an abstract discipline. Examples include exploration of sorting algorithms and binary arithmetic. Whilst subjects such as these are clearly grounded in core computer science, their value is diminished if they are unable to excite and draw in a broader and more diverse audience than has typically explored these subjects independently.

A key aspect of modern teaching practices is therefore not just to deliver and share new knowledge, but also to facilitate learning by deepening engagement and participation. One approach to achieving this is to make the content meaningful in some way to the learners. It is this approach that Sonic Pi attempts to take.

CODE AS A MUSICAL INSTRUMENT

Sonic Pi is a powerful new kind of musical instrument with a novel interface. Instead of plucking strings, blowing into mouthpieces or hitting things with sticks, you write and modify code. This new style of music making has been termed 'live coding',[1] and the number of musicians producing music in this way is growing dramatically and even gaining mainstream attention. For example, the *Rolling Stone* magazine covered a recent Sonic Pi performance at Moogfest[2] USA:

> [The set –] which sounded like Electric Café-era Kraftwerk, a little bit of Aphex Twin skitter and some Eighties electro – was constructed through typing and deleting lines of code. The shadowy DJ sets, knob-tweaking noise and fogbank ambient of many Moogfest performers was completely demystified and turned into simple numbers and letters that you could see in action. Dubbed 'the live coding synth for everyone,' it truly seemed less like a performance and more like an invitation to code your own adventure.[3]

The critical idea here is not just the representation of musical process with a formal language precise enough to be executed by a computer – it is the ability to modify it whilst it is executing. This enables the transformation of a tool typically used for composition into one that also enables performance. Through the act of writing and modifying code, a live coding musician can convert thoughts into musical events as fluidly as a jazz musician can improvise. It's also important to note that the limitations of this approach are not just the computational constraints of the executing machine. Clearly a more powerful computer can execute at a faster rate than a low-powered machine. The existence of 'Dark MIDI' demonstrates just how complex a score can become with today's hardware, with MIDI files containing thousands of notes that can be used to create new compositions. However, when we move from composition to performance, we also transition from code as purely a sequence of instructions for a computer into code as a medium which also may directly act as a human interface. We are therefore invited to ask questions such as:

- ▣ How easy is it to turn musical thoughts into code?
- ▣ How much time does it take to type the code for an idea?
- ▣ How easy is it to find an error?

Additionally, if we project the code for the audience to read during a performance, we are also invited to ask:

- ▣ How easy is it for the audience to understand what the code is doing?

As we shall see, these questions turn out to be just as important in a classroom context as they are in a performance venue.

CLASSROOM-FOCUSED DESIGN

From the very first iteration, Sonic Pi was designed for and iterated within the classroom. The first version was implemented specifically for classroom collaboration with then teacher Carrie Anne Philbin, who is now Director of Education at the Raspberry Pi Foundation. The many constraints of working within a classroom context created an instant impact on the initial designs of the Sonic Pi interface and language. For example, it was immediately clear that reducing the amount of instruction required to go from starting the system to running the first program and creating the first sounds was a critical factor. Time spent creating projects, navigating file systems and writing boiler-plate code, before any meaningful output was created, acted as friction that reduced the efficacy of the learning situation and reduced pupil engagement. Similarly, when things weren't working, perhaps due to incorrect code being entered, time spent having to understand what had gone wrong and what steps might be taken to fix the situation was also difficult. A high priority was therefore placed on reducing the time to the first running program and the time taken to triage and fix issues. The level of success in achieving these design goals could immediately be determined by direct observation of pupils using the system in the classroom.

The first trial of Sonic Pi took place a month after development had started, with seven weekly lessons. A new version of Sonic Pi was developed every week, based on observations from the previous week and also in anticipation of the features needed to deliver the next lesson. The features themselves came directly from discussions between Carrie Anne and the author, based on the requirements of the new UK computing curriculum.

The process with which new lessons and software features were created can be visualised as a "partnership workflow", with this iterative coding design finally cycling back to feed into the initial one. The nature of this process wove the design element of Sonic Pi directly with the delivery of the lessons. This allowed the process to directly react to observations in the classroom and directly feed active reflection back into the design at the earliest possible opportunity.

Within this responsive iterative process, it was quickly discovered that the effectiveness of the delivery was not purely a function of delivering the curriculum, but also of the motivational impact of the tasks the pupils were performing. For example, one lesson attempted to teach functions and variables. The pupils quickly became disengaged with the material, often asking questions such as 'Why are we doing this?' They then proceeded to create many meaningless variables with the names of their favourite pop stars or food. Interestingly, it seems that they were attempting to insert their own meaning into an activity forced upon them that was void of meaning for them. This point may need a little further clarification. Whilst concepts such as variables and functions are incredibly meaningful to the practice of programming, they are merely tools to manage complexity. Their real meaning is therefore only easily understood in the context of complex code. Until a pupil has created a sufficiently complex program, they are typically not needed – and therefore, when they are taught separately in their own right, it is much harder to communicate this meaning to a beginner. Instead, when the meaning drove the introduction of concepts, the pupils reacted extremely positively. For example, instead of teaching iteration and lists, it was more effective to teach bass riffs. Pupils were much more interested in the idea of making their own bass riff, which in turn required them to master the core computing concepts of lists (a sequence of notes) and iteration (a means of doing something with each note in the list).

It is the author's belief that building effective education software needs an effective collaboration between technology and education. Software developers working directly with educators in the classroom has provided Sonic Pi with an extremely fertile context for this collaboration. This has enabled a design process that is freer to ask the question 'How can pupils educate the software's design process?' rather than 'How can we educate pupils to use the software?'

A SIMPLE INTERFACE

In order to attempt to meet the strict simplicity constraints described above, the graphical user interface (GUI) was designed to be as simple and straightforward as possible. On opening the application, you are greeted with a text editor environment, which feels like a simple version of Word. There is a large area in which to enter text, a row of buttons with clear actions to perform and a message window that is used by Sonic Pi to write messages to the user. There is also a large help section at the bottom of the window containing a full tutorial (translated to multiple languages) in addition to example compositions, and detailed information about the built-in sounds that may be used. There is no requirement to create a project, to configure the system on launch or even to manually save your work – all of this is done automatically so that the users can get straight to coding and making music. Additionally, the interaction workflow was designed to be both simple to work through and simple to teach. The user needs only to write code into the editor and click the Run button in order to hear the composition. To stop the program from running, the user can click the Stop button. As the program executes, the message window describes what it is doing step-by-step. Also, errors are clearly communicated to the user, with a large box that appears below the coding area describing the problem encountered.

An example of the many areas where priority has been placed on simple interaction workflows is saving work. One of the buttons enables users to save the contents of the code area to an external text file. This was just created to enable sharing of code between users and also with the teacher for evaluation purposes. However, this button is not needed for basic usage. Sonic Pi automatically saves the contents of the code so that if the user closes the application (or if it were to crash), they can re-open the application and their previous work will not be lost. This behaviour matches expectations, which can be found in mobile operating systems, where apps are often expected to launch in the same state with which they were closed.

A SIMPLE LANGUAGE

A core design decision for Sonic Pi's language is to implement and build upon a very simple core set of instructions. The main inspiration for this was Logo, developed by Papert (1993). The Logo system was developed to engage learners with programming concepts and employed three key strategies: a similarly simple set of instructions, a means of composition and a meaningful form of expression. Let us briefly look at each of these in turn.

Firstly, the operations you could perform were very simple and easy to describe to anybody – students and teachers alike. They were:

- Pen Down
- Pen Forward
- Pen Rotate
- Pen Up

These commands can therefore be strung together into a sequence of operations, such as this small program for drawing a square:

```
PENDOWN ; start drawing
FD 50 ; forward 50
RT 90 ; rotating clockwise 90 degrees
FD 50 ; forward 50
RT 90 ; rotating clockwise 90 degrees
FD 50 ; forward 50
RT 90 ; rotating clockwise 90 degrees
FD 50 ; forward 50
RT 90 ; rotating clockwise 90 degrees
PENUP ; stop drawing
```

These four simple commands are very easy for anybody to learn and start using to draw. In fact, similar systems are still being used to teach computing concepts at a very early age. A common adaptation has been to replace the idea of drawing with the manipulation of a physical robotic vehicle, such as the early BigTrak and the more recent Beebots. However, in addition to being very simple, they are also very powerful when strung together, enabling the possibility of drawing extremely sophisticated imagery from four basic commands.

In a similar fashion to Logo, Sonic Pi represents process using imperative code – a series of instructions for the computer to carry out. At their core these instructions can be distilled down to three kinds:

■　which synthesisers to trigger or control
■　how long to wait before the next instruction
■　which studio effects to use (reverb, flanger, distortion etc).

Let us explore each of these in turn. First is the ability to trigger sounds. There are two ways of doing this: playing the built-in synthesisers or triggering pre-recorded samples. To play the most basic sound you just need the following code:

```
play 70
```

This instructs Sonic Pi to play note 70. If you launch the Sonic Pi app, type the code in to the editor and press the Run button, you'll hear a basic beep. Even at this early point, from an education perspective, there are many learning opportunities to explore. For example, we can discuss instructions to the computer as parameterisable functions. In this case, the function is called 'play' and the parameter is '70'. This then invites the question: what purpose do function parameters serve? The answer is loud and clear: to enable different behaviour. In the case of our 'play' function, the parameter defines how high or low the note will be. We can then easily experiment with this concept by trying different numbers. For example: 'play 40' or 'play 90'; what about 'play 72.345'? At this point, we can start talking about an important computer science concept: abstraction. In this case, the number is our abstraction – specifically the property that it can go up and down (with higher and lower values). Once we have a property like this, we just need to find examples in the real world that also share this property, and we can then start to model one with the other.

In the musical world, pitch also has the property that it can go up and down and so a higher note can be represented by a higher number. With Sonic Pi, this idea becomes instantly tractable and meaningful to them. For example, if they want to play bass notes, they simply need to choose low numbers.

Sonic Pi doesn't just support the ability to play notes – you can also trigger any pre-recorded sound. This is made available by the function 'sample'. For example, to play a recorded version of the famous 'Amen Break', we just need the following code:

```
sample :loop_amen
```

The ':loop_amen' sample is one of many built-in pre-recorded sounds. However, you are entirely free to record your own sounds and use those. This is possible by passing the path to the stored wav, aif or flac file representing the recording:

```
sample "/path/to/sample.wav"
```

At this point, with just two commands, we can play any note and any recorded sound. More importantly, children can do this with ease, and teachers can map their efforts directly to core computer science concepts. Next, we might want to play multiple notes – sounds one after another through time – to create melodies and rhythms. We therefore need to learn a third command: 'sleep'. This instructs Sonic Pi to wait for the specified amount of time before carrying out the next instruction:

```
play 70
sleep 1
play 75
sleep 0.5
play 82
sample :ambi_lunar_land
```

The snippet of code above plays three notes, one after another, and also a sample at exactly the same time as the final note. This is because if you don't call 'sleep' between two lines of code, Sonic Pi will trigger them at the same time. With 'play', 'sample' and 'sleep', we now have the basics of melody and rhythm in a form simple enough for children to play with. We need to explore one more concept to finish our tour of the basic semantics of Sonic Pi: the ability to add studio-quality effects. This is possible by using the 'with_fx' function and wrapping it around the parts of the code you want the effect to manipulate:

```
with_fx :reverb do
  sample :drum_roll
end
```

One of the most powerful parts of the FX system is that you can put any code between the 'do' and 'end' part of 'with_fx' and all of it will be passed through the effect unit. For example, we can combine all three of our core abstractions with one simple example:

```
with_fx :reverb, room: 1 do
 sample :drum_cymbal_open
 play 70
 sleep 1
 play 75
 sleep 0.5
 play 82
end
```

We now have our core musical abstractions to match the basic drawing abstractions of Logo:

- 'play' – play one of the built-in synthesiser voices with a given note
- 'sample' – play any pre-recorded sound
- 'sleep' – wait for a specific amount of time
- 'with_fx' – play the enclosed code through a studio FX unit.

TEACHING PROGRAMMING WITH MUSIC

With the four basic musical building blocks described above, we can start to explore the standard programming language concepts in a new and engaging way. For example, instead of teaching concrete data structures such as lists, we can teach bass riffs (a list of notes). We can therefore define our notes as a basic list and assign it to a variable for later use:

```
riff = [:C1, :E3, :D5, :C2]
```

Another important aspect of the computing curriculum is repeating sections of code with iteration. However, instead of just teaching iteration, we can instead teach drum loops (repeated sample triggers). The following repeats our drum rhythm eight times:

```
8.times do
 sample :bd_haus
 sleep 1
 sample :drum_cowbell
 sample :drum_snare_hard
 sleep 0.5
 sample :drum_snare_hard
 sleep 0.5
end
```

Finally, instead of functions, we can teach sections of music (using named functions). For example, we can define two sections of music as functions 'section_a' and 'section_b'. Once these are defined, we're free to work with them as new building blocks for our performances and compositions, such as repeating 'section_a' twice before and after playing 'section_b':

```
define :section_a do
 play 70
 sleep 1
 play 82
end

define :section_b do
 play 75
 sleep 1
 play 75
end

2.times do
 section_a
end

section_b
2.times do
 section_a
end
```

PROGRAMMING AS PERFORMANCE

Whilst this chapter has mainly focused on using music as a mechanism to engage users with computer science concepts, it is important to stress the benefit of inverting this and looking at using computer science to engage and create new pathways into music making. More recent versions of Sonic Pi have placed a very strong emphasis on music making, specifically enabling it to be an increasingly powerful performance tool. There are already a large number of known education organisations worldwide that teach Sonic Pi purely as a musical instrument, with lessons leading up to a final performance. In 2014, the Digital R&D Fund for the Arts funded the 'Sonic Pi: Live & Coding' project,[4] which set out to create an arts-led impact within school music lessons leading up to a week-long live coding summer school hosted at Cambridge Junction. This was a collaborative partnership between the arts, research and technology. This enabled the inclusion of artists within the classroom, with researchers assessing the educational impact, and all activities and experiences feeding directly back into the ongoing design of Sonic Pi. This project provided a number of interesting insights that directly highlighted the close relationship between education and performance. It turned out that many of the design decisions taken to improve the education experience were very useful when using Sonic Pi as a performance tool. For example, the fast and helpful feedback of errors is useful for quick debugging in the classroom, yet also essential for fixing problems whilst on stage performing in front of an audience. In turn, many of the features that were added to enable richer musical experiences, such as the ability to play pre-recorded samples or to add studio effects such as reverb, turned out to deepen the engagement of the users in the classroom. Additionally, the act of teaching can be perceived as a performance, and performances can be perceived as opportunities to educate. This latter statement is even more important in the cases where the performer is using an instrument that the audience has never seen or experienced before, which is almost certainly the case with code at the time of writing. For a deeper evaluation of the 'Sonic Pi: Live & Coding' project, in addition to a more formal treatment of the educational aspects of Sonic Pi, see: Burnard, Aaron and Blackwell. (in press).

CONCLUSIONS

This chapter has introduced the concept of using live coded music as a means for creating engagement in the classroom, specifically for computer science lessons. However, it has also expanded on this idea to consider live coded music within music lessons and as a performance instrument in its own right. Finally, whilst these three applications might seem distinct, it has been observed that there are a number of core software design principles that are at the heart of each of them. These design principles focus on the concepts of core simplicity, effective communication, fast feedback and clear learning pathways. It is the author's belief that truly engaging educational software can be created when all of these principles are considered in a holistic fashion directly at the intersection of technology, education and the arts.

ACKNOWLEDGEMENTS

The author would like to thank the Raspberry Pi Foundation and pi-top for their continued support for the Sonic Pi project.

NOTES

1 http://toplap.org
2 http://sched.moogfest.com/event/6mE0/synthesize-sounds-with-live-code-in-sonic-pi
3 http://www.rollingstone.com/music/live-reviews/moogfest-2016-was-it-actually-the-future-of-music-20160523#ixzz4DkLStGwJ
4 http://www.sonicpiliveandcoding.com

REFERENCES

Burnard, P., Aaron, S. and Blackwell, A.F. (in press). Using coding to connect new digital innovative learning communities: Developing Sonic Pi, a new open source software tool. Presentation at SEMPRE 2014 – Researching Music, Education, Technology: Critical Insights. Society for Education and Music Psychology Research.

Papert, S. (1993). *The Children's Machine: Rethinking School in the Age of the Computer*. NY: Basic Books.

MINECRAFT AS A FRAMEWORK FOR ENGAGEMENT

Joel Mills

CONTEXT

"Nice T-shirt."

"Thanks; do you play Minecraft?"

"Yes, I'm building a castle in the sky so that I can defend it more easily from the others on the server."

"Wow! Sounds awesome. And what are you basing your design on?"

This was the start of a conversation with a year 5 pupil (aged 9 to 10 years) at a school[1] I was visiting whilst wearing a limited edition *Minecraft* T-shirt for my visit. The pupil was a stranger to me; I had never visited the school before and he had never met me before, yet we had a common bond. A conversation started because I was wearing a *Minecraft* T-shirt. A conversation that started so easily and quickly evolved into design, creativity, problem solving, challenges and the merits of "command blocks".

BACKGROUND

Minecraft, the video game, has been described in many ways: "a sandbox game", "virtual LEGO", "a building block game". Between May 2009, when *Minecraft* started being developed by independent game developer Mojang, and its official release in November 2014, it reached millions of people through a community of beta testers and developers who had access to the software. Mojang's release of the beta to the wider community, under a particularly open end user licensing agreement (EULA), allowed users to tweak the code behind the game and write modifications or "mods" that changed the behaviour or characteristics of the game for their own purposes.

> If you've bought the game, you may play around with it and modify it. I'd appreciate it if you didn't use this for griefing,[2] though, and remember not to distribute the changes.
>
> Any tools you write for the game from scratch belong to you. You're free to do whatever you want with screenshots and videos of the game, but don't just rip art resources and pass them around. Plugins for the game also belong to you and you can do whatever you want with them, including selling them for money.
>
> Mojang (2011)

This open EULA was the key to the success of *Minecraft* as a development tool and provided an entry point for it in education, as it allowed other companies, such as Teacher Gaming, to develop a modded version, *MinecraftEdu*, which introduced various teacher-centric controls for managing *Minecraft* in a classroom situation. *Minecraft* became established in the classroom as a creative tool allowing pupils to explore ideas and concepts across the UK national curriculum through downloadable worlds created by teachers and pupils from across the globe. One project, CultureTECH, took the adoption of *MinecraftEdu* a stage further by distributing it to every secondary school in Northern Ireland as a means of engaging people across the curriculum.

> The level of engagement is the first thing you notice," said Mark Nagurski, chief executive of CultureTECH. "This is work that the kids really want to do and if you're able to harness that enthusiasm, energy and creativity you end up with a pretty significant learning opportunity."
>
> Stuart (2015)

As Teacher Gaming developed their modded version alongside, but a few versions behind, the 'vanilla' version being developed by Mojang, they incorporated third-party mods into their releases. Both ComputerCraft and WorldEdit became part of the core *MinecraftEdu* product, allowing teachers to use these mods within the game with no additional administration requirements. ComputerCraft changed the view of *Minecraft* in the classroom as it tapped into the core of the ICTD (Information Communication Technology for Development) curriculum in the UK and the governmental drive to introduce programming or 'coding' to all children, as *Minecraft* allowed pupils to create simple computer programs that controlled a virtual robot called a 'turtle' to perform repetitive tasks of mining and building automatically. Through ComputerCraft, *Minecraft* became a way to engage young people with coding in a format they understood and enjoyed. Unlike the days of the first BBC Model B computers in schools – where there was one computer in the class, possibly in the school, which was "programmed" using the BASIC programming language and controlled a single "plotting robot" on the floor – *Minecraft* and ComputerCraft brought the technology to all through a graphical interface that made programming accessible.

One thing is for sure: it is a very popular game. *Minecraft*, in all its formats, has been downloaded over 100 million times.

BACKGROUND TO THE THREE PROJECTS

Our three projects that form the basis of our framework for engagement are *HullCraft: History Makers*, *MolCraft* and *The University of Hull Library*. HullCraft: History Makers was an extension of an existing engagement project run by the Hull History Centre to digitise a new collection of archival material from the work of local architect Francis Johnson and bring it to a wider audience. They were already bringing families into the archives on weekend family fun days and encouraging people to draw or paint pictures and build models in LEGO using the archival material as reference. It was therefore a natural extension to continue the building in the virtual world through the use of *Minecraft*, and engage a wider audience beyond the 9am to 4pm time frame of a monthly family workshop. The HullCraft: History Makers world comprised a reconstruction of the Hull History Centre at spawn,[3] which gave the context for the project. It served both as a hub for the players to access different worlds attached to the project and as a virtual interface for the History Centre itself. This project was funded by an independent grant for three years.

The MolCraft project was conceived by Professor Mark Lorch at the University of Hull as an alternative way of providing evidence for the third-year undergraduates in their Final Project module. He gave them the option to build a portfolio of evidence, and, through discussion with the students, they agreed that they would create a world in *Minecraft* based on the proteins and amino acids they had been studying. What evolved was how, through game-based learning (GBL), the students created a world that could be used as a teaching and engagement tool for younger players. With pedagogic support from the Technology Enhanced Learning team in the university, the students created a fully playable adventure map, which was used in a variety of science fairs and school engagement activities. Funding was secured from the Royal Society of Chemistry to enable the necessary servers to be purchased to host the world map as a live server. The map was finally distributed as an Open Educational Resource from the MinecraftEdu World Library.

The third project was an in-house project that developed from an idea in the Technology Enhanced Learning team to recreate the university campus, starting with its newest build, the newly refurbished Brynmor-Jones Library (BJL). As a result of the refurbishment, the BJL had a full set of architectural plans, which were made available to the *Minecraft* build team. Through a combination of the plans and photographic and video walk-through recordings, the team were able to create a replica library – to scale, in astonishing detail for a *Minecraft* build.

The library is a hub of the university and is a centre for learning on the campus. It is a blend of older, art deco architecture in one wing of the building, which contains meeting rooms, teaching spaces and the art gallery, and the more modern multi-storey block that contains the majority of the library content.

With two 'feature' entrances and split across mezzanine floors in one part of the library, the building can be somewhat confusing for new students and staff, so one of the reasons for undertaking this build was to use this as the starting point for a much larger university build that would function as an orientation and induction exercise for new staff and students. The BJL build is still in its infancy at the time of writing, and its impact on audiences has yet to be fully realised. The reason for its inclusion in this chapter is that the Library build is the culmination of all of the university *Minecraft* builds in a single environment and is the destination of our *Minecraft* community at the university, acting as a single point of entry into university *Minecraft*. The reason it exists is because of the other projects that have gone before it.

THE FRAMEWORK FOR ENGAGEMENT

"Just one more block" is the cry that goes up at the end of many *Minecraft* workshops, such is the complete engrossment of the players in their latest build/contraption/battle/ exploration in the game. Like many successful video games, *Minecraft* immerses players deeper and deeper into the world of the game; minutes turn into hours and, just as in the game itself, day turns into night before you know it. Games are immersive: in *Minecraft*, players often spend weeks and even years creating builds and maps in minute detail. When crafting or building, players enter a state of consciousness that is known as "flow". It is during this enhanced state, where the player hovers between the challenge presented and the skill level they currently have, that time seems to pass unobserved. The sandwich is half eaten, the tea has gone cold, but the player plays on.

Minecraft projects are often collaborative, but complex builds retain an element of individual commitment; players dedicate themselves for their own personal motivations: pride, achievement, satisfaction, completion, competition. McGonigal reflects on why such motivation may exist, saying:

> If the goal is truly compelling, and if the feedback is motivating enough, we will keep wrestling with the game's limitations – creatively, sincerely, and enthusiastically – for a very long time. We will play until we utterly exhaust our own abilities, or until we exhaust the challenge. And we will take the game seriously because there is nothing trivial about playing a good game. The game matters.
>
> McGonigal (2011)

The game does matter: just ask any parent who has to endure/engage with endless discussions on Stampy's[4] latest adventures, or the new Mini-game by DanTDM.[5] *Minecraft* players are enthusiastic and passionate and will talk at length about the various intricacies of the game, new updates, events or YouTube content they have discovered, shared or created. It is tapping in to this passion that is the key to using *Minecraft* as an engagement framework.

The projects used a *digital engagement framework* (see Figure 10.1), which was adapted for use with *Minecraft* and GBL.

HOW DID THEY ENGAGE?

HullCraft: History Makers

As the project was initially an add-on to existing History Centre activities, HullCraft started out as just a website domain that was purchased,[6] on which a Wordpress blog was run that hosted a number of scanned archival plans and drawings by the architect Francis Johnson. Participants in the project then downloaded the scans onto their home computers and used them to recreate the structures on their own copies of *Minecraft* on their consoles, tablets or PCs. The project then encouraged further participation through awarding "digital badges" on the website for uploading pictures or screenshots of their creations. There were three different levels of badge that could be earned, depending on the complexity of the build that they undertook: the simplest level 1 builds were single-storey designs, whilst the most complex level 3 builds were complex structures such as churches.

Once project funding had been obtained, it was possible to pay for and host our own *Minecraft* server on which to build the HullCraft world. A small team of builders recreated the Hull History Centre (HHC) as a focal point for the *Minecraft* world from which players could explore and interact with non-player characters (NPCs). Other worlds were added to the server using plugins such as Multiverse,[7] which allowed the player to have different experiences all within the same server.

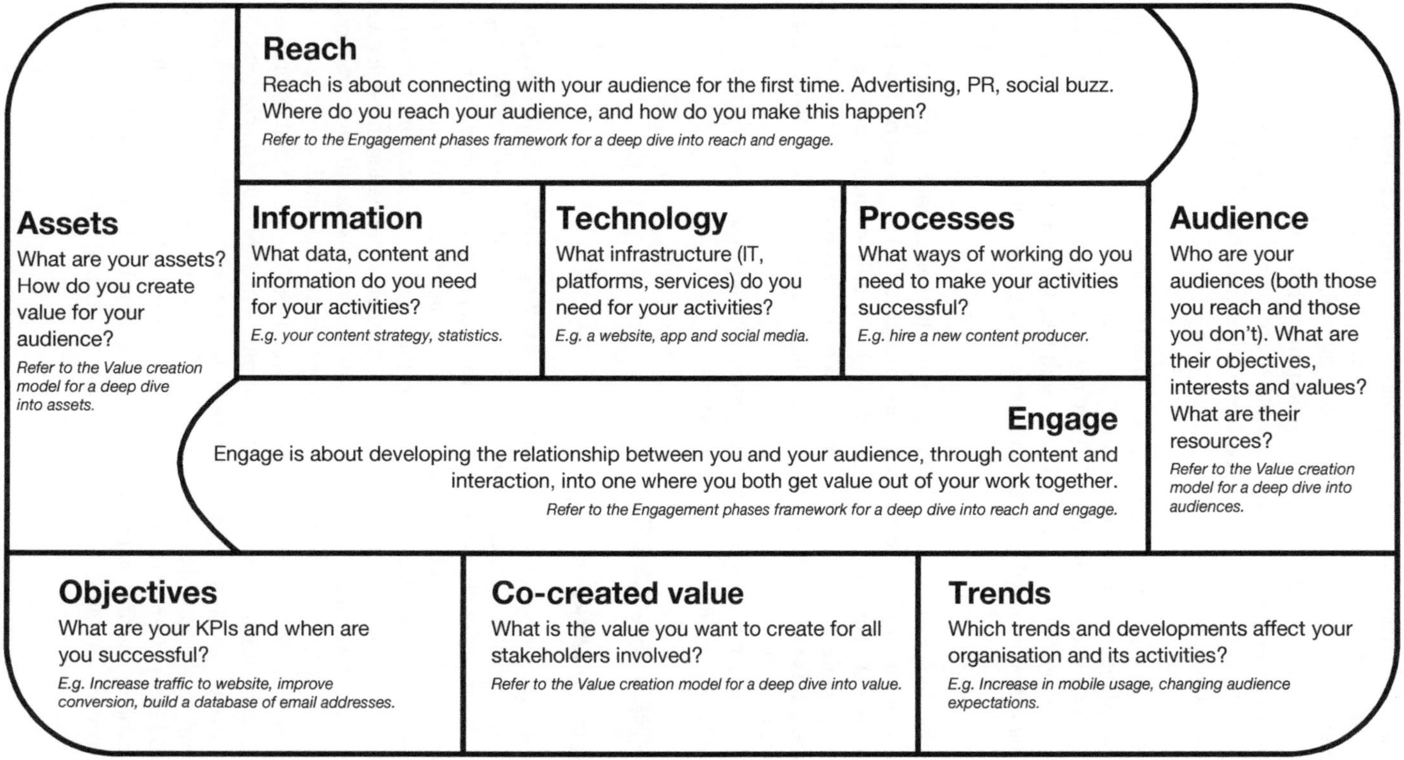

Reach

Reach is about connecting with your audience for the first time. Advertising, PR, social buzz. Where do you reach your audience, and how do you make this happen?
Refer to the Engagement phases framework for a deep dive into reach and engage.

Assets

What are your assets? How do you create value for your audience?
Refer to the Value creation model for a deep dive into assets.

Information

What data, content and information do you need for your activities?
E.g. your content strategy, statistics.

Technology

What infrastructure (IT, platforms, services) do you need for your activities?
E.g. a website, app and social media.

Processes

What ways of working do you need to make your activities successful?
E.g. hire a new content producer.

Audience

Who are your audiences (both those you reach and those you don't). What are their objectives, interests and values? What are their resources?
Refer to the Value creation model for a deep dive into audiences.

Engage

Engage is about developing the relationship between you and your audience, through content and interaction, into one where you both get value out of your work together.
Refer to the Engagement phases framework for a deep dive into reach and engage.

Objectives

What are your KPIs and when are you successful?
E.g. Increase traffic to website, improve conversion, build a database of email addresses.

Co-created value

What is the value you want to create for all stakeholders involved?
Refer to the Value creation model for a deep dive into value.

Trends

Which trends and developments affect your organisation and its activities?
E.g. Increase in mobile usage, changing audience expectations.

Figure 10.1 Digital engagement framework (adapted from Visser and Richardson (2016))

A separate space called PlotWorld was set up, and specialist plugins such as PlotMe broke up the space into allotment-like plots that could be claimed by a player for their own use. Players were encouraged to use these plots to build the designs that they had downloaded from the website and show off their building and creative skills. No restrictions were put on the plots – so, of course, not only did we get some of Francis Johnson's creations built, but we also got our fair share of fantasy castles, pixel art and strange contraptions being made from redstone. (In *Minecraft*, redstone bricks can be used to create structures that work on electricity.[8]) All part of the freedom, creativity and experimentation that *Minecraft* allows.

Once the server had become established and the necessary anti-griefing tools had been put in place to prevent "*Minecraft* vandalism", the server was opened up for open workshops, where people could bring their own laptop to a family day at the History Centre and build in the HullCraft world with their parents or friends.

MolCraft

Engagement with MolCraft happened on two levels: Firstly, the undergraduates creating the map and evidencing their understanding of the concepts of amino acids and protein molecules through the application of *Minecraft* and secondly, though the playing of the resulting map by younger players at schools and science fairs.

To achieve the end goal, the digital engagement framework requires information, understanding of the technology, and processes to generate specific and efficient work-flows. These are core to the framework and underpin both the reach potential and the engagement of the project.

The undergraduates who worked on the map were all able to collaborate from home using *MinecraftEdu* on their PCs. The ability for the students to have their own space to work on and develop game concepts directly on a server map was essential in building the technical workflows required to transform the molecule structures downloaded from the national protein database, through the various pieces of software, to end up with *Minecraft* schematics that could then be used to build the world. *Minecraft* provides both server and clients, and, through the options for hosting servers online, it allows asynchronous or synchronous collaboration opportunities for the gamer. More information on the exact workflow used in this project can be found on the University of Hull website.[9]

WHAT EVIDENCE WAS THERE THAT THEY WORKED?

Each of the projects had different measures of impact, according to the nature of the project

Measure of success 1: server logs

For online, hosted *Minecraft* servers, a simple way to determine the success of a *Minecraft* project is to count the number of unique players who have logged in to the server. Whilst there are several websites that will provide statistical analysis for a server on a paid-for basis, it is possible to determine the number of unique players on a server by simply downloading the "Player Data" folder from the server for the home "world". For the HullCraft: History Makers project, we had over 170 unique players joining the server.

MolCraft has had over 1000 unique players who have entered the world and explored the molecules within, and it is available as a download for the *MinecraftEdu* version through the World Library.

Measure of success 2: registration websites

HullCraft set up its own website before it even had an online server, as a way of engaging people with the archive material from the project. Through the website, people could download plans and drawings from the archive; they were then asked to recreate the drawings in *Minecraft* and submit their photographs or screenshots back to the website as "proof", whereby they would then get a digital badge of achievement. Part of the process of submission required the users to register for the website in order for them to submit their photographs and claim their badges. Through this, we were able to get useful evidence of engagement. In the initial year of setting up HullCraft, over 130 subscribers to the website created an account, submitted a picture or left a comment.

Measure of success 3: subscribers

Some projects lend themselves to being measured through their number of subscribers, readers or viewers. YouTubers measure their own success in terms of subscriber numbers, with the most successful 'Tubers, like Stampy[10] or DanTDM,[11] having numbers in the millions.

MolCraft featured in an article on The Conversation[12] and, at the time of writing, has had nearly 50,000 readers, 279 tweets on Twitter, 488 shares on Facebook and 88 on LinkedIn. Through this article, MolCraft quickly gained exposure and was reposted across the internet.[13] This exposure resulted in invitations to events, workshops and conferences across the country and is a key part of the framework for successful engagement using *Minecraft*.

Measure of success 4: event or workshop feedback

Collecting meaningful feedback at events is often done through online questionnaires, smiley-face polls or simple paper-based feedback forms, but often the true measure of success is overhearing those conversations at the end of a workshop that are never documented formally. "That was simply the best session we have had since starting university," was a comment I heard at the end of the workshop where I delivered *Minecraft* to Archaeology and History undergraduates in a *Minecraft* world where they reconstructed the deserted medieval village of Wharram Percy. *Minecraft* creates meaningful and engaging experiences by its very nature; it is important that project teams recognise that anyone who attends a *Minecraft* in education project is already likely to be interested in *Minecraft*, so can the positive feedback at the end of a *Minecraft*-related workshop really be attributed to the project, or is it down to the game? Or a combination of both? What we do know is that in *Minecraft*-related lessons you get the students asking to continue the work outside the classroom, and the cry "Hold on, just one more block!" goes up when you announce you are switching off the server at the end of a session.

Measure of success 5: exposure

Any framework for engagement must include a strong social media and online presence. Twitter, Facebook, blogs and YouTube all have the potential to go "viral", attracting wide circulation for the project. By linking the social media with a common hashtag, website URL or Twitter handle, you create trackbacks, reciprocal links and reposts/retweets that build project interest. All of the university projects use Twitter, Instagram and YouTube to generate interest and engage a wider audience, who might not actually play *Minecraft*, with the project. In the case of HullCraft, it was advantageous to have the website at www. hullcraft.com, where we hosted a Wordpress site with a blog. This allowed the project to have a voice through the blog, and link in plugins such as "auto-tweet" blog posts,[14] which turn every blog post into a tweet through a linked Twitter account.

Through the use of social media and articles published online on The Conversation, MolCraft too generated much interest in the press and at conferences,[15] and generated exposure for the project and further reach of the use of *Minecraft* at the university.

MolCraft was delivered at a series of science events at the University of Hull, where it received much attention from the young people and their parents. In addition, MolCraft was showcased to a wider gaming audience at Insomnia, one of the UKs largest video gaming events, as part of a collaboration of *Minecraft* in education projects where several players and parents again expressed interest in how it could use *Minecraft* to support science.

The project has also been used in schools in London as part of the GCSE (General Certificate of Secondary Education) curriculum[16] and is also available via the MinecraftEdu World Library for students and teachers to download. The key to the reach of MolCraft is due to both its innovative approach to science and the focussed media exposure it has gained.

RESULTS IN THEORY

Minecraft has the power to reach large audiences due to the scale of its success. With over 100 million downloads across multiple gaming platforms, there is no question that it is huge and is still growing. Since Microsoft acquired it, they have pushed the educational angle of the game hard, with a dedicated website[17] featuring many of the best educational maps, tools and educators from across the globe. They have also piloted a "Minecraft Mentors" programme[18] of selected individuals who have shown particular dedication, knowledge and range of how *Minecraft* can be used in education to act as support mentors to those who are new to *Minecraft* in education.

Microsoft have also taken the bold move to purchase *MinecraftEdu* from Teacher Gaming and replace it with their own version, *Minecraft Education Edition* – a version of *Minecraft* completely written for the education market in the C++ language, which makes it more compatible with the Windows 10 version, console and tablet versions. *Minecraft Education Edition*, or *MinecraftEE* as it is known, is a game changer as its licensing model allows pupils to download it on their devices at home and log in with their school Microsoft account, thus connecting their school building projects with working at home without any extra cost to the pupil. In this way, Microsoft are demonstrating their commitment to *Minecraft* as a platform for engagement both at school and at home.

RESULTS IN PRACTICE

Growing your target audience beyond the project is a key part of a framework for engagement using *Minecraft*. What starts out as a university project can quickly extend into the local community and serve as an aspirational model for younger children. HullCraft created local interest in the community and was featured in the local press, on local radio and at the BBC.[19] A nearby primary school that had heard about HullCraft approached the university to help them set up and run a *Minecraft* Club,[20] which would run educational after-school activities in *Minecraft* as a reward for pupils with improved behaviour. *Minecraft* in this context had the power to change a community. It reached far beyond the initial scope of the project goals and engaged people who were not part of the target audience. *Minecraft* starts conversations – about building, exploring, contraptions, dragons and underworlds. It inspires people to try, to experiment, to test, to be bold, to be creative, to fail. A game that was released with no instruction manual, but has grown to epic proportions, has no doubt touched the minds of a generation. MolCraft is not without controversy, with some academics criticising the use of computer games in science and suggesting that it is not real learning.[21] The research, however, suggests otherwise, and goes further to suggest that playing 30 minutes of video games daily actually increased brain plasticity and functioning in the areas of spatial reasoning, strategy, planning, memory and motor skills (Kuhn et. al., 2014).

What is not in doubt is that through the development of engagement projects using *Minecraft*, the University of Hull has gained a reputation for innovation in the curriculum and as a leader in the field of GBL in higher education, recognised through awards, accolades and appearances at conferences. The university continues to push the boundaries of GBL and innovative use of *Minecraft* in the curriculum, and to extend its network of partners in this area of research. Through the successes of these projects, it is hoped that other educators can identify opportunities for learning in their own communities and develop projects that engage, develop and inspire young people.

WHAT WAS LEFT UNRESOLVED?

Microsoft's homogenisation of platforms and versions is at the exclusion of the very open nature of *Minecraft* that it was born with. As stated earlier in this chapter, the EULA from Mojang was incredibly open and forward thinking, allowing the end user to modify and develop unique customised experiences of the game through coding mods, thus bringing a higher level of engagement with *Minecraft* that went well beyond the initial game and into coding, programming and computer science. Hack spaces featured methods to connect *Minecraft* with Raspberry Pi computers, or Oculus Rift VR machines, or with 3D printers to create maker-spaces and home craft workshops.

The new versions of *Minecraft* are closed to developers and the modding community. Microsoft, in their own FAQ section for *MinecraftEE*, state that "Mods are not currently supported in Minecraft: Education Edition," and content seems to be available only in the form of paid-for downloadable content on the Windows 10 version. This is a huge blow for the education community, as it would appear that not only is the rich and varied world of modding being excluded from future project work, but also all of the maps and worlds created for *MinecraftEdu* and the PC/Mac Java versions – as it will not be possible to convert them to the new versions written in C++, and there is no sign of a conversion tool in development.

So whilst, in theory, *Minecraft* continues to be a great platform to engage people with educational material through creative play, experiential learning and collaborative projects, some of the very tools that made it open, accessible and desirable are being channelled down a more specific, focussed path. What remains to be seen is how the education community will respond to the new versions, and in what new ways they will engage their students. Or perhaps the right question to ask is just how students will show us how to be creative and exciting using these new tools – for they will lead the way, not us.

What works for one project may not directly translate onto another, even in the same field of study. HullCraft evolved into several other off-shoot projects, which is often the nature of *Minecraft*, some of which were more successful than others. This is where the co-created value of the digital engagement framework applies to *Minecraft* projects. Through the success of the HullCraft: History Makers project, the university received funding for another history project, recreating the world and work of renaissance Hull poet Andrew Marvell using *Minecraft* as a conduit for engagement. This project was a co-creation of work between the History department and children from the local community who were attempting to recreate parts of renaissance Hull and integrate the poetry of Marvell. The project was more one-dimensional than the HullCraft project, and lacked the same creative freedom that inspired the children to build freely in the PlotWorlds on HullCraft. The result was poorly attended workshops and little post-workshop activity on the server.

What appeared to be a recipe for successful engagement was clearly not a recipe for success just by using *Minecraft* to bring new audiences to historical poetry. Whilst much effort was made in publicising and creating the right environment for the Marvell workshops, the initial interest in the concept was lacking in the target audience. This is what is known in game-based learning as 'chocolate covered broccoli' – a metaphor for getting people to engage with material that they would otherwise not swallow. Whilst this approach can work in some classroom-based learning situations, with a captive audience and a playable *Minecraft* map, in most cases the resulting learning is shallow and the learners quickly disengage. In the case of the Marvell project, there was not much initial interest from the target audience, and the event attracted a younger group of participants between the ages of 8 and 12. The result was that the material prepared by the History department was too advanced for the age of the learner, and adjustments had to be made to differentiate the learning for the younger age group.

There are lessons to be learned here: simply building a project in *Minecraft* does not mean "they will come".

NOTES

1 Mills, J. (2016), visit to Alne School in Easingwold, North Yorkshire, England, 31 October 2016.
2 "Griefing" is a term for a type of bullying that can happen in *Minecraft*.
3 Spawn points are the starting point in a Minecraft world. When a player dies in the game they "respawn" at spawn.
4 Stampy is a pseudonym for Joseph Garrett – also known as Stampy the Cat and Stampy Longnose. He is a YouTuber, a person who produces YouTube content, with over 8 million subscribers and over 2 billion views of his videos at the time of writing, making him one of the most popular and widespread content creators on the planet.
5 DanTDM is a pseudonym for Daniel Middleton, another very popular YouTuber who, started out making *Minecraft* videos of himself playing mini-games on *Minecraft* servers.

6   www.HullCraft.com
7   https://dev.bukkit.org/projects/multiverse-core
8   http://www.dummies.com/games/engineering-with-redstone-in-minecraft/
9   http://www2.hull.ac.uk/science/scienceoutreach/molcraft.aspx
10 https://www.youtube.com/user/stampylonghead
11 https://www.youtube.com/user/TheDiamondMinecart
12 https://theconversation.com/how-minecraft-could-help-teach-chemistrys-building-blocks-of-life-49449
13 http://www2.hull.ac.uk/science/scienceoutreach/MolCraft.aspx
14 https://www.joedolson.com/wp-to-twitter/
15 http://www.hullcraft.com/events/
16 https://www.gov.uk/national-curriculum/overview
17 https://education.minecraft.net
18 https://education.microsoft.com/minecraftmentors
19 https://twitter.com/bbcmidigital/status/660787609141161984
20 http://www.hu17.net/2015/09/17/mayor-of-beverley-opens-minecraft-club-at-local-primary-school/
21 Comments submitted in response to MolCraft article on The Conversation, referred to earlier.

REFERENCES

Kuhn, S., T. Gleich, R. C. Lorenz, U. Lindenberger and J. Gallinat (2014). "Playing Super Mario induces structural brain plasticity: gray matter changes resulting from training with a commercial video game". *Mol Psychiatry* 19(2), 265–271.

McGonigal, J. (2011). *Reality is broken: Why games make us better and how they can change the world*, London: Penguin.

Mojang (2011). "Minecraft EULA 2011" Accessed from http://wayback.archive.org/web/20110408232718/http://www.minecraft.net/copyright.jsp.

Stuart, K. (2015). "Minecraft free for every secondary school in Northern Ireland". *The Guardian*. Accessed from http://www.theguardian.com/technology/2015/mar/25/minecraft-free-secondary-school-northern-island.

Visser, J. and J. Richardson (2016). "Digital engagement framework version 3". Digital Engagement Framework. Accessed from http://digitalengagementframework.com/digenfra3/wp-content/uploads/2016/02/Digital-engagement-framework-worksheet-v3.pdf.

CHAPTER 11

SOLE CODING

Towards a practitioner-led development framework for the teaching of computational thinking

Anne Preston, Chris Carr, Shaimaa Lazem, Bradley Pursglove, Ahmed Kharrufa, Patrick Olivier and Sugata Mitra

INTRODUCTION

In 1993, Michael G. Fullan, the well-known educational author and authority on educational reform, published a paper called "Why Teachers Must Become Change Agents". This widely cited work argued that "to have any chance of making teaching a noble and effective profession – teachers must combine the mantle of moral purpose with the skills of change agentry" (p. 2). By "moral purpose", Fullan meant "making a difference", and at the paper's heart was a call for a new conceptualisation of professionalism which put the untapped resources of teachers as the central driver for change in the future of education systems.

Twenty years later, another award-winning commentator, Professor Sugata Mitra, was taking to the educational stage. He also offered a vision on the future of learning, only this time the teacher was almost nowhere to be seen. "The teacher sets the process in motion and then she stands back in awe and watches as learning happens," claimed Mitra in his 2013 TED talk, ideas from which earned him the first $1 million TED prize (Mitra, 2013a).

Mitra asks what teachers are preparing pupils for. This is contextualised in his well-known work on *minimally invasive education* (Mitra, 2003) and, most recently, *self organised learning environments* (SOLE), described as "the first step towards preparing our children for a future we can barely imagine" (Mitra, 2013a).

SOLE grows out of the results of research called the "Hole in the Wall experiments" (Mitra, 2003, 2005), where ATM-like Internet-connected computers were placed in walls in the streets of Indian slums. Local children left entirely unsupervised were observed (from afar) to teach themselves how to use the computer and the Internet, and teach themselves about various subjects of their choosing. Research showed that children could become computer literate and achieve scores comparable with those of children who studied the computer curriculum and other subjects (Inamdar, 2004; Mitra, 2005). Results in other experiments showed that children performed 'hard' problems better in groups than they did individually and were capable of researching effectively using the Internet (Inamdar & Kulkarni, 2007; Mitra & Dangwal, 2010; Mitra & Quiroga, 2012). In sum, these experiments demonstrated that children could learn in groups, with the Internet and without a teacher.

Today, Mitra's work in India continues and, beyond that immediate context, also translates into the concept of SOLE, a space where "educators encourage students to work as a community to answer their own vibrant questions using the Internet" (Mitra, 2014). SOLE shares commonalities with personalised and student-led learning, but is distinguishable through its focus on emphasising the convergence of social, intellectual, academic, conceptual and physical space that is needed in order for learning to take place, rather than prescribing specific teaching methods. Its universal methodological principles are to stimulate curiosity and engagement in learning content, a social and collaborative atmosphere and peer interest. SOLE-based learning is stimulated by the introduction of a 'Big Question' – an often unanswerable question which initiates big picture thinking and allows children to go off in a range of directions.

Through facilitating SOLE spaces, the principles of curiosity, collaboration and peer interest are fuelled by adult encouragement and admiration, but not by direct intervention. Thus, based on the 'Hole in the Wall' experiments, SOLE follows 'minimal invasion' from the teacher, whose role is changed from transmitter to facilitator of learning content.

SOLE is not an isolated solution to access to education in the developing world, but it builds on research into children's innate curiosity and ability to learn independently of a teacher using computers, and the vital role that technology can play in improving learning outcomes and quality of education. The notion of minimal teacher 'invasion' links to the enacting of the learning process during a SOLE, but does not limit the role, expertise and craft of the teacher in the design for learning and its assessment. Therefore, as Mitra recently said, "the absence of the teacher can be a pedagogical tool" (2013b).

SOLE AS CHANGE ENABLER

In this chapter, the Big Question we ask is this: What are the implications of SOLE for creating the coding generation? In doing so, we critically engage with the big picture of the future contribution of primary teachers in the development of the UK primary computing curriculum. Our work is motivated by how innovations in classroom practice like SOLE can leverage the *priming* of primary aged children into a more holistic and deeper understanding of coding through computational thinking. Computational thinking as defined by Wing (2006) is a set of thinking patterns that includes understanding problems with appropriate representation, reasoning at multiple levels of abstraction, and developing automated solutions (i.e. solutions that could be implemented using computers). Our work is based on the premise that computational thinking is an essential skill that should be mastered by the computer programmer (the future coding generation). Central to our approach is that non-computing specialist teachers can be the agents for change in creating the coding generation. SOLE is adopted as both the object and subject of pupil *and* teacher development. We position SOLE as a powerful enabler for teachers to inquire into the role of computing in their own and their pupils' development, and, more broadly, as a way to engage in deeper discussions about the pedagogical implications of curriculum change.

Fullan's model of educational change focuses on the roles and strategies of various types of change agents and asks the Big Question: What can different stakeholders do to promote change that addresses their needs and priorities? To enable us to move beyond a descriptive account of the implications of SOLE, we used Fullan's work to provide us with a holistic conceptual approach for framing our work. The chapter is organised around four core capacities identified by Fullan as required for engagement with curriculum change: personal vision; mastery; inquiry; and collaboration (1993).

These capacities provide a way through which we, the SOLECODE research team, planned, designed, implemented and reflected on the use of SOLE to teach pupils about computational thinking in a six-week after-school club in a primary school in the North East of England in November to December 2015. The SOLECODE team included a primary teacher in his first year of teaching, an educational researcher specialising in SOLE, two computing science researchers, a software programmer and a human–computer interaction expert, with advice from Prof. Sugata Mitra.

WHY SOLECODE?

In September 2014, computational thinking was introduced to all stages of the UK Computing National Curriculum. As a way of advising on the change to the teaching of computer science, Computing at School[1] produced a number of guides, including one which put computational thinking at its heart. The guide is presented as helping teachers cope with change and overcome the challenges of bringing this new subject into schools, and helping them learn new vocabulary and skills, and a new way of teaching (Csizmadia et al., 2015).

Late 2014 was also the time of the inauguration of SOLE Central, a new research centre set up to extend intellectual understandings of the concept and broaden the scope of SOLE-based research. Researchers in the centre had been reflecting for some time on how a vision of the UK Computing National Curriculum, and particularly computational thinking, could be taught by non-computing subject specialists. A few months later, when a SOLE Central researcher was contacted via Twitter by a local primary teacher, Chris, who wanted to share news that he had started his own after-school 'SOLE club', the seed for the project was sown.

Planning and designing for the club involved synthesising our personal visions and working collaboratively to think about the role and relevance of SOLE, our research practice and its relationship to computational thinking. Implementing a SOLECODE learning design involved further collaboration and discussion about what worked and didn't work. In this sense, we were able to develop a sense of mastery over teaching computational thinking through SOLE, particularly by reflecting together, re-sharing and revisiting our personal visions as a form of inquiry. Evaluation involved a specific inquiry into the facilitation of SOLECODE and focused in on Chris's own views feeding into his development and change agentry.

PERSONAL VISIONS

> Working on personal visions means examining and re-examining why we came into teaching. Asking "What difference am I trying to make personally?" is a good place to start.
>
> (Fullan, 1993, p. 13)

Chris's initial interest in SOLECODE was rooted in his belief in the importance of creativity in teaching and learning:

> Rather than the old methods of teaching, where the teacher stands at the front and delivers knowledge, for me teaching is about sparking pupils' interest and creativity – with an idea, a concept or a metaphor. I want to support my pupils to take ownership over their own learning and their own creativity. Learning is not just about acquiring a discipline knowledge base – it also has a social purpose. This is important at primary level because it is so important at tertiary level – taking ownership of one's own learning is a lifelong skill. At tertiary level, my own experience was that I lacked the ability to think about my own learning, stand up, present my ideas and defend them. The earlier you can introduce the skills and ideas to children so that they are in charge of and responsible for their own learning, the better. I'm not there to ensure they pass the test or do well, I'm there to give them the tools to do so and to achieve what they can.

From the perspective of the SOLE Central researchers, there was also a sense of a personal vision for the project, informed by their own conceptions and experiences (related to moral purpose) of teaching and learning as students, teachers and researchers of computing science and education. The researchers had a shared vision on SOLE integration, which was to extend its intellectual understandings through partnership working and to explore how SOLEs are made material in local contexts.

From the conception of the project, the SOLE Central team and Chris worked together closely to co-design the initial outlines for the SOLE sessions and emerged as the 'SOLECODE research team'. Our shared vision was one in which the talk around learning computing and computers was turned upside down. We wanted to challenge the popular notion that technological and computing knowledge was something magical and mysterious, needing to be learned for a better future. Our vision placed the child as the protagonist who interrogates the computer's ability to think, knows its computational limitations, and personally builds one better than we have now.

COLLABORATION

> … the actions of individuals and small groups working on new conceptions intersect to produce breakthroughs.
>
> (Fullan, 1993, p. 17)

Our aim for SOLECODE was that it could become an example of a learning environment with a power structure and dynamics very different from those of the traditional classroom. SOLECODE was a judgement-free conceptual and physical space where:

■   an after-school club took place with no grades associated with it;

■   teacher(s) were not subject experts;

■   the problems explored in the sessions did not have a solution (by experts);

■   pupils could quit at any point; and

■   progression (in its very pragmatic sense) in this environment was attributed to the intrinsic motivations and engagement of the teacher and the pupils.

We decided that the sessions should take place in a regular classroom, using the original classroom layout already set out for different configurations for group work, Each table (six in total) had a laptop with Internet access, and the Big Question for each week was displayed on a large whiteboard. The reduced number of computers and the shared board were part of the SOLE guidelines to create a collaborative environment (Mitra, 2014). The children were free to work with whomever they chose and could change groups at any time. A sharing and collaborative attitude was encouraged, and the children were reminded of this at the start of each SOLE.

Our plan included the Big Question, suggested facilitation and debrief questions. We (Chris and the other 'assistant facilitators' from SOLE Central) modified the plans 'on the fly' during the sessions. After each SOLECODE session, we also had an open conversation, where the children's engagement and our facilitation practice were discussed.

Through our examination and discussion about existing methods used in primary teaching, Chris's interest in creativity, and other materials we found which were being used in the teaching of computational thinking, we decided to explore SOLE as a complex system for knowledge production rather than focusing on one aspect (i.e. a 'teacher-less' environment). Using the concept of 'learning design', we introduced several elements to our outlines to embrace the dynamic nature of this environment. This included offering various material resources to be used by the children to produce the outcomes. This was one of the main departures we made from the original SOLE approach: the introduction of material resources and the use of them by the children in answering the Big Questions.

■ **Figure 11.1** The SOLECODE club in action

What is a thought? What is thinking? Can a computer think for itself?

In the first two sessions, we asked the children, respectively: What is a thought? What is thinking? In the second session, a further Big Question emerged from the children: Can a computer think for itself? The children had the option of producing their answers using pen and paper, MS Word or MS PowerPoint, and could explore in any direction they wished. These Big Questions had the objective of motivating the children to establish an analogy (or lack thereof) between human thinking and computer thinking. We thus embraced the classic view of creating the computer to replace the human.

What is a computer bug?

The third session proposed the concept of 'metaphors'. The children were encouraged to produce the answer to the question in LEGO bricks.

NON-PROGRAMMABLE LEGO BRICKS

We introduced LEGO bricks as a resource to produce SOLE outcomes (regularly produced in schools using pen and paper, or MS Office). The choice of non-programmable LEGOs was aimed at encouraging conceptual thought processes rather than learning a programming tool. We envisioned that the LEGO affordances would encourage the children to think about modules and abstractions more than working on paper or a Word document.

■ **Figure 11.2** A computer bug

We designed this SOLECODE session to introduce the concept of metaphors as a method for expressing ideas and thoughts, in order to help the children get comfortable building LEGO models that were 'far from perfect' and imagining stories around them. Inspiration for this was also informed by Mitra's early work on using the notion of computer bugs in a minimally invasive educational environment to teach programming. Moreover, he also used computer bugs as a training tool in the development of a diagnostic method for computer programming training which involved trainees detecting bugs purposely put into a computer program (Mitra & Pawar, 1982).

What is the P vs. NP problem?

The fourth SOLECODE session introduced the notion that 'computers cannot do everything we want them to do'. In this session, we decided to challenge some of the perceptions around the capability of computers. Continuing with the theme of creativity and put simply, this Big Question asks whether computers can be taught to think for themselves. The question has at its base one of seven Millennium Prize Problems set out by the Clay Mathematics Institute, referred to as the problem of P vs. NP. Introducing this problem engaged the children in a major area of research around the search for solutions to problems that seem easy to make up but require an intractable amount of time to solve. P is the class of computing problems solved in polynomial time – which is easy for a computer. NP is the class of computing problems that could be solved in polynomial time by a non-deterministic Turing machine – so a computer could easily verify its solution, but there is no efficient way of obtaining the solution in the first place. The Millennium Prize Problem therefore asks whether a problem whose solution could be *verified* in polynomial time could be also *solved* in polynomial time.

3-COLOURED GRAPH PROBLEM

A graph consists of connected blank areas (Figure 11.3). A graph is x-coloured if x is the minimum number of colours that could be used to colour in the blank areas so that no two adjacent areas (i.e. sharing a border) have the same colour. The children were given several sheets for multiple graph examples and were asked to find out whether these graphs were 2-coloured or 3-coloured. The multiple sheets were provided to encourage them to try several different solutions. The use of the graphs (equivalent to paper-based colouring maps) was introduced to the children as one way in which people try to represent computational thinking.

The children first explored the question with only the Internet made available to them as an external material resource. We then integrated a classical graph colouring problem as a practical example for P and NP problems, taken from a series of resources from CS Unplugged called "The Poor Cartographer".[2] The use of the graphs (equivalent to paper-based colouring maps) was introduced to the children as one way in which people try to represent computational thinking.

■ **Figure 11.3** An example for a 3-colourable graph with the correct minimum number of colours

Our aim was to make the problem tangible by offering examples for simple and complex problems. We wanted to encourage the children to grasp where complexity comes from when it comes to computing. The overall aim was to encourage the children to find the rules they used to solve the problem for themselves. In later SOLECODE sessions, we hope that they would use these to engage in applying them when addressing further Big Questions.

What does the computer of the future look like which could solve the P vs. NP problem?

The fifth and sixth SOLECODE sessions focused on 'making the computer of the future' (the hardware and software). Our computational thinking aim was to encourage the children to engage in learning about the computer from the 'inside' as well as engage in discussions about solving a complex problem (P vs. NP). We therefore invited the children to respond by designing the computer of the future, one that could solve the P vs. NP problem using LEGO bricks (see Figure 11.4). In addition to the bricks, we provided the children with a keyword sticker list from UK National Computing Curriculum, which could be used (if they chose) to help with Internet searches and the construction with the computer. Empty stickers were provided so they could label their own computer pieces.

The UK Department for Education (2013) says, "A high quality computing education equips pupils to use computational thinking and creativity to understand and change the world" (p. 217). Echoing this, SOLECODE was co-designed to encourage the children to adopt a critical perspective towards computing and impact the *route* rather than the rate through which they learned how to code. Our design does not aim to discourage children by the 'bugs' they encounter at the beginning of their learning – rather it is designed to trigger curiosity to learn why these errors happen and how they can fix them in a self-organised way. Figure 11.5 shows a visual outline of all six SOLECODE sessions reported here. SOLECODE 7 is an additional session which we envisage adding to future sessions.

■ **Figure 11.4** A computer of the future

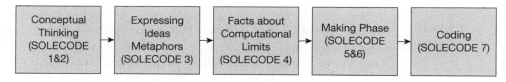

■ **Figure 11.5** An outline of the SOLECODE learning design

The SOLECODErs

We initially had 24 children aged between 9 and 10 years old (Key Stage 2) sign up to the after-school club, whose abilities were marked by their class teachers as follows: six high ability, 12 middle-ability, six low-ability and one special educational needs. Twenty children participated up until the last two sessions (ten males and ten females).

INQUIRY

> inquiry – indicates that formation and enactment of personal purpose are not static matters but, rather, a perennial quest.
>
> (Fullan, 1993)

Our SOLECODE learning design, based on SOLE principles, provided the instructional ingredients for teaching computational thinking. However, this was only one part of the project. In implementing it, our primary interest and focus was on developing SOLECODE as a mediational tool – as an enabler for the teachers' change agentry.

■ **Figure 11.6** The SOLECODE generation

This meant exploring the notion of pedagogical intent in the enactment of our shared vision. For this, our collaborative inquiry, led by Chris, was central.

Chris's initial interest in SOLECODE was rooted in how it embraced current changes in education, but this also came with a number of questions:

> The government says that the new Computing Science National Curriculum has a real freedom for teachers to decide how best to teach. Taking this into consideration and the radical changes spurred on by innovations in technology, I'm intrigued about the idea of teaching in a chaotic child led environment like SOLECODE. Although exciting, it does bring a plethora of new questions such as: How do I know learning is taking place? How do I assess progress and attainment? In what ways do I evidence this new type of learning?

As part of the collaborative inquiry, Chris identified two key areas that he wanted to explore, revisit and discuss during the SOLECODE sessions:

1) Develop an understanding and competence in the delivery of SOLECODE.

> I'm concerned about how the delivery of SOLECODE will be very different from my day-to-day teaching role. With the children being in such control of the direction of the lesson, I'm going to have to map out and adapt my questioning to ensure the children cover the topics and learning required before progressing to the next session.

2) Develop an understanding of what learning in a 'chaotic' SOLE-like setting looks like.

> I think my role of teacher is going to drastically change in SOLECODE; I'm going to have to step back and assume the role of a mediator. I'm worried that by giving the children completely free rein, it will be too chaotic and they'll learn nothing.

Everyone is engaged – no one is sitting back doing nothing – they are all focusing on what they've decided their job is, be it LEGO, be it researching, be it writing something – the whole class is fully engaged.

I'm sitting in – even though I'm sitting back, I know from my experience of sitting there that I'm engaging in conversation and everybody is sitting there listening to what a student is saying on the table, because we are all kind of looking at him and it has completely opened up to a big discussion, which I think is so important – you can see I'm not even standing in front of the board – I'm just letting it happen through discussion and findings.

The left one – this is following on from the discussion back into the activities – this links to supported and independent working – it is very important as a teacher to support if there is anything going wrong–be it technical with the laptop or be it a misconception, I'm there to guide, be it though questioning, or talking about the autonomy. In the other one, I'm leaning over because the support was obviously important for him to then be able to work independently.

This is important because it is important that the children have a wide range of resources, but I think the engagement, group involvement, whole class discussion and teacher support lead to independent working – although the resources are important, I don't care how the work is produced as long as we get to this end point, be it through LEGO, computer work or writing.

■ **Figure 11.7** SOLECODE Diamond Ranking Activity 1

Over a number of sessions, these areas became a central part of the inquiry and fed into the implementation. Often, they provided a specific focus for the post-session conversations, where we reviewed individual sessions and made plans for how we might modify the next and develop facilitation techniques. After the second SOLECODE session, Chris wanted to devote some specific time to explore his development, so we decided to document the activity in the sessions using photographs. The idea was drawn from participatory approaches to research which use visual methods to build shared understandings of concepts and activities (Clark et al., 2013).

Chris ranked photographs taken by other members of the SOLECODE team as a way of exploring and clarifying his growing facilitation of the sessions and particularly the nature and quality of the children's learning. This activity revealed a number of interesting points about engagement and different teacher–pupil and pupil–pupil interactions emerging in the SOLECODE environment.

Figure 11.7 zooms in on a closer look at the images with Chris' commentary, where he chose to rank the photographs according to two concepts: engagement and narrative of events.

In the last SOLECODE session, Chris documented the proceedings by taking photographs himself (Figure 11.8), then, in discussion with another member of the team, performed another ranking exercise. This revealed a further focus on engagement, but also a deeper discussion about the role of the teacher. This deeper discussion demonstrated a more significant focus on how the learning environment and, in particular, the facilitation of the SOLECODE sessions, were inextricably linked to progression and the nature of learning outcomes.

MASTERY

> Beyond exposure to new ideas, we have to know where they fit, and we have to become skilled in them, not just like them.
>
> (Fullan, 1993)

Fullan's characterisation of mastery as a process of becoming skilled in ideas and not just liking them is just as relevant now as it was more than twenty years ago. This is echoed in the concluding remarks in the guidance for primary teachers Computing At School (Berry, 2013):

> It's a really exciting time to be a primary school teacher, too. Don't be daunted by the changes in the move from ICT to computing. Rather, see this as an opportunity to develop your own knowledge about computing and to learn to program, if you've never had the chance before. Although this might sound like hard work, it's actually great fun. You'll find that you make better use of the technology you have at home and in school, and also that you start to think a bit differently, looking at systems and problems in the same way a computer scientist does.

The SOLECODE project provides insights into how the translation of ideas into actions can take place through collaboration and inquiry. The SOLECODE learning design was to a large extent informed by Chris's personal belief that teaching is about sparking pupils' interest and creativity. By working together, the SOLECODE team began to think differently about computing in and out of school, as well as the research lab, to create the SOLECODE learning design.

I ranked the photos here on the basis of how successful the session had been taking into consideration the learning outcomes. In the top photo you can see that there are no adults and there is lots of different activity – there's no teacher present but the children are still absorbed in what they are doing, they are still engaged and still motivated. Whole-class engagement is important – as a teacher it tells me that the SOLECODE session has been pitched at the right level, that the children understand, that the activity is suitable for them, that they like it and are enjoying it. It confirms to me that I've picked nice resources and ones which are accessible to them and that the Big Question is not too difficult because they are not sitting back doing nothing.

I know from the session that the student on the laptop is feeding information to the girls who are then creating the output through LEGO. There are further examples of consolidation in this photo where the children are explaining their ideas to other team members.

This photo is ranked lower because there is an adult in the picture – I think that the children would be automatically engaged because there are adults present so they know they have to do work.

In this photo, where another facilitator is there, these are important because through facilitation you can get a good indication of their understanding – through their conversation you can gain an insight into their progress.

This row is all about the completion of the task, it's ranked lower not because this is not important, but because it is just a lower ranked indicator that the session has gone well – at the outcome stage in the SOLECODE, it is all about consolidating ideas and tying the learning up. The outcome demonstrates the children's awareness that the learning has happened: you have got the best of the children at this point, you know their understanding, you know what research they've done, you know what difficulties they are having, you know how they are working as a class, as a group and as an individual – the outcome is a summary of all of that. From the girls' expressions here, they don't seem in any way engaged. It is a snapshot and on the row higher up there is another photo of them all engaged, but I would be devastated at that picture if someone else had taken it. I think these students had been engaged in creating, but I ask myself: do they fully understand the activity and can they explain their computer in terms of the Big Question? Can they answer questions? Can they go further to explain their learning? This is a new area I would like to focus in on…

Figure 11.8 SOLECODE Diamond Ranking Activity 2

Chris's inquiry showed that for the teacher, SOLECODE became a mediational tool for understanding the teaching and learning of computational thinking as a situated process. SOLECODE became a physical and intellectual space to extend on understandings about the teacher development in computing, from being exclusively based on skill development in the mastery of subject knowledge, to being about *appropriation*. Appropriation is closely tied to Fullan's definition of mastery and moral purpose. According to Wertsch, appropriation is a "process of taking something that belongs to others and make it one's own"; this is contrasted with mastery, which is "knowing *how to* use an artefact" (1998, p. 53). Here, artefacts are physical and intellectual "signs, symbols and tools" (Instefjord, 2015, p. 157) – a category to which we believe SOLE belongs. The process of appropriation begins with "an initial contact with something that is not familiar to us", and as we progress in using new artefacts we begin to "investigate the different aspects of how the artefact mediates" and "learn new ways to use it and we discover new functions that we did not recognize in the beginning" (Instefjord, 2015, p. 158). In time, this artefact becomes appropriated and we no longer need help from others.

CONCLUSION

To conclude, we return to our Big Question posed at the beginning of this chapter: What are the implications of SOLE for creating the coding generation? Our inquiry has shown that SOLECODE provided a context for the development of new ideas about the teaching of computational thinking in ways that have yet to be explored in computing education in the UK and elsewhere. But, as Chris concludes, change agentry does not come without challenges: it demands creativity, trial and error, and personal strength. Ultimately, these are all values that the future coding generation made up of teachers and pupils also need to learn:

> I remember sitting in a training session being told that we had to teach children about algorithms and coding, and we all just kind of looked at each other. I remember some very vague lesson plans were handed to us that we were not at all confident in teaching. What I've learned from my SOLECODE experience is that it is not as scary as you might think it would be to teach something like computing science when you don't feel 100 per cent sure about what it is. I've learned along with the kids: I've learned to embrace that fear of 'not knowing all' and just get on with it, experiment and learn by trialling things – teachers can be self-organised learners too!

We thank Amberley Primary School pupils and staff for being part of this project. The SOLECODE project was jointly funded by a UK–Egypt joint fund (Newton–Mosharafa) and the Digital Economy Research Centre at Open Lab, Newcastle University, UK. Ethical guidelines for Newcastle University were followed. Written informed parental consent was provided for work reported in this publication and its accompanying images.

NOTES

1 https://www.computingatschool.org.uk
2 http://csunplugged.org

REFERENCES

Berry, M. (2013). Computing in the national curriculum: A guide for primary teachers. Computing at School. Accessed from: http://www.computingatschool.org.uk/data/uploads/CASPrimaryComputing.pdf.

Clark, J., Laing, K., Tiplady, L., and Woolner, P. (2013). Making connections: Theory and practice of using visual methods to aid participation in research. Newcastle University: Research Centre for Learning and Teaching. Accessed from: http://eprint.ncl.ac.uk/file_store/production/190964/23811F02-9772-42F3-B124-AD0830449ED7.pdf.

Csizmadia, A., Curzon, P., Dorling, M., Humphreys, S., Ng, T., Selby, C., and Woollard, J. (2015). Computational thinking: A guide for teachers. *Communications of the ACM, 60*(4), 55–62.

Department for Education (DfE) (UK). (2013). Statutory guidance: National curriculum in England: computing programmes of study. Accessed from: https://www.gov.uk/government/publications/national-curriculum-in-england-computing programmes-of-study/national-curriculum-in-england-computing-programmes-of-study.

Fullan, M. G. (1993). Why teachers must become change agents. *Educational leadership, 50*, 12–17.

Inamdar, P. (2004). Computer skills development by children using 'hole in the wall' facilities in rural India. *Australasian Journal of Educational Technology, 20*(3), 337–350.

Inamdar, P., and Kulkarni, A. (2007). Hole-in-the-wall computer kiosks foster mathematics achievement: A comparative study. *Educational Technology & Society, 10*(2), 170–179.

Instefjord, E. (2015). Appropriation of digital competence in teacher education. *Nordic Journal of Digital Literacy, 10*, 155–171. Accessed from: https://www.idunn.no/dk/2014/04/appropriation_of_digitalcompetence_in_teacher_education.

Mitra, S. (2003). Minimally invasive education: A progress report on the 'hole-in-the-wall' experiments. *British Journal of Educational Technology, 34*(3), 367–371.

Mitra, S. (2005). Self organising systems for mass computer literacy: Findings from the 'Hole in the Wall' experiments. *International Journal of Development Issues, 4*(1), 71–81.

Mitra, S. (2013a). Build a school in the Cloud. *TED 2013*. Accessed from: https://youtu.be/y3jYVe1RGaU.

Mitra, S. (2013b). The future of learning. Accessed from https://youtu.be/xNzt_xaVYa0.

Mitra, S. (2014). SOLE toolkit: How to bring self-organised learning environments to your community. Newcastle University. Accessed from: https://s3-eu-west-1.amazonaws.com/school-in-the-cloud-production-assets/toolkit/SOLE_Toolkit_Web_2.6.pdf.

Mitra, S., and Dangwal, R. (2010). Limits to self-organising systems of learning: The Kalikuppam experiment. *British Journal of Educational Technology, 41*(5), 672–688.

Mitra, S., and Pawar, R. S. (1982). Diagnostic computer-assisted-instruction: A methodology for the teaching of computer languages. Sixth Western Educational Computing Conference, San Diego, Calif.

Mitra, S., and Quiroga, M. (2012). Children and the Internet: A preliminary study in Uruguay. *International Journal of Humanities and Social Science, 2*(15), 123–129.

Wertsch, J. V. (1998). *Mind as action.* New York and Oxford: Oxford University Press.

Wing, J. M. (2006). Computational thinking. *Communications of the ACM, 49*(3), 33–35.

PART III

CODING AND THE WIDER CURRICULUM

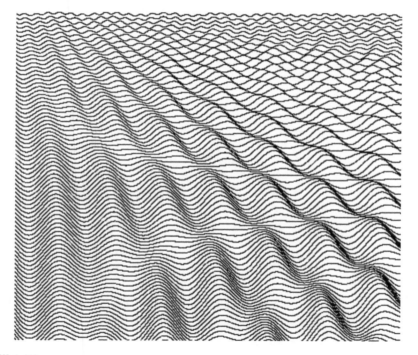

PART III
CODING AND THE WIDER CURRICULUM

POSSIBLE

The Raspberry Pi – a world of opportunities

Simon Marsden and David Hill

INTRODUCTION

If you work in a school or other educational establishment, you have probably heard of the Raspberry Pi. It was released in 2012, and increasingly sophisticated models of the "credit card" sized devices have been produced ever since. The Raspberry Pis are exceptionally affordable devices and now have a host of add-ons that will pretty much cater for any project that you might wish to carry out. They are also exceptionally powerful and reliable.

Before we carry on, we think we should state: we really love Raspberry Pis; however, we will be suggesting alternative approaches on a route to being able to fully appreciate just how amazing this device is.

Although we will be pointing out some ideas that you might wish to try out, we will not be giving step-by-step instructions as to how to implement these ideas. There is a really good reason for this. If you just browse, you will find instructions online for more Raspberry Pi projects than you could ever hope to make in a lifetime! These online tutorials are far more likely to be up to date and appropriate for you and the devices you are using over time. Everything else we mention is also easy to find online. The key thing is to know the right questions to ask; and to help you ask the right questions, you need to know a little about what you can (or can't) do with a Raspberry Pi.

If we are suggesting that you just browse for all the answers you could ever want to ask about a Raspberry Pi, why on earth are we writing this chapter? Well the simple truth is that, whilst we go into many schools, we see the same thing in nearly all.

THE RASPBERRY PIS ARE IN THE CUPBOARD, NOT BEING USED!

This needs some exploration, so please bear with us whilst we explain why we think this is the case and what we should do about it.

The first thing that most people do when they get a Raspberry Pi is to hook it up to monitor, keyboard and mouse to have a look at what the operating system is – to see it "working". On an individual basis, in preparation for understanding and working with the Raspberry Pi in a school environment, this is not a bad place for the teacher, child or technician to start. However, unless you specifically want to use software such as the Raspberry Pi version of *Minecraft* (perhaps with Python) and you have carefully considered how you will manage the logistics of, efficiently, setting up the Raspberry Pi, it is not a great way to start with a class of children.

The reason we say this is because to most people/children this will just be another computer running another operating system. Most of the software that you might want to use at this stage is software that you could install on your normal machines, for example Scratch or Python. It is fine to set up a Pi to do a classroom demo by way of introduction, but if you want to use a different operating system, there is a much easier and more user friendly way to do so, which we will outline later on. From a classroom perspective, setting up a Raspberry Pi for each child is a recipe for a fairly frustrating and fruitless time, unless they can be permanently set up or sufficient time is set aside for the session.

Why is this not an approach that we would endorse?

Firstly, the Raspberry Pis come with an HDMI socket for connecting to a monitor. Most schools will still have VGA monitors, so a convertor or new monitors will be needed. Secondly, most schools will not be able to set up the Raspberry Pis permanently, so you will be taking to bits a room of working computers running one operating system to set up another computer to run a different operating system. At the end of a lesson, you will be reasonably lucky to have got all the machines working and networked, and the children doing something meaningful! You will then have to get the children to take it all apart to put the room back to the state it was in before you started. We will leave you to imagine the chaos that you might have, and to draw your own conclusions as to why so many Raspberry Pis are in the cupboards!

VIRTUAL MACHINES

With the power of modern computers, the above approach seems even more bizarre when you can run different operating systems in a virtual machine (VirtualBox or VMware). This approach allows you to have a machine stored as a file in your computer that you can run in a window or full-screen. You can run Windows on a Mac, or vice versa, for example. Virtual machines are widely used by people who need access to several operating systems but do not want the inconvenience of having to do so on several machines.

The beauty of a virtual machine is that you can let the children have full admin access to the machine, so that they can tinker and discover without fear of breaking the host operating system. If they do "break" the virtual machine, you just need to replace the virtual machine file with a backup file and it will be as good as new. A virtual machine will boot up very quickly (around 15 seconds on a typical machine) and can be shut down with a few clicks of the mouse. At the end of a lesson using a virtual machine, the room will be exactly as it was when you entered it! If you just want the children to have a sandpit to play in to discover how a computer operating system works, this is the approach that we would adopt – it has been proven to work in one of our schools over several years of use. We would currently recommend using VirtualBox.[1] There are several flavours of the Linux operating system that you can download to create your virtual machine. If you want it to look and behave like a Raspberry Pi, Debian would be the operating system of choice, although you might find Ubuntu slightly easier to use. You can just put Debian or Ubuntu (or others) on any spare or older machines as their primary operating system.

COMMUNICATING WITH THE PI

But this isn't the Raspberry Pi, is it? No, but then just using the Raspberry Pi as a cheap computer is not taking into account the most amazing thing that it can do (although a Raspberry Pi 3 with 1.2GHz Quad-Core 64-bit CPU, WiFi and Bluetooth would make a very attractive machine at an amazing price). The Raspberry Pi can communicate with physical objects such as lights, sensors and motors whilst retaining all the functionality of a computer that you can log in to and control from anywhere in the world!

Did we say anywhere in the world? Yes, and out of it too. Several projects have put Raspberry Pis up in balloons to photograph near space. At the time of writing, the second British astronaut in space, Tim Peake, is using the Raspberry Pi to run computer science based experiments, which school children designed, on the Space Station.

The best way to start using a Raspberry Pi is with a small project that you, as a teacher, technician or child, feel confident that you can organise. As mentioned earlier, there are literally thousands of projects online that allow you to just follow the instructions, such as those that involve sensing movement (using passive infrared (PIR) sensors), or the detecting of the opening of a door using reed switches (the little white blocks that you see on windows for home burglar alarms). All of the bits and pieces that you need for these projects can be easily bought online at the many Raspberry Pi based sites, and in high street electronics shops.

Before you start a project, though, it would help you to have a little bit of knowledge about the following. You don't need a Raspberry Pi for these; however, you will need a machine running Linux for the first one, or you could use an online emulator.[2] Look around for projects that you want to carry out, and you will have a lot more desire to complete those projects – you will learn all you need to know along the way.

Linux

In the early days of computers, there weren't any desktops with icons to click on. To use them, you had to type text commands in. These were entered on what was called the *command line* – it is still there in different operating systems, just sometimes hidden away. The Raspberry Pi uses the Linux operating system. You know when it's ready for a command, as it displays a sign (called a *prompt*). Before this prompt comes some useful information: your username, the name of the computer and the current directory you are in. You don't need to be a super hacker to use the commands – however, it is useful to know a few in order to get around. What we are *not* going to do is tell you every command you can use, as you can find these online. Some commands have options, called *switches*, which change how the command works. As there are a lot of these, it is perfectly normal, and a good idea, to create your own cheat sheet of the commands and switches you find most useful.

Some of the most useful commands are shown in Table 12.1. The "$" symbol preceding each command is the prompt.

GPIO

What makes the Raspberry Pi special are the GPIO (General-Purpose Input/Output) pins on the edge. These allow it to physically connect to other things. What each pin is useful for will depend on the type of Pi you have.

▨ **Table 12.1** Useful Linux commands

$ ls	Lists everything in the directory (or folder if you prefer) you are in.
$ cd	Changes directory. What you type after this determines where you go . . .
$ cd nameofdirectoryinfolder	Takes you to that directory (as long as it exists in the directory you are in).
$ cd /	Takes you to the topmost directory.
$ cd ~	Takes you to your home directory.
$ cd ..	Takes you up a directory.
$ cd /pathtoadirectory	If you know the full path to a directory, you can type it in, remembering to start with a "/".
$ pwd	Shows you the full path of the directory you are in (print the working directory).
$ mkdir newDirectory	Makes a folder called "newDirectory" in your current working directory.
$ sudo	When you log in to your Pi, it is as an ordinary user. Linux is quite strict on security, and sometimes you don't have the right permissions to run a file or open a directory. If you add "sudo" in front of a command, it assumes you are a super user for that one command and allows you to run it.

For example, the Raspberry Pi 3 has two pins that output 5V, two that output 3.3V, eight ground pins and 26 GPIO pins (think of them like switches you can turn on or off (input) or get the Pi to turn on or off (output)). It is important when using these pins to follow any instructions carefully, or know exactly what you are doing, because if you connect things up incorrectly it is possible that you will damage your Pi!

If this makes you nervous, there are a host of add-on boards (called *HATs* – Hardware Attached on Top) that you can use to simplify things. These automatically configure the GPIOs and make life easier for you. They will also usually come with some examples of Python scripts that show you how to use the inputs and outputs of the board. For example, the Explorer Hat Pro allows you to safely connect and control motors should you want to build, say, a vehicle, and has a mini breadboard where you can attach LEDs without the worry of using wires to create a circuit.

Scratch

If you are not already aware of Scratch, it is a simple computing language that uses blocks (or jigsaw pieces) to create programs. It is perfect for starting to teach programming at primary school. You can use it online through a web browser, or download it to a computer. Scratch is already included in most of the operating systems used on Raspberry Pi (including NOOBS). If you are not familiar with Scratch, go to scratch.mit.edu and have a look at some of the millions of projects that have been posted there. Using Scratch on the

Raspberry Pi allows you to control things connected to it using the GPIO pins. You can do this using the Scratch GPIO server (click on Scratch's Edit menu and choose "Enable GPIO server" – no more clues). Suddenly you go from programming things to happen on screen to making things happen in real life (e.g. light up, move. . .) – which is one of the KS2 attainment targets in the Computing and Design Technology (DT) curriculums.

Python

Python is a text based computing language. Whilst it may seem a big jump from Scratch to Python, it isn't. It uses the same concepts you use when you write a program in Scratch, such as variables and conditional statements. It is a natural progression for those children who've started to master Scratch to move on to.

Python requires the syntax to be exact to work, so it helps teach skills like resilience and debugging – which can be easily related to English and its syntax.

Like with Scratch, you can write programs (although they are usually called *scripts*, but don't worry about the difference!) to control things connected to the Pi. But, unlike with Scratch, you can also write scripts that interact with other programs on the Pi, such as *Minecraft*. A free, cut down version of *Minecraft* is included in the Pi operating system. Again, you don't need to be a coding expert here. There are plenty of examples online of how to use Python to create and manipulate things in *Minecraft*.

You will need to know how to run a Python script, and which version of Python you have installed, at the very least. Of course, as your skills and knowledge develop, you will be able to tweak the scripts to do exactly what you want them to do. All you need to do is apply the computational thinking and programming concepts.

PROJECTS – HOW TO GET STARTED

The key to successfully using a Raspberry Pi project in the classroom is to have a real reason for doing it. In other words: use a Raspberry Pi to solve a problem, rather than generating a problem to solve using a Pi. You don't have to know everything before you start. Just start, get stuck and then find the answer online. Once you have finished one project, you will be more confident about starting another, perhaps more complicated, one.

A big tip is to build a project that you intend to keep. Think long term, as a demonstration piece. It doesn't have to sit in the classroom – as we've already mentioned, it can sit anywhere as long as you can remotely log in to it: for example, a weather station or a bird box camera.

These projects often take several hours, days or weeks from concept to realisation. You can scaffold this into meaningful lessons and long term projects with the children, but don't expect to conquer the world in one lesson – you will end up disillusioned and the Raspberry Pis will end up back in the cupboards. As one of our well known colleagues, Miles Berry from Roehampton, tweeted recently: "Wouldn't robotics be great if you could get rid of the fiddly bits?" Well, you can, if you don't take the projects to bits every lesson and you set them up to last.

An example of the sorts of projects we have been talking about is a robotic arm. Maplin, a national electronics firm, sell a robotic arm for under £40. It comes with software to control it that runs on Windows, but in its basic form is not programmable and is quite limited in scope.

Simon Marsden recounts his personal journey in setting up a Raspberry Pi project involving a robotic arm.

As soon as I saw this, I wanted to run it from a Raspberry Pi. Now, considering myself ahead of the game, I was sure that absolutely no one else had thought of this. I was, of course, wrong! There were already several projects that had managed to get the Raspberry Pi working with the arm using a PyUSB (Python to USB) module. Then, to put icing on the cake, I found a primary school that had used Scratch to talk to Python to talk to the arm. Again, we are not going to steal anyone else's thunder; if you want to have a go at this, you will find it online.

This Raspberry Pi robot arm setup was used several times as a demonstration learning tool with pupils, students and teachers, to good effect. However, as with all technology, it can have a habit of letting you down occasionally. The worst case of this for Simon was during an explanation of the new technologies in schools to a lecture theatre of trainee teachers.

This created a new problem for Simon to solve.

I didn't want to keep setting up the arm and the Raspberry Pi every time I wanted to demonstrate it. After much deliberation, I decided to set up an auto-answering videoconference into my office whilst remotely accessing the Raspberry Pi to control the robotic arm.

The videoconferencing bit can be done with the Raspberry Pi, but I used Skype for functionality and quality. You can set up Skype to auto-answer everyone in your address book. If you have only one person in your address book, no one else can get in. Just set up a separate account for the Raspberry Pi project.

There is some slightly more technical explanation of how you set up a machine that you can talk to remotely. This is all clearly outlined online, but your technical support will be doing this with your current machines, so they might be a starting point in your journey.

Once I had successfully set up my network connections, I had the ability to log in to the Raspberry Pi, and control the robot arm from anywhere with a connection to the Internet – no more risky failures of trying to set up a demonstration for a lecture. Failure, trying to impress someone with this in the evening in the middle of winter – it was pitch black in the office!

Another example is to get the Raspberry Pi to turn a lamp on. This proved to be very easy, as there is a company that sells a board that connects to the Raspberry Pi and allows you to use it to turn the light on with a Python script. The board talks to a remote plug similar to the remote plugs that you can buy from any electronics shop.

So, success again. Now I can log in to this Raspberry Pi from anywhere in the world, day or night, and control a robot in much the same way that you would control a robot in space – all for less than £100. Oh, and it is now June and this has been working since November! Not last November, but the one before! For a year and a half, without it failing or having to be rebooted. That is really impressive for a computer that costs so little! Have you got a machine that you haven't had to reboot in that time?

This one project can be used to demonstrate or scaffold activities using basic Scratch commands, networking, remote control, robotics, Python, security, remote access; I am sure you can think of some more.

Don't feel the Raspberry Pi is just tethered to a computing curriculum, though. A project can help towards the attainment targets of other areas, together with helping to develop skills such as resilience, resourcefulness, reflection and reciprocity

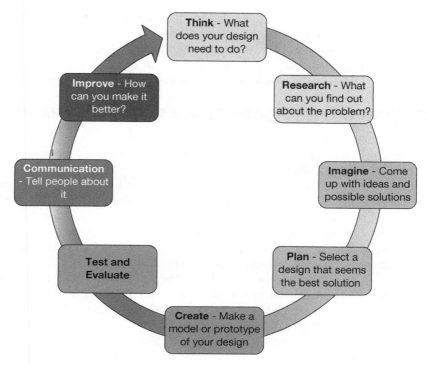

■ **Figure 12.1** Engineering design process

(amongst others). Any project needs to be approached as an iterative process, like following the engineering design process, as illustrated in Figure 12.1.

Let's imagine the problem of wanting to identify what local wildlife uses the school grounds as part of a science project. One problem they will encounter is how to know what comes when they're not around: time-lapse camera with Pi. . . DT controlling. . . Maths time. . . English reports. . .

In a classroom setting, we could envisage a number of such projects, visible either within the room or via a camera from another location around the school. The pupils can then access the projects via SSH (Secure Shell) and VNC (virtual network computing) to control and program them. As the devices are computers on the network, the technicians can manage the security and housekeeping of these machines in just the same way as any other machines are managed in the school network – backing them up, keeping them updated, deleting old files (all of which can be automated) etc.

The great thing about setting up projects like this is that they are reusable, and therefore are cost and time effective. The pupils can learn valuable concepts efficiently, and then apply these to their own projects as their skill and understanding develops.

Pupils' projects should similarly be thought of as long term. It's better to have one well-thought-out class project with the one remaining Raspberry Pi running over several weeks or months, rather than getting one LED light working in a one hour lesson on 20 Raspberry Pis!

Remember: everything that has been mentioned is easy to find out about on the Internet. It was never the intention to give a recipe book, but rather an approach to working with the Raspberry Pi (or micro:bit or Arduino for that matter). Good luck, and enjoy the Raspberry Pi journey – it is one well worth taking.

We'll just finish off the chapter by looking at some pointers for network connections.

NETWORKING AND COMMUNICATION WITH THE PI

You can network the Raspberry Pi with either wireless or cable. The latest model comes with wireless built in, but you can buy inexpensive dongles for older models that give comparable levels of connectivity. .

As with all operating systems, once the machine is connected, it can be logged into and managed remotely. You just need to know its IP address and to have some software that handles the communication. The IP address is usually assigned dynamically, whether you connect at home, in school, in a cafe etc., when you access the router to join the network. The problem here is that if you have a dynamic IP address, you won't know if it has changed since you last logged in to the machine.

There are two ways around this. The first is to assign a static IP address. This is the best if you are at home or school and are using the machine locally. If you wish to access the Pi over the Internet, your network manager can assign you a static IP that can be used locally but can also be accessed externally.

If you want to set up a machine at home to have access from the Internet, you have to either buy a static IP from your Internet service provider, or use a web based service that allows your machine to tell it what its current IP is at regular intervals. The service then points any requests to the IP address that it currently holds on the machine. Please note: you might have to tell your router to point things at the right machine if you are doing this at home, as most home router solutions turn off any server functionality by default. Each vendor will have clearly documented instructions for allowing external access to machines in your home.

So, setting up a machine to be accessed over the Internet does involve a few more steps, but within the same network you just need to know the IP address of the machine you want to talk to. In Linux, you would just type 'ifconfig' in the shell to find what it is.

SSH

There are several ways to talk to a machine when you know its IP address. SSH (Secure Shell) is one of these ways. There are many explanations of how to set up SSH Server on a Raspberry Pi (guess where). As you are probably gathering, it is not difficult to find the answers: you just have to know how to ask the right questions. SSH allows you to talk directly to the Raspberry Pi by command line (actually, most operating systems will allow you to SSH into them or from them). Once connected, it is just as if you were in the shell on the machine.

VNC

VNC (Virtual Network Computing) gives an updating image in the window of the connecting computer linked to the Raspberry Pi. For applications which require a more graphical approach, such as the robot arm project mentioned earlier, VNC is more suitable.

VNC is a great way to access the Raspberry Pi, because you don't need the Pi to be connected to a keyboard, mouse or monitor. The virtual network image is a replica of what you would see if the Pi was connected to a monitor, but just within a window on the computer you are using to access the Pi.

Deadheading the Pi

You might like to just set up a Pi by connecting it with a network lead into your laptop or desktop. This has the added advantage of not needing power, or a keyboard, mouse or monitor (like connecting over a network as outlined above). You will need to set up your machine to do this, and that is dependent on the host operating system – but this is widely explained online and not difficult. The Pi will need to have a static IP address and access via SSH or VNC as outlined above. You may want to set these up with the Pi attached to a monitor etc. in the first place.

NOTES

1 www.virtualbox.org
2 http://bellard.org/jslinux/

KIDS, CODING AND COMPUTATIONAL TINKERING

David Miller and Mark Horneff

INTRODUCTION

> I'm not enrolling my son in coding lessons because I want him to learn to code. Instead, I want to make sure he understands enough about the language of computing that he's in control of the machines that power our world. I want him to develop a critical literacy around computers so that he understands the logic behind all of the predictive algorithms that now auto-curate most of the information, knowledge, and media he consumes. I want him to have enough of an understanding of computers and the way they work that he can make informed and thoughtful choices about how he can best contribute to the world in which he lives.
>
> (Shapiro 2016)

Children are voracious consumers of all things digital: computers, internet, digital games, mobile technologies. They are completely at home in the digital world – digital natives living digital lives (Prensky 2001) – meeting, creating, communicating, sharing, within expanding and evolving digital environments. Although there still exists a significant divide between the digital haves and have nots, digital media is nonetheless becoming a ubiquitous feature of children's lives, and digital games a near integral part of their environments.

Fifty years ago, Seymour Papert had a vision that computers would become enmeshed in the very fabric of children's lives, and that children would ultimately program computers. Logo, his then revolutionary programming language, was the very first designed for children; with its famous turtle, Papert brought programming to millions of children. He spoke with remarkable prescience about children using computers as instruments for learning, for enhancing creativity and for fostering thinking skills. He even described (Papert 1980) how children would program computers to control robots, to compose music and to design games, suggesting that, through the process of programming, and debugging their code, children would come to reflect more deeply on their own thinking and digital creativity (Kolodner et al. 2004).

While one aspect of Papert's vision has become all too real – the ubiquity of digital media, and their increasing use in almost every aspect of our lives from early childhood onwards – the more significant thrust of his vision fell away. Despite an early excitement around children learning to code, the enthusiasm for Logo (and the turtle) would not last. Ironically, the demise of children coding corresponded to the rise in schools of ICT – Information and Communication Technology. Rather than instruments for making and creating as Papert had envisioned, computers came to be seen as machines for accessing information, for consuming and manipulating data. In the process, programming became a limited interest activity for 'techies', more appealing to boys than to girls.

Much time has been lost. The shift away from children learning to code meant whole generations of kids growing up to be passive consumers of technology rather than digital creators. There seemed to be little encouragement in schools to transition young people from being passive consumers of new media to becoming innovative thinkers, doers and makers.

Thankfully, decades later, Papert's vision has sparked into life once more. With the recognition of problem solving and thinking skills as key aptitudes of the twenty-first-century learner, the potential of programming to support computational thinking skills has gained increasing traction in the intervening decades. And from the simple textual programming languages of the 1960s and 1970s, there has been an explosion of new technologies that make use of graphical, child-friendly user interfaces. Programs such as Scratch allow drag-and-drop picture-based programming commands on a computer or mobile phone screen, thereby giving children, even very young children, their first experience of coding to create mini-animations or games.

But what has driven this shift? There has clearly been an economic imperative. Jobs requiring coding skills continue to outnumber the graduates who can fill these posts. Code.org, the US non-profit that has been instrumental in pushing the coding agenda globally, regularly updates its website with information on the widening skills gap. And there have been numerous reports coming out of the UK that equally point up the detriment to economies of not equipping young people for the digital age. Maggie Philbin, in her report "Digital Skills for Tomorrow's World",[1] stated the case clearly: "We have to make sure everyone in the UK is equipped for the digital revolution. Not just a fortunate few." That this needs saying 50 years after Papert is an indication of just how far we have yet to go, but the report does valuably underscore the need for collective action to "change perception, build confidence and demonstrate the value of collectively nurturing a truly digital generation". The conclusion? That without such common purpose, we will stifle our own potential, fail our young people and choke economic growth.

However, the economic argument is only one driver of the move towards children learning to code. Another significant influence on coding going mainstream has come from the Maker Movement.[2] At the 2014 National Day of Making, President Obama proclaimed, "I am calling on people across the country to join us in sparking creativity and encouraging invention in their communities." New open source and entry level hardware projects, such as 3D printers, Arduino microcontrollers, the Raspberry Pi and the BBC micro:bit, are being invented at an unprecedented rate, and children, families and teachers around the world are being drawn to these exciting new creative technologies. Over the last five years, the Maker Movement (and its younger sibling, the Hackathon) has built an energetic community of global, and collaborative, problem-solvers. Libraries, museums, after-school clubs, non-profit and independent for-profit alike have all become impromptu makerspaces and crucibles for creativity and communal endeavour.

This enthusiasm for the creative potential of new technologies is having its impact on the educational landscape. However, despite the increasing visibility of these essentially DIY movements, and the general accessibility of computers inside and outside the classroom, most children still use their (increasingly mobile) devices to consume commercial media. So, at the school level, how do teachers help children to be creative with the technologies that have become so integral to their lives? How do we develop the computational literacy that will not only help them to succeed in the work environments of the future, but also further their social, emotional and intellectual well-being?

COMPUTATIONAL THINKING

There has been much discussion about computational thinking since Professor Jeannette Wing coined the term in 2006. In a short essay for *Communications of the Association for Computing Machinery*, Wing defined computational thinking as "solving problems, designing systems, and understanding human behavior, by drawing on the concepts fundamental to computer science". She went on: "Computational thinking includes a range of mental tools that reflect the breadth of the field of computer science" (Wing 2006). Wing's essay has prompted a range of responses over the years, and the definition of computational thinking has broadened. Google's online resource Exploring Computational Thinking defines it as "a problem solving process that includes a number of characteristics, such as logically ordering and analyzing data and creating solutions using a series of ordered steps (or algorithms), and dispositions, such as the ability to confidently deal with complexity and open-ended problems".[3] It goes on to say that, beyond computer science, computational thinking is now understood as supporting problem-solving across all disciplines, including maths, science and the humanities. Pupils who learn computational thinking across the curriculum will begin to see a relationship not only between subjects, but between school and life beyond the classroom. Indeed, computational thinking has become the guiding principle in how schools approach the teaching of computer science.

This leads neatly back to Papert. For him, the goal was "to use computational thinking to forge ideas". In other words, to decouple it from code. Learning, Papert says, is "much more related to love, than to logic". In an interview with Dan Schwartz,[4] he said, "Anyone who has witnessed a toddler using a computer has probably experienced a sense of awe at that child's facility with what for adults can be an infinitely frustrating gadget." He went on: "It's one thing for a child to play a computer game; it's another thing altogether for a child to build his or her own game."

And this, according to Papert, is where the computer's impact lies as a medium of learning. It drives and broadens children's natural curiosity to explore and experiment, to build and imagine, to reason and evaluate. For Papert, learning about computer science should be based on projects that have relevance for the learner; the learning should have a social and cultural context that resonates; learning to code, like learning to write, becomes meaningful and authentic when it increases a pupil's ability to contribute creatively, to express themselves and share within their communities: school, home, friends, clubs.

Among these purposeful, relevant social contexts is the computer game. Over recent years, there has been a significant move towards the acceptance of digital games for learning in school and other academic settings. For example, at the 2013 White House Science Fair, a computer game designed by a middle school pupil won first place out of many other school STEM projects (Curtin 2013). The 13-year-old's game, *The Dark Labyrinth*, was coded on Kodu, a free tool provided by Microsoft that enables kids to build their own video games. Later in the chapter, we shall to explore how storytelling blended with computer games can be a highly motivating activity for children learning programming skills.

The beauty of the visually appealing interfaces in Kodu, Scratch and Alice, for example, is that they bring a child-like authenticity and emotional resonance to what for children is something abstract and unrelatable. For example, Scratch, the drag-and-drop programming language developed at MIT Media Lab, provides blocks arranged by colour based on their function. This encourages pupils to associate similar programming blocks with each other, and, since the blocks are shaped like jigsaw pieces, only syntactically logical blocks can fit together. Programming becomes something physical and aesthetic, concrete rather than merely abstract. This system also neatly eases the pain of debugging. As Papert (1980) pointed out in *Mindstorms*, modular form representation of a process makes it easier to debug.

STARTING FROM SCRATCH (AND LOGO)

As its name suggests, Scratch was inspired by music – in particular, the popular practice among DJs of creating percussive or rhythmical sound effects when making and remixing tracks. In aligning their new programming language with youth culture, the originators at MIT Media Lab heralded their determination that Scratch would draw on the spirit and culture of the young. Like Kodu, Scratch was designed to provide an entry level to computer programming that would allow players to create graphics, games, animations and simulations. Such possibilities marked a shift in focus from maths and science towards self-expression and creativity, thereby significantly broadening the appeal of programming as a playfully creative endeavour.

Because of the simplicity of the interface, and because it requires only the dexterity to use a mouse, even very young children can use Scratch to create their own games and animations. Importantly, children may also use their own, or digitally manipulated, images in the creation of their 'programmed' artefacts. This ability to personalise the experience is a key aspect of the program's appeal. By drawing on children's interests and aesthetic preferences, created artefacts become invested with personal meaning and emotional significance. And with emotion comes the desire to share – for their creation to be valued by peers and teachers.

Like Logo before it, Scratch makes an object the focus of learning – from turtle to orange cat. However, whereas Logo is syntax-based, Scratch offers learners the LEGO-like experience of assembling building bricks of code, in the process making programming more child-accessible. What both achieve is that, in learning to code (with input and support from teachers, parents and peers), children learn to assimilate new ideas and concepts, to articulate processes and procedures, to think about how they learn.

In interacting with a computer, children are 'writing' commands to move graphical ('physical') objects, rather than abstractly manipulating number arrays or symbols. Programming the computer means programming the turtle or cat. Having, as Papert (1980) put it, an "object-to-think-with" (an object-to-tinker-with) means that children are encouraged to move from a simple view of right and wrong, to seeing their program as something to be worked on, to be fixed, in the same way that they might fix a collapsed sandcastle, or rebuild a broken LEGO fortress. Having something tangible to program also means that the child is more likely to see their learning as relevant, rooted and purposeful. An object in the physical or digital world helps a child identify with what's being learned, and therefore the object takes on a personal and cultural resonance, as well as a social and physical presence too.

LEARNING TO CODE, LEARNING TO CREATE

Making and sharing online are as much about collaboration and social skills as they are about technical proficiency. As such, learning to program in today's classroom is seen as a key literacy skill rather than an esoteric dark art! The question is, how do teachers create new and innovative contexts for creative coding? How do they leverage the current curriculum to create authentic opportunities for creative collaboration?

While instructional software has long been a part of a teacher's armoury, video games, as has previously been noted, have only recently come to be seen as rich learning environments in their own right. Recent research exploring the outcomes of learning game design showed that through these tasks learners were able to engage in and learn programming. For example, using GameMaker, and building on the work of Papert and others, Baytak and Land (2010) conducted an investigation into how children designed computer games as artefacts that reflected their understanding of health and nutrition concepts. The study found that in the process of programming their own computer games, children became "active participants and problem solvers". They also found that collaboration was a key element in the learning process and that the children actively shared their designs and helped one another, thereby taking ownership of their own learning. Collaboration wasn't just limited to design aspects, however. Questions over curricular content and peer testing were all part of the iterative learning process. Thus, as Rieber et al. (1998) put it, "Children become deeply invested in their learning when they feel empowered to choose what they learn and the ways in which they learn."

In another study by Kafai (2006), a class of ten-year-old children designed and programmed their own fraction games in Logo. They met every day to design games that would teach fractions to a group of younger pupils in their school. Over a period of six months, the children created their own characters, storylines, game themes and interactions. Although there was no great difference between boys and girls as to the quality of the games, there were, as might be expected, significant gender differences in design aspects around feedback, characters, game goals and context. Boys tended towards fantasy, lots of characters and punishment for wrong answers, whereas girls opted for fewer characters, an absence of punishment, and adventure over fantasy. In their programming of interactions and animations, boys and girls were able to draw on their own preferences for the digital games and stories that they played, or were drawn to, in their leisure time.

As Kafai (2006) points out, what's important about these learning experiences is that the learner is involved in the design decisions and develops technological fluency through the process of designing and making. "Just as fluency in language means much more than knowing facts about the language, technological fluency involves not only knowing how to use new technological tools but also knowing how to make things of significance with those tools and most important, develop new ways of thinking based on use of those tools." In this way, activities around making games for learning, as opposed to playing games for learning, encourages young gamers to be producers, not merely consumers, of digital artefacts. In creating an artefact to solve a real-world problem, children are encouraged to think, and solve, computationally.

And it's not just limited to STEM subjects. A project by Burke and Kafai (2010) that combined storytelling and programming investigated how writing computer programs could help children develop their storytelling and creative writing abilities. Starting from the premise that "writing to program can also serve as programming to write", the study looked at the shared features of programming and storytelling: sequence, structure, and precision in expression. Using Scratch, children created their own digital stories as a way to understand the process of expanding an idea into a conventional story arc. Each of the digital stories was created through sequentially based, object-oriented programming. The program 'objects' were the stories' sprites, or characters, and a variety of background 'sets'. Each had specific functions and procedures attached, which contributed to a clear storyline.

In the initial stages of the project, the researchers discovered that storytelling was a very effective way to introduce programming to children precisely because it didn't focus on the technical components of the software, or on the programming elements. Instead, the key was starting with features of storytelling – notions of 'setting', 'climax', 'character', 'antagonist', 'protagonist' – that the children were already familiar with from English and Language Arts classes. Once the children's creativity was firmly anchored to storytelling, rather than 'learning to program', gradually over time, the children grew more confident about developing storylines to incorporate programming aspects such as debugging scripts and integrating coding sequences. As the programming elements began to feature more prominently, they became the narrative driver for the children, but also caused some difficulties in the creative process. Tinkering with code predictably proved more challenging than playing around with storyline! Children soon discovered that programming, like writing, is an iterative process, involving tinkering and revision. This was a very positive experience of creative symbiosis between a programming language and the language of storytelling, where, echoing Papert, the object-to-think-with was the story. Having a narrative, rather than a purely technical, reason to debug codes and test new scripts proved a highly motivating way to learn programming. By the end of this project, the researchers reported that 90 per cent of the children felt they knew more about programming.

Similarly, a study by Kelleher and Pausch (2007) that used Storytelling Alice found that storytelling, and the need for multiple scenes, was a natural way to explore, and motivate, pupils' use of methods. For example, some characters' actions (like jumping through a window) required pupils to use methods that take parameters. In others, repeated actions like petting a dog, or bouncing a ball, involve repeating motions that naturally motivated the use of loops. Pupils discovered that certain characters could have methods which others didn't: for example, the character of a teacher could have a reprimand method, which a pupil character wouldn't! Using storytelling as the driver for learning to program, the study found that 87 per cent created a program with multiple methods; and, in their first two hours of programming, several were using loops and/or creating methods that take parameters.

FROM BLOCK-BASED TO TEXT-BASED PROGRAMMING

So, where programs like Scratch promote an understanding of programming logic, and support self-directed learning by encouraging users to tinker with commands without failing or breaking the results, and programs like Alice provide 3D storytelling capability with draggable widgets representing character behaviours, what about code learning environments where the inputs are text-based, rather than block-based? What are the impacts on learners and learning when the blocks are removed, and the focus moves from programming logic to programming syntax? How should pupils be taught to program in a way that they learn the processes of problem-solving inherent to programming?

Many, if not most, non-specialist teachers find text-based programming difficult. From the intuition and logic of building blocks and drag-and-drop, suddenly pupils (and teachers) come up against the syntactic rules of Python or JavaScript. It's like going from painting or drawing a scene to having to describe it using perfectly written English. However, teachers discover that through blending problem-solving with teaching methodologies derived from other subjects, they can help their pupils make the transition from graphical to text-based programming.

For example, let's look at the learning of language and literacy skills as a route to text-based programming (Dorling and White 2015). Teachers, particularly at primary level, spend much time developing children's understanding of how language works. From word-level awareness – spelling patterns, the relationships between sounds and symbols – to sentence-level skills, where learners create meaningful contexts out of word-level understanding, children come to understand the unique forms and rules of writing. Two broad areas of competency are worked on: writing mechanics and writing process. Writing mechanics involve everything from physically producing text to spelling correctly and using accurate grammar, and appropriate syntax and punctuation. Writing process involves planning, constructing and editing text. Together these approaches reinforce and develop pupils' abilities in language and literacy. Many of these skills and approaches can be successfully transferred to the teaching of text-based programming languages.

For example, starting with a block-based programming environment like Scratch, because it encodes the grammar of the language into the individual blocks through the name, shape and colour, pupils can be encouraged to talk through or translate in writing what each block is contributing to the overall program. Conversely, they might match code blocks with corresponding text-based programming concepts and excerpts of code. Indeed, in a recent study, pupils declared block-based representation as closer to English than its text-based counterpart. One pupil observed, "With blocks, it's in English, it's like pretty, like, more easier to understand and read." Another highlighted the difference, saying: "Java is not in English, it's in Java language, and the blocks are in English, it's easier to understand." A third pupil explained: "[the blocks] are basically a translation of what [the JavaScript] is doing, in, I guess, English for lack of better words. It is describing what [the JavaScript] is doing, but it's describing it in an English form. . . like a conversion" (Weintrop and Wilensky 2015).

However, a major drawback with the use of block-based programming is its perceived lack of authenticity. Many pupils don't see these graphical interfaces as anything like how they would code in a real-world situation. While they recognise Scratch and similar programs as useful introductory tools, many are keen to develop skills that can be used beyond the classroom, for example in future careers or further computer science coursework.

Our own Studio, Kuato Studios, developed a game which addressed the issue of pupils wishing to code using a real programming language, JavaScript. In *Code Warriors*, pupils see their code at all times, rather than having it encoded into graphical blocks. The game takes a chess-like mechanic, and gives pupils two different views. One, the code editor view, is where pupils plan and execute their moves. The other is the arena view, where pupils watch their, and their opponents', code play out. Depending on how they have coded their robots, they will see their Code Warriors move across atmospheric arenas taking out enemy robots, or moving toward their opponents' core to delete it – the ultimate aim of the game. In the arena view, pupils see an animation of their coded algorithms running in the background, so that the code and its execution are visible at the same time. Like a story, pupils can 'read' their code as it plays out in dramatic narrative fashion!

Although it is not a full text-based programming environment, pupils nonetheless author small snippets of code to define the behaviour of their robots. In the code editor view, they can tinker, undo and debug, paying all due attention to the rules of both syntax *and* logic. Whereas in a block-based program, pupils won't have to worry about parentheses, and brackets, in *Code Warriors*, pupils must pay attention to these elements. A misplaced comma or semicolon means their script won't execute. As in real programming environments, we included an autocomplete function to assist pupils with syntax, and an easily browsed small library of valid commands. And where a bug exists in a specific line of code, the line will turn red. It's up to the pupil to find and correct the bug.

Because *Code Warriors* is an asynchronous multi-player game, pupils can be both competitor and collaborator. In testing the game in schools, we discovered that many pupils chose to work in pairs, often with their opponents! In this way, pupils supported each other's learning, demonstrating how to solve a particular challenge, or how to accomplish a specific game task. Although not solving real-world problems, pupils felt that they were programming, and therefore creating, the game they were playing. The next step would be for them to create and code new challenges, or develop existing challenges, using existing game assets.

Creating new games, and modifying existing games, has been taken a step further by the hyper-popular *Minecraft*, a sandbox game that uses three-dimensional textured cubes in a variety of gameplay modes: survival, creative and adventure modes. Players can build alone or together on a shared server, through exploring, gathering resources and crafting. Like *Code Warriors*, because of the immersive nature of the game, the player has a real sense of presence in the game world. Recently, *Minecraft* has been extended and enhanced using 'mods' ('modifications') – additional chunks of code that are added to the game. ScriptCraft and LearnToMod are examples of mods that allow players to program in JavaScript from within the game. Using simple JavaScript statements, players can extend the game in interesting ways – add new objects, change game behaviours, create mini-games and challenges.

TANGIBLE COMPUTING – CUDDLY CODING

Although the idea of tangible computing has been around since the 1970s or earlier, it is a rapidly developing space that shows significant potential for helping young children learn to program. Removing the need for keyboard and mouse, and obviating the necessity for time spent in front of a screen, tangible computing encourages children to learn through interacting with physical objects – robots, cubes, spheres, toys. Bringing computer programming into the physical world as a collaborative creative activity has also helped bridge the gap between abstract computation and the learning abilities, and collaborative instincts, of children.

Researchers are only beginning to explore the exciting possibilities of programming in and with the physical world. However, let's look at some of the more significant games and languages. And where better to begin than with Papert? It was his conviction that programming should be brought into children's physical worlds that led to the creation of the Logo turtle, and Logo programming language. Papert's original turtle was a robot the size of a basketball and shaped like a dome. In response to simple Logo commands, the 'turtle' would move FORWARD, BACKWARD, LEFT and RIGHT across the floor. Fitted with a pen, and placed on a large sheet of paper, the turtle could be programmed to draw pictures. Children learned to 'teach' the turtle to draw basic shapes: triangles, squares, circles, even letters.

Fast forward to the present day, and there is a growing industry around computers embedded into plush toys, programmable LEGO bricks that can sense environment and control motors, spherical robots that can be programmed with mobile phones.

Let's look first at programmable plush toys, and a project called Plushbot, described by its originators, Huang and Eisenberg, as "a software system that enables children to design and create plush toys incorporating computational elements (microprocessor, sensors, and actuators)" (Huang and Eisenberg 2011). Plushbot takes soft materials like stuffing and felt, and adds robotic parts including the popular LilyPad Arduino microcontrollers, conductive thread, a battery and various sensors to create soft toys that can be programmed to play music, change colour (via LED lights) and move. Although the LilyPad Arduino is usually programmed using standard Arduino language, the designers of Plushbot wanted to provide a low threshold for beginners, and so employed Modkit, a visual programming environment that, like Scratch, makes use of drag-and-drop 'blocks' of code to control and execute the desired behaviours of sensors and components. In playing and making with Plushbot, children are not only engaging with, tinkering with, computational concepts and practices, they are also learning about engineering – designing functional circuits by connecting alligator clips to batteries, switches and LEDs for example – and learning about handicrafts by knotting thread ends and sewing these to fabric. Crafting, engineering and computing: a marriage of learning domains across a range of media and conditions. Although still in its early stages of development, Plushbot suggests a whole new direction for inspiring children in making and coding. It is only a matter of time before there emerges a Plushbot community, sharing creations online, offering tutorials and technical support, and leveraging the web to create Plushbot maker spaces for similarly minded creators and crafters. It is worth noting that in the years since MIT Media Lab launched its Scratch programming language and online community in 2007, literally millions of projects have been shared on the Scratch website by children from eight years and upwards, with thousands of new projects added each day.

Another, less cuddly but no less inspiring, blend of programming and real-world play is in robotics, a playful and tangible way for children to engage simultaneously with technology and engineering concepts. Robotics kits like LEGO Mindstorms help children develop a deeper understanding of mathematical concepts such as number, size and shape in much the same way that they do using traditional materials like pattern blocks, beads and balls (Resnick, 2013). With its sensors, mechanisms and LEGO bricks, it can be used to build robots, interactive houses, and even animate characters from the *Star Wars* franchise. Equally, robotics activities and manipulatives encourage the development of fine motor skills and hand-eye coordination while simultaneously fostering collaborative teamwork (Lee et al., 2013).

For younger children, a curriculum called Tangible K, being developed at Tufts University, is exploring robotics as a tool to engage children in developing computational thinking and learning about the engineering design process (Bers 2010). Instead of a mouse and a keyboard, children aged between 4 and 7 build their programs using connectable wooden blocks. A camera takes a picture of the labelled blocks and the program is then downloaded into a robotic artefact constructed by the child using a LEGO-based robotic construction kit. This approach offers an opportunity to understand and separate the intellectual act of computer programming from modern graphical user interfaces and complex mechanical constructions. In turn, it provides a means to better understand the developmental capabilities of young children with respect to computer programming and robotics.

CONCLUSION

We have come a long way from the opening paragraph of this chapter, in which an interested dad declared that he wanted his child to understand enough about the language of computing to ensure they were more in control of the machines that power our world. We hope we have illustrated how many and varied are the routes to that understanding, from the graphical education environments like Scratch and Kodu, to text-based games like *Code Warriors* and *Minecraft*, to the possibilities offered by plush toys and robotics, and from storytelling to construction kits. What all routes share is active participation in learning – be it at school, attending code clubs, at home with friends, with Mum and Dad at the kitchen table – and with that active participation, the inherent desire in all children to play, create and share. Anyone designing learning experiences that teach computational thinking, or delivering programmes that teach coding skills to young people, must ensure that participation, collaboration, creativity and sharing are at the heart of the experience. Equally, the learning narrative must be free of gender bias. For too long, computer science has been accompanied by narratives around nerds or superhero geeks. The ability to think computationally, and to design and create digital artefacts, is vital for *all* children growing up in this digitally powered world. While not all children will go on to become computer programmers, we will at least have helped them to make informed and thoughtful choices about how best they can contribute to the world in which they live.

NOTES

1 "Digital Skills for Tomorrow's World", the independent report of the UK Digital Skills Taskforce 2014.
2 Often heralded as a new industrial revolution – combining, in community settings, the spirit of old school do-it-yourself with modern technologies.
3 https://www.google.com/edu/resources/programs/exploring-computational-thinking/
4 Ghost in the machine: Seymour Papert on how computers fundamentally change the way kids learn, http://www.papert.org/articles/GhostInTheMachine.html.

REFERENCES

Baytak, A. and Land, S. M. (2010). A case study of educational game design by kids and for kids. *Procedia Social and Behavioral Sciences, 2*, 5242–5246.
Bers, M. U. (2010). The TangibleK robotics program: Applied computational thinking for young children. *Early Childhood Research and Practice, 12(2)*, 1–20.
Burke, Q. and Kafai, Y. B. (2010). Programming & storytelling: Opportunities for learning about coding & composition *Proceedings of the 9th International Conference on Interaction Design and Children*.

Curtin, C. (2013). Young Kodu designer showcases at 2013 White House Science Fair. Microsoft. Accessed from https://blogs.microsoft.com/firehose/2013/04/24/young-kodu-designer-showcases-at-2013-white-house-science-fair.

Dorling, M. and White, D. (2015). Scratch: a way to Logo and Python. 46th SIGCSE (Special Interest Group on Computer Science Education) Technical Symposium, Kansas City, Missouri. Accessed from http://ispython.com/wp/wp-content/uploads/2014/11/Asigsce17_titled.pdf.

Huang, Y. and Eisenberg, M. (2011). Plushbot: An application for the design of programmable, interactive stuffed toys. In Tangible, Embedded, and Embodied Interaction conference (TEI 2011), 22–26 January, Funchal, Portugal, pp. 257–260. Accessed from http://l3d.cs.colorado.edu/~ctg/pubs/TEI11PlushBot.pdf.

Kafai, Y. B. (2006). Playing and making games for learning: Instructionist and constructionist perspectives for game studies. *Games and Culture, 1(1)*, 36–40.

Kelleher, C. and Pausch, R. (2007). Using storytelling to motivate programming, *Communications of the ACM, 50(7)*, 59–64.

Kolodner, J. L., Owensby, J. N. and Guzdial, M. (2004). Case-based learning aids. In D. H. Jonassen (Ed.), *Handbook of research for educational communications and technology* (2nd ed., pp. 829–862). Mahwah, NJ: Lawrence Erlbaum Associates Inc.

Lee, K., Sullivan, A. and Bers, M. U. (2013). Collaboration by design: Using robotics to foster social interaction in kindergarten. *Computers in the Schools, 30(3)*, 271–281.

Papert, S. (1980). *Mindstorms: Children, computers, and powerful ideas.* New York: Basic Books.

Prensky, M. (2001). Digital natives, digital immigrants. *On the Horizon, 9(5)*, 1–6.

Resnick, M. (2013). Learn to code, code to learn. EdSurge, May. Accessed from https://www.edsurge.com/news/2013-05-08-learn-to-code-code-to-learn.

Rieber, L. P., Luke, N. and Smith, J. (1998). Project KID designer: Constructivism at work through play. *Meridian: A Middle School Computer Technologies Journal, 1(1)*, 1–9.

Shapiro, J. (2016). President Obama wants every kid to learn coding – for all the wrong reasons. *Forbes*, 31 January.

Weintrop, D. and Wilensky, U. (2015). To block or not to block, that is the question: Students' perceptions of blocks-based programming. Interaction Design and Children (IDC), 21–25 June, Medford, Mass. Accessed from https://pdfs.semanticscholar.org/1f60/cf1dc9f caf2df8467cb76acf7e837e084916.pdf.

Wing, J. (2006). Computational thinking. *Communications of the ACM, 49(3)*, 33–35.

COLLABORATIVE CODER POETS

Bill Liao

CODING IS A LANGUAGE SKILL

The reason why the instructions we give computers are called languages is because they are actual languages with which we as humans can "speak" to computers. All mainstream coding languages are, in a way, dialects of American English; and, just like in English, it is vital to learn how to use the tools of language to construct new and elegantly efficient, impactful material.

English and even creative writing classes the world over have an unhealthy focus on analysis of the moods and intentions of historical authors. It would be better to have a powerful focus on the figures of rhetoric used to deliver such amazing writing as is found in *Hamlet* than to try to analyse Shakespeare's view of equality. For, with a grasp of the former, one can create new and impactful rhetoric that might sway the modern world towards a joyously just equality for all.

In all subjects it is important for young people to feel comfortable in developing a set of creative tools that allow them to explore new ideas in an imaginative manner.

■ **Figure 14.1** CoderDojo – amazing projects

Source: Paul Kelly at Docklands Photo Agency.

In creative writing, those tools are the figures of Rhetoric. In coding, those tools are not so easily formalised in one phrase. Coding languages are relatively new and rely heavily on English mental construction. There are also numerous languages for different tasks, each with its own peculiar syntactical quirks, and also open source resources (see Appendix 2).

While it is possible to create an app for an iPhone in JavaScript, it is not nearly as useful to do so as it is in Apple's new programming language Swift, so a focus for learning code must be on equipping the learner for efficient discovery. Here, coding departs from all other language skills in that the entire canon of function can be found in various forms and forums online. There are no dusty tomes to elucidate the proper use of "{}" in C, and no plays in the park to give a view on the best choices of compilers or interpreters. The ability to search, asking the right questions, online; the ability to operate a search engine collaboratively; the ability to sleuth out your own answers and then share them – these are vital in finding and using the tools of construction of code.

CREATIVITY IN SCHOOL

That construction is of little import if there is no stimulation of the other great meaning of "creative": to bring forth substance from the void – to imagine otherwise. To sweat out the new form of inspiration wherever you find it, and to think divergently. Sir Ken Robinson demonstrated in his beautiful RSA (Royal Society of Arts) animate talk[1] that schools cause a significant reduction in divergent thinking over time.

It is fairly obvious that much of the school context is necessitated by the need to keep pupils' attention on the teacher. This continual submission to control often has a nasty side-effect in that it punishes divergent thinking. Thus creativity suffers. In CoderDojo, there are no teachers, and thus the learner must seek self-motivation.

There is one rule for learners – "be cool" – and so there is the ability to be highly divergent and unrestricted in the context. Subtle cues are used to inspire the desired emergent phenomenon of learning through creativity and collaboration. These can be found in the CoderDojo *Ethos, Culture, Happiness and Outcomes* manual.[2]

All forms of art and creativity in the purely cultural sense are encouraged in CoderDojo, as a way of further stimulating divergent and creative thinking. It is a shame that in many schools such endeavours are now often purely elective. This would be less dissatisfying were it not for the loss of efficiency in many schools of engendering proficiency in maths and science at the same time as relegating art.

Overall, it can be reasonably argued that humans learn more outside school than they do inside. Even doctorates for professions such as medicine and law cannot deliver real-world experience. They do, though, try to ensure that the practitioners they produce are of an acceptable standard to entrust the public to, with an overwhelming majority of good results. Engineering graduates do better than creative lay-people at construction. It is a very good thing that structural engineers routinely outperform kindergarteners at the Marshmallow Challenge.[3]

It should also be apparent that creative disciplines need a method of inspiring creativity. Language learning that does not rely on traditional academic school methods or infrastructure is thus free to become more expansive and encouraging, and above all it can be made to cause self-directed behaviour. What is not commonly understood is that the design of the interaction, if implemented correctly, can result in simple rules that allow creative learning to be an unrestricted emergent phenomenon.

■ **Figure 14.2** Supporting pupils

Source: Paul Kelly at Docklands Photo Agency.

Older and more traditional didactic and rote-learning models do not allow for such creative output and creative and collaborative learning.

The traditional academic model has some contextual cornerstones that are very difficult to adapt to the world of young people learning code.

"Pedagogy" is a term that has a wholly inconsistent etymology for a modern mind. It comes from *pedagogue*, Latin from Greek *paidagōgos*, denoting a slave who accompanied a male child to school. Even without the odious connotations of sexism and slavery, the term means "to lead" and therefore for the pupil to be led.

CODERDOJO MENTORSHIP

There is a reason why CoderDojo resists the urge to have a pedagogy and to eschew the labels of "pupil" or "teacher", and it is to empower the learner through supportive mentorship. "Mentor" comes to us from a very different place in Greek mythology: *Mentōr* was the name of the great adviser of the young Telemachus in Homer's *Odyssey*, and was not in charge of Telemachus as much as in support of him.

CoderDojo avoids standardised testing in favour of medals of achievement awarded by peers rather than any other external authority. The achievement of badges of merit is highly motivational to learners and thus a useful artifice. The rating of learners against each other is motivational for only a select few, and so to serve the greater good it is best to allow for achievement to be recognised in different structures. CoderDojo does not seek to be a certification body – it rather seeks to have learners generate a portfolio of excellent work, which should allow their prowess to be self-evident.

Academia tends to subtly punish failure and to generate fear around failing. Here it is useful to make a distinction between merely getting something wrong and not putting sufficient effort into the skills that might enable one to get it right. The first is to be celebrated, as to learn, in coding especially, it is imperative to make mistakes and correct them. Debugging code is thus both inevitable and essential. In the martial art of Kendo, to which the "Dojo" component of "CoderDojo" has been ascribed – a Kendo Dojo is a "temple of learning", and Kendo has been freely taught globally for over 800 years – there is a lovely series of actions, or "Kata", that all contain deliberate errors or "teaching mistakes" from which a young learner can quickly discern the proper form by correcting the master. Debugging is a way of life to be celebrated, dismal though it may feel at the time, rather than denigrated, as is so often the case with mistakes in a purely academic setting.

This leads us to a further incongruity between learning to code and the traditional methods. All great coders stand on the shoulders of those who went before them, and thus, through the magic of open source, plagiarism (preferably with attribution in the comments, and who has time to make such comments?) is rife in the coding world. While there can be great merit in understanding a principle through recoding something from scratch, there is speedier efficacy in cutting and pasting code wholesale to achieve a desired outcome.

There is just not the kind of taboo around this that there is in other settings – it is often the best, if not only, way to make something that works. It is important too to foster the idea of sharing what you have wrought so that others may use it. Plagiarism in coding is almost indistinguishable from open source – indeed while failure to attribute may still be a sin in coding, it really is a forgivable one, and more so if you are also allowing your code to be used at will.

Coding is a discipline that does not match any current academic pedagogy well. Any sufficiently great artefact that is coded is also likely to have been written collaboratively, with perhaps large self-organising groups using modern collaborative tools. This cooperation needs to be fostered early if it is to thrive, and two of the traditional control aspects of the education classroom are just not equipped to handle this: silence and lectures. It is almost impossible to collaborate in silence, and so CoderDojos are noisy places a lot of the time. If there is quiet, it is usually because a problem is particularly interesting, or because the Dojos have been structured to require a quieter environment for that particular problem solving activity.

Lecturing and lectures do occur in some CoderDojos, and the practice is not strongly encouraged. For pure efficacy, many Dojos have a newbie table, where a young ninja mentor (a club member who has been involved with CoderDojo for several months/years) might hold sway for 20 minutes or so, to get newcomers over the initial state of complete bewilderment that so often afflicts humans when faced with new technology. This is more about allowing young new learners to be able to fit in, rather than to gain a deep insight into a particular topic. The context of the master lecturing from the lectern and illustrating with a whiteboard is cumbersome. Imagine trying to learn a physical martial art from a lecture and diagram – to produce collaborative coders with the highest levels of creative skills in coding languages, and also possessed of economy of expression in these languages, requires immersive involvement. The goal is *creative language*, economically expressed – this is the definition of poetry, and, as collaboration, not lecturing, is the *sine qua non* of CoderDojo, thus can produce generations of collaborative coder poets.

NERFED CODING LANGUAGES

Much has been made of the various languages that purport to make coding easier for young people to learn using colourful and visual tools. There is a term in the video gaming industry whose etymology refers to a foam ball that was popular in the seventies and is now usually found in the form of a dart-shaped bullet fired by a Nerf gun, often seen in automated USB form on the desks of computer programmers who also moonlight as warriors in late-night video gaming sessions. When a particularly overpowering weapon is discovered, in multi-player versions of these games, the game developer will often seek to overcome the imbalance caused by such weapons through the simple expedient of reducing their power to render them less harmful. This much-hated practice has been dubbed "nerfing", and such dulled weapons are said to have been "nerfed".

Ultimately, such nerfed artefacts prove themselves to be of limited utility, no matter how easy they may be to adopt or how many pretty colours they may display. With such nerfed coding languages designed for kids, the school system can give kids a taste of what is possible in coding, because no expertise is needed to sit them down in front of a game-like environment and have them dabble. This leads to a false sense of progress and, worse, is patronising to the young learner. We regularly witness young learners tackling extremely dry material in learning to code in real development environments, not needing to be spoonfed and kept safe.

Young learners generally cannot build anything with deep utility for others, which is actually powerful, using nerfed tools. We are looking with interest, though, at the new initiative from Apple that combines very easy-to-understand animation with their Swift programming language, where it is actually possible to export the results of a coding session in the nerfed environment back into Xcode and thereby create a real app for general use or even for sale on the app store.

Nerfed tools only go so far, and are more reassuring to the teachers than they are able to keep a young learner interested enough to develop an actual passion for coding. Powerful action begets passion, not the inverse, and so for powerful actions that inspire passion young learners need powerful, not nerfed, tools. It is easy to pass an online language course and thus be measured and approved of, while not actually being able to talk your way out of being mugged at a French train station. It is also a testament to the inefficacy of nerfed materials that a large proportion of such tools end up sitting unused on a shelf. To rely on such tools is not likely to make an education system fit to call itself capable of teaching code.

CODERDOJOS WORLDWIDE

At the time of writing (July 2016), there are 1150 CoderDojos in 66 countries across the world. and CoderDojos have existed for precisely five years. While the independent style and self-organising nature of CoderDojo does not lend itself to absolutes in terms of academic rigour and analysis, there is an overabundance of anecdotal and circumstantial evidence that learners at CoderDojos are enthusiastically engaged, are extremely diverse, and operate with both a sense of, and attendance level of, real gender equality.

From CoderDojo 0 – the first and still operational CoderDojo – there have been numerous new Dojos calved off and set running; and in the growing population of CoderDojo ninjas there are those who have gone on to study computer science and many who have set up their own businesses. There are those who have taken code into other disciplines, and many who have released software to the public. There have been many positive social outcomes, ranging from mentors and parents finding better jobs to alternately able learners finding at last a place to truly fit in: one young paraplegic remarked, when asked what the best thing about CoderDojo was, that "my wheelchair is invisible here". There are also many who have come back to CoderDojo as mentors, and it is expected that in years to come others will come back as parents themselves.

To come in every Saturday and see, hear and feel the buzz in the CoderDojo space of CoderDojo 0 is a joy. Beholding young learners stepping up and developing and sharing mastery and, at the same time, having a lot of jolly good fun. What is demonstrated is that young learners can tackle the most difficult and advanced coding tasks by figuring things out together. This is so well demonstrated to those in the global CoderDojo community that, upon being asked to create a book for young learners, they insisted that it be recommended that readers of the book[4] work in small teams and not individually.

It should be no surprise to those who study language learning that younger learners are sponges, and that the younger they begin the journey with real programming tools and languages, the faster they progress. Another Saturday joy to behold is the sight of an 11- or 12-year-old girl leading a session for older boys who have come to programming just a year or two later and who find it much more difficult to make progress. If there is anything for mainstream education to adopt from CoderDojo, it is that learner-led learning is hugely empowering and efficacious in the age of the Internet.

There is something delightfully respectful in allowing those who come to learn to also share what they have mastered with those who have not yet achieved mastery. There is all too often an assumption that the learner is somehow also incapable. Thus many systems of education are both dominating and disempowering in one swoop. This is not

▪ **Figure 14.3** Working with pupils in Docklands, London

Source: Paul Kelly at Docklands Photo Agency.

generally the fault of those who are engaged at the coalface of the classroom. It is built into the fabric of the system and forms an integral part of the context.

Stanley Milgram[5] demonstrated, through a series of ethically questionable experiments, that context is decisive in controlling how humans behave towards one another and how they behave in a given circumstance. CoderDojo is, at its core, a created context in which learning and the love of learning emerge lightly and liberally to the benefit of the young learners. To focus on the content and ignore the context would be a grave mistake, because it is also the reason why CoderDojo expands and thrives globally without the need for massive amounts of funding; this is also core to the level of inclusion CoderDojo is capable of globally.

CoderDojo was established because it was simultaneously observed that the world was running short of talented computer programmers while at exactly the same time young people were both desperate to learn how to code (and thereby manipulate the technology infusing every aspect of their lives and that they depended on daily) and also that they were having difficulties in learning to code in schools in any meaningful and fun way. In fact, coding as a group activity was not to be found anywhere for an age demographic in which language skills were easy for them to onboard. Also, those who did learn to code spending hours alone in front of a screen with little outside support, often did so at the expense of other vital social skills.

The original CoderDojo was experimenting with what might or might not work to get young learners coding. There were some overarching principles that had to be adopted. CoderDojo had to be low cost and highly efficient. As at the outset, a decision was made that it would be free to all comers under the age of 17. It was reasoned that charging for services created an inequality between those who had and those who had not.

■ **Figure 14.4** Coding partnerships around the world

Source: CoderDojo

In order to provide a space, free industry partnerships were formed with relevant companies, and the first of these was the highly appropriate National Software Centre in Cork, Ireland. Yet, surprisingly, many other companies who got involved were not actually totally dependent on coding to make their businesses work at all. CoderDojos get free spaces and resources from an amazing array of corporate partners, from banks to supermarkets and more. Also, many CoderDojos are partnered with community groups, churches and schools.

All the components of the CoderDojo methodology scale well, because a lot was done with few resources from the very start. This has led to some interesting results as well as unintended positive consequences. For instance, in order to provide a safe environment for the young learners, CoderDojos insist that the parent of the learners stay in the room throughout the session and that they join in wherever possible. This has created a unique dynamic, has helped support CoderDojo organisers/champions and in the long run has led to greater sustainability. The collaborative nature of the CoderDojo community is supported at every level, and this also helps the young learners to collaborate. Also, while CoderDojo is free, it is not a "free ride". Everyone who is involved has the sense that they are contributing parts that in the end make up the whole.

Reciprocity is at the heart of CoderDojo philosophy because CoderDojo is growing talent for both society and industry. This creates a natural fit between CoderDojo and its partners. This also occurs between the Dojos and the young learners, as they are expected to mentor as well as learn as they develop. This mentoring develops a wider range of skills other than just coding, allowing children to feel it is cool to contribute, to support others and to learn new things.

The collaborative and reciprocal aspects of CoderDojo are also important in making it incredibly economical and scalable. This is good news, because CoderDojo seeks to tackle at least two, if not more, intractable problems by sharing resources between those who are burdened with said problems. Society and industry need more talented makers, and talented makers need a place to become talented in the first place. Individually, these global problems are intractable, yet collaboratively they can be solved.

As with many good things, there are also a range of side benefits that were not anticipated in the original CoderDojo design. Every time parents become friends, or a mentor gets a job, or a young learner develops a new social interest as a result of attending CoderDojo, there is a lot of joy unleashed. This was not part of the original purpose of getting young learners coding, yet these and many other delightful side effects are very present to all involved. It is anticipated that many more good things will result from the journey, to give every young learner the ability to express their creativity as a collaborative coder poet.

NOTES

1 https://www.youtube.com/watch?v=zDZFcDGpL4U
2 https://kata.coderdojo.com/images/6/62/CoderDojo-ECHO.pdf
3 www.tomwujec.com/design-projects/marshmallow-challenge/
4 https://www.amazon.co.uk/CoderDojo-My-First-Website-Nano/dp/1405278730
5 https://www.simplypsychology.org/milgram.html

APPENDIX 1

Glossary

A selection of useful words to add to your coding vocabulary.

Absolute value　the magnitude of a number regardless of its sign. For example, 6 and −6 have the same absolute value of 6.

AND　an operator used in an IF/THEN statement when giving the computer more than one condition to test.

```
IF x < 0 AND y > 10 THEN PRINT "you are outside the permitted area"
```

Array　a set of variables containing several pieces of data.

Artificial intelligence (AI)　the property of a synthetic system that allows it to behave in some way that a human observer would consider intelligent.

Boolean logic　a form of algebra that uses 'true' and 'false' statements, named after the nineteenth-century mathematician George Boole. This algebra works well with the binary numbering system, as true and false statements can be coded 1 and 0.

Bug　a mistake in a program.

Casual games　games that have short narratives and few rules, and can easily be played in 8–10 minutes.

CLS　command to clear the screen.

Cluster　a set of data that share some common characteristics, often called a cloud of data, or a class of data; used in computer learning to allocate data to a particular category, frequently in non-supervised learning.

Code　to create a series of steps in developing a program or an action within a program.

Computational thinking　an approach to problem solving for situations where the solution is a process. This term is generally used in the context of identifying foundational ideas from computer science, programming and software engineering that are relevant for school pupils to explore.

Computer science　the theoretical foundations of computing; this provides the tools to enable us to develop efficient and effective digital systems, covering a large range of sub-disciplines such as algorithm efficiency, network design, computer security, interface design, and the design and implementation of programming languages.

Cursor a flashing shape on the screen which shows where the next character will be displayed.

Data a list of items stored by the computer, to be read with the command READ. These items can be words or numbers.

Deep neural network a complex neural network with many interacting processing layers capable of learning to do complex tasks.

DIM sets the size for an array. For example, DIM A$(20) would allow 30 items of data in string A$. DIM B(3,7) would set up a two-dimensional array for 21 items of data arranged in three rows and seven columns.

END command to stop the code running.

ELSE the instruction used when an IF/THEN statement is not true. In the example below, when X is greater than zero, the IF/THEN is true, but if it is less than or equal to zero it is not.

```
IF X > 0 THEN PRINT "You win" ELSE PRINT "You lose"
```

FOR/TO/NEXT in coding, this is called a 'loop'. The code instructs the computer to repeat a set of instructions a number of times. In the example below, the PRINT "Coding is FUN" is repeated 100 times.

```
FOR A = 1 TO 100
PRINT "Coding is FUN"
NEXT A
```

Genetic algorithm a supervised learning computer technique used in artificial intelligence, which mimics natural selection to uncover good solutions to computational problems. The process is driven by a simulation of evolutionary pressure and survival of the fittest.

GOTO a command that sends you to a particular line number in the code. For example, GOTO 50 would tell the computer to go to line 50 and continue running the code from this point.

IF/THEN a decision statement. IF is used when you want to test a condition and then carry out an instruction. The following symbols are used to test data: = (equal), <> (not equal), > (greater), < (less than), >= (greater than or equal to), <= (less than or equal to). The example below checks to see whether A is bigger than B in numerical value. If this is true, it prints 'Game over'.

```
IF A > B THEN PRINT "Game over"
```

INPUT a command that allows the user to store data in a named variable. For example, with the code INPUT A$, the computer would wait for the user to type in a string. This string would be stored in the variable A$. If, later in the code, you had the command PRINT A$, the computer would print this string on the screen. If the command was INPUT A, this command would wait for the user to enter a *numerical* value which similarly would be stored as A.

INT a function that converts numerical values to integers, by ignoring all the numbers after the decimal point. For example: INT (2.78) = 2.

**LEFT$**   a function for string 'slicing', which is used in many computer languages to manipulate string variables. LEFT$ takes a given number of characters from the left part of a string. If, for example A$ = 'Win and Lose', the following code will only print 'Win'

```
LET A$ = "Win and Lose"
B$ = LEFT$(A$, 3)
PRINT B$
```

LEN   counts the number of characters in a string. In the following example, LEN returns an answer of 12, as you need to remember 'spaces' are also characters.

```
LET A$ = "Win and Lose"
PRINT LEN(A$)
```

LET   allows a value to be assigned to a given variable, which can be a string or a numerical variable.

Machine learning   computer programs that mimic learning by example, by modifying the connections or by using rules within a system to usefully classify given training data.

MID$ takes a given number of characters from part of a string. For example, the following code would print 'and'.

```
LET A$ = "Win and Lose"
B$ = MID$(A$, 5,7)
PRINT B$
```

Multidimensional data   the extension of the idea of a 2D point in space (X,Y) to a higher dimension space where an individual point may have many hundreds of coordinate values (X,Y,. . .) to define its position.

Neural network   a collection of neurons (biological or computational) that are connected together to form an often complex series of interlinked structures that process information.

Neuron   the special type of nerve cell that makes up the structure of a biological brain. The switch-like properties of a biological neuron are often copied in code for artificial intelligence systems.

OR   this decision operator is used in an IF/THEN statement in a similar way to the AND command, but is less stringent as both conditions do not need to be true. In the example below, the print message about being outside your permitted area would appear when either condition was true.

```
IF x < 0 OR y > 10 THEN PRINT "you're outside the permitted area"
```

Pixels   small squares on the computer screen.

PLOT   this command colours a pixel at certain co-ordinates on the screen. In some coding languages, the command is PSET x,y.

PRINT   a command that tells the computer to display data on the screen.

Programming   another term with many meanings, ranging from writing the source code of a computer program, to the broad enterprise of designing and implementing a digital system.

RAM   Random Access Memory. This is memory storage in a computer where code and data are stored. All the information in RAM is automatically erased when the computer is turned off.

REM   short for 'remark'; this is used to put explanatory notes in a program.

RND   a function that generates and returns a random number.

Robotics   the study and construction of technology which is able to affect change in the real world through means of actuators controlled by intelligent software systems.

ROM   Read Only Memory. This memory storage is permanent, set by the manufacturer, containing the computer's operating system.

Rule base   a set of IF/THEN type rules that are used by an artificial intelligence to make decisions. For example: IF (COLD) THEN (SWITCH ON THE HEATER).

RUN   a command that instructs the computer to execute the code.

Software engineering   the broad discipline of designing and developing large digital systems, with an emphasis on methodologies for developing and maintaining software that meets the users' needs, in a timely manner.

String   a group of characters stored under a variable name. e.g. 'Sinclair' or 'ZX81'.

Training data   sets, often large, of examples of labelled input and output pairings used to train an artificial intelligence system, e.g. a labelled set of data of images of chairs, or a set of temperature data where each temperature is labelled as cold, warm or hot.

Unplugged activities   the demonstration of computer science principles without the use of a computer, which can be used to prepare a class in understanding basic concepts before they start to write code.

Video console games   games designed to be played on a particular brand of video console rather than on a computer. With the rise of hand-held devices, many video console game apps can now be downloaded and played without the use of the console. Video games generally have multi-structured levels of rules.

APPENDIX 2

Coding resources

TEACHING CODING TO THE YOUNGEST PUPILS

Tynker – https://www.tynker.com/

Kodable – https://www.kodable.com/

Cargo-Bot – http://twolivesleft.com/CargoBot/

Scratch Jr – http://www.scratchjr.org/

LightBot Jr – http://lightbot.com/

Robot Turtles – http://www.robotturtles.com/

TEACHING CODING TO AGE 8 AND UP

Hopscotch – http://www.gethopscotch.com/

Scratch – https://scratch.mit.edu/

ChipmunkBASIC – http://www.nicholson.com/rhn/basic/

Codarica – http://www.codarica.com/

LightBot – http://lightbot.com/

Alice – http://www.alice.org/index.php

Kodu – http://www.kodugamelab.com/

Gamestar Mechanic – http://gamestarmechanic.com/

GameMaker – https://www.yoyogames.com/gamemaker

SpaceChem – http://www.zachtronics.com/spacechem/

Code Combat – https://codecombat.com/

MinecraftEdu – http://education.minecraft.net/minecraftedu/

Codea – http://twolivesleft.com/Codea/

Code Monkey Island – http://codemonkeyplanet.com/

Code Warriors – http://codewarriorsgame.com/

HARDWARE FOR PUPILS

Raspberry Pi – https://www.raspberrypi.org/

Kano – http://uk.kano.me/

Hummingbird Robotics Kit – http://www.hummingbirdkit.com/

LEGO Mindstorms – http://www.lego.com/en-us/mindstorms/

Dash and Dot – https://www.makewonder.com/dash

Sphero – http://www.sphero.com/

PROGRAMMABLE TOYS

Programmable Rover – https://smartlabtoys.com/

Robot Turtles – http://www.robotturtles.com/

Code Master Board Game – http://www.thinkfun.com/

Code Monkey Island – http://codemonkeyplanet.com/

Ozobot Bit – http://ozobot.com/

Bitsbox – https://bitsbox.com/

Sphero Ball – http://www.sphero.com/

LEGO Mindstorms – http://www.lego.com/da-dk/mindstorms/

Puzzlets Cork the Volcano – https://www.digitaldreamlabs.com/

Minecraft Server Design – http://www.youthdigital.com/

Sphero BB-8 App-Enabled Droid – http://www.sphero.com/starwars

APPENDIX 3

Coding art

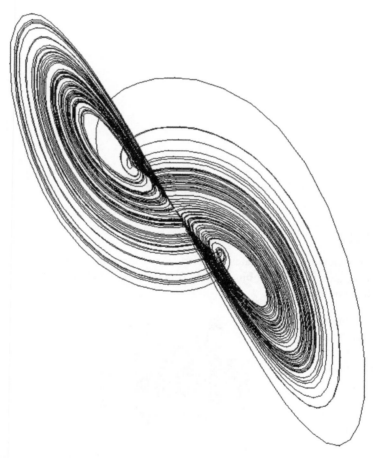

Figure A.1 The butterfly effect

In this section are some short snippets of code that will allow you to generate the computer art seen in this book. You are encouraged to experiment and explore this code by changing the numbers (parameters) to generate your own computer art.

BUTTERFLY EFFECT

The meteorologist Edward Lorenz was the first person to explain how long-term weather predictions may not be possible. He used his three differential equations[1] (i, j and k in the code below) to suggest that the fluttering of a butterfly's wing could produce large fluctuations in the weather. His work implied that there are limits to predictability when using computer coding. To generate the image in the book, use a=10; b=28; and c=8/3 in the following code.

```
cls
graphics 0
input "a = ";a : input "b = ";b : input "c = ";c
x = 1 : y = 1 : z = 1
graphics moveto 350,350
for g = 1 to 10000
i = a*(y-x)
j = x*(b-z)-y
k = x*y-(c)*z
p = x+(i*0.01)
q = y+(j*0.01)
r = z+(k*0.01)
w = (11*p+350)
 v = (11*q+350)
x = p : y = q : z = r
graphics lineto w,v
next g
```

PIXEL ART

The following code creates pixel art 'Space Invader' in an 11 by 8 grid. To create your own pixel art, edit the binary DATA code with '1' (space fill) and '0' (space empty) in different places.

```
00100000100
00010001000
00111111100
01101110110
11111111111
10111111101
10100000101
00011011000
```

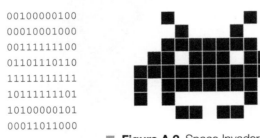

■ **Figure A.2** Space Invader binary code

```
graphics 0
dim h$(10)
data "00100000100","00010001000","00111111100","01101110110"
data "11111111111","10111111101","10100000101","00011011000"
graphics window 20,20,800,800
graphics color 0,0,0
x = 200 : y = 200
for b = 1 to 8
read h$
for a = 1 to 11
p$ = mid$(h$,a,1)
if p$ = "1" then graphics fillrect x,y,x+20,y+20
x = x+21
next a
y = y+21 : x = 200
next b
```

SPIRAL ART – DESCENT TO THE CENTRE

Using the trigonometry functions of sine and cosine, you can create the illusion of spi-ralling into a three-dimensional point on the screen. This code spirals squares, but it is possible to write code to spiral any shape. To do this, you will need to edit the code on the line with the command 'fillrect'.

```
graphics 0
graphics moveto 100,100
graphics window 20,20,800,800
graphics color 0,0,0
for z = 1 to 80
for a = 0 to 160
g = (2*a)*cos(a/4)
h = (2*a)*sin(a/4)
x = g*4000/(z-4000)
y = h*4000/(z-4000)
if a = 20 then graphics moveto x+400,y+400
graphics fillrect x+400,y+400,x+400+(a/3.8),y+400+(a/3.8)
next a
next z
```

WAVES

As with spiral art, this short snippet of code also uses trigonometry to generate waves and ripples. It is suggested that you start experimenting by using small values for a and b, such as 1 and 2 respectively.

```
graphics 0
c=500: d=250
input "a = ";a : input "b = ";b
for y = 600 to 5000 step 50
for x = 1 to 700 step 0.05
REM axis and scale
p = (x- d)
q = (y- d)/10
graphics pset p, q+(y/c)*sin(a*p/20)+(y/c)*sin(b*p/10/(y/c))
next x
next y
```

JULIA – MONSTER FOOTPRINTS

In honour of the research carried out by Pierre Fatou and Gaston Julia, in the days before the benefit of computers, the collection of functions to create these images are given the name 'Julia sets'.[2] You are invited to experiment with small values of a and b, such as a= −0.8 and b=0.2, to create beautiful coding art in colour.

```
graphics 0
input "a = ";a : input "b = ";b
for y = 90 to 410 step 0.4
for x = 70 to 430 step 0.4
REM axis and scale
p = (x-250)/120
q = (y-250)/120
n = 0
100 n = n+1
r = (p*p)-(q*q)+a
s = (2*p*q)+b
p = r
q = s
REM n iterations
if n < 20 and (p*p)+(q*q) < 500 then goto 100
c = (p*p)+(q*q)
if c < 4 then graphics pset x,y
REM colours
if c > 4 and c < 5000 then graphics color 100,0,0 : graphics pset x,y
if c < 50000 and c > 5000 then graphics color 0,100,0 : graphics pset x,y
if c < 100000 and c > 50000 then graphics color 0,0,100 : graphics pset x,y
graphics color 0,0,0
next x
next y
```

SQUARES: FROM ORDER TO RANDOMNESS

This piece of art starts off in ordered lines and gradually moves to a random array of squares. By changing the values of m, n and p in the following code, you can create pictures of this form. The degree of randomness around the position of the squares is also generated by the use of the random number generator function 'rnd'. You may wish to experiment by changing the 'rnd' value to increase or decrease the degree of randomness observed in the resulting picture.

```
graphics 0
graphics moveto 100,20
for y = 20 to 800 step 35
for x = 100 to 740 step 30
if y < 249 then graphics moveto x,y
n=30000: m=10000: p=150
REM define drawing starting point
a = (x)*cos(-y/n+rnd(2)/p)-(y)*sin(-y/n+rnd(2)/p)  b=(x)*sin(y/n+rnd(8)/
p)+(y)*cos(y/n+rnd(8)/p)
if y > 249 and y < 449 then graphics moveto a,b
c = (x)*cos(-y/m+rnd(7)/p)-(y)*sin(-y/m+rnd(7)/p)
d = (x)*sin(y/m+rnd(5)/p)+(y)*cos(y/m+rnd(5)/p)
if y > 449 then graphics moveto c,d
if y < 249 then graphics lineto x,y : graphics lineto x,y+10 : graphics
lineto x+10,y+10 : graphics lineto x+10,y : graphics lineto x,y
if y > 449 and x > y/2 then graphics lineto c,d : graphics lineto c,d+10 :
graphics lineto c+10,d+10 : graphics lineto c+10,d : graphics lineto c,d
if y > 249 and y < 449 and x > y/3 then graphics lineto a,b : graphics
lineto a,b+10 : graphics lineto a+10,b+10 : graphics lineto a+10,b :
graphics lineto a,b
next x
next y
```

LISSAJOUS FIGURES

A range of interesting-shaped curves were investigated by Jules Antoine Lissajous[3] around 1855. You are invited to experiment with a range of values for a and b to see the beauty that can be generated from such simple code.

```
graphics 0
input "a= ";a
input "b= ";b
for n = 1 to 50000
x = 250+200*sin(n/120)
y = 250+200*sin(a*n/120+b)
REM for/next loop is used to slow down the code
for s = 1 to 100000 : next s
graphics pset x,y
next n
```

FRACTAL FERN

The beauty of the natural world cannot be represented by Euclidian geometry such as triangles, squares, pentagons, etc. In 1975, Benoit Mandelbrot[4] unified hundreds of years of mathematical research in the area of fractal geometry. Michael Barnsley took these concepts to create a geometrical vision of the world that could be replicated by a computer. He coined the term 'SuperFractal'.[5] His work is seen in many computer game animations to enable a replication of the natural world. The following code uses Barnsley's ideas to draw a fern. You can experiment with the initial values in the following code to create other natural biological objects.

```
graphics 0
dim a(4),b(4),c(4),d(4),e(4),f(4)
REM initial values
a(1) = 0.85 : a(2) = -0.15 : a(3) = 0.2 : a(4) = 0
b(1) = 0.04 : b(2) = 0.28 : b(3) = -0.26 : b(4) = 0
c(1) = 0 : c(2) = 0 : c(3) = 0 : c(4) = 0
d(1) = -0.04 : d(2) = 0.26 : d(3) = 0.23 : d(4) = 0
e(1) = 0.85 : e(2) = 0.24 : e(3) = 0.22 : e(4) = 0.16
f(1) = 1.6 : f(2) = 0.44 : f(3) = 1.6 : f(4) = 0
REM starting point
xold = 0.1 : yold = 0.1
input " How many points to plot (>1000) ";p
for i = 1 to p
REM for/next to slow code
for e = 1 to 10000 : next e
REM generate random numbers
r = rnd(1)
REM create probabilities
if r < 0.01 then k = 4
if r > 0.01 and r < 0.08 then k = 3
if r > 0.08 and r < 0.15 then k = 2
if r > 0.15 then k = 1
REM define fractal matrix
newx = a(k)*xold+b(k)*yold+c(k)
newy = d(k)*xold+e(k)*yold+f(k)
REM plot values
if i > 50 then graphics pset(300-35*newx), (450-35*newy)
xold = newx
yold = newy
next i
```

▨ **Figure A.3** Fractal fern

RANDOM PACK OF CARDS

Code to simulate a random pack of cards and calculate the chance that any two out of three named cards will be next to each other in the deck.[6]

```
REM input data for decks of cards
data "1","2","3","4","5","6","7","8","9","T","J","Q","K"
data "1","2","3","4","5","6","7","8","9","T","J","Q","K"
```

```basic
data "1","2","3","4","5","6","7","8","9","T","J","Q","K"
data "1","2","3","4","5","6","7","8","9","T","J","Q","K"
dim a$(60)

REM ordered deck a$
for n = 1 to 52
read a$(n)
next n
for t = 1 to 10000
REM shuffle by swapping random cards
for m = 1 to 52
b$ = a$(m)
c = rnd(52)+1
a$(m) = a$(c)
a$(c) = b$
next m

REM create whole deck string c$
for p = 1 to 52
c$ = c$+a$(p)
next p
REM print out deck of cards
print c$

REM checking for a snap
for q = 1 to 52
s = 0
d$ = mid$(c$,q,1)
e$ = mid$(c$,q+1,1)
if d$ = e$ then s = s+1 : print "snap ";d$;e$
next q

REM 2 out of 3 named cards next to each other
for r = 2 to 51
print "pick cards " : input f$ : input g$ : input h$
for r = 1 to 51
if mid$(c$,r,1) = f$ and g$ = mid$(c$,r+1,1) then print "match ";f$;g$
if mid$(c$,r,1) = h$ and g$ = mid$(c$,r+1,1) then print "match ";h$;g$
if mid$(c$,r,1) = h$ and f$ = mid$(c$,r+1,1) then print "match ";h$;f$
if mid$(c$,r,1) = f$ and h$ = mid$(c$,r+1,1) then print "match ";f$;h$
if mid$(c$,r,1) = g$ and f$ = mid$(c$,r+1,1) then print "match ";g$;f$
if mid$(c$,r,1) = g$ and h$ = mid$(c$,r+1,1) then print "match ";g$;h$
next r
if x > 0 then y = y+1
x = 0
c$ = ""
next t
print t;" ";y/t
```

NOTES

1 http://www-history.mcs.st-and.ac.uk/Biographies/Lorenz_Edward.html
2 https://en.wikipedia.org/wiki/Julia_set
3 http://mathworld.wolfram.com/LissajousCurve.html
4 http://www-groups.dcs.st-and.ac.uk/history/Biographies/Mandelbrot.html
5 http://superfractals.com/wpfiles/
6 Humble, S. (2016). Street maths: What's the chance of that? In: Silva, J.S, ed., *Recreational Mathematics* (pp. 161–166). Lisbon: Associacao Ludus, or accessed at: drmaths.org.

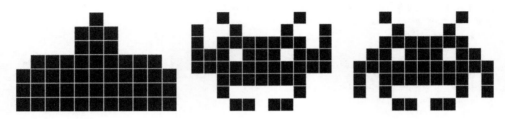

■ **Figure A.4** Game over

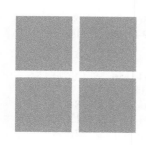

INDEX